Introduction

This is a different kind of book about gardening. It contains a wealth of things you need to know about growing better vegetables and fruits in Minnesota but it tells you even more than that.

This is a book for the person who wants to enjoy, really enjoy, the warm glow of accomplishment and the feeling of self-sufficient contentment that come from growing one's own food.

It is a book to consult, to read on a cold winter night, to enjoy as much as a chat with another gardener. It is a book for the beginning gardener who wants the lore and tips that some people get from Uncle Ed or Grandma or Dad — those oldtimers whose plants always seem to thrive and produce fall bounty overflowing their larders. And it is a book for Ed, Grandma and Dad, too; they will want to compare their experiences with those of the authors.

This book tells you how to enjoy gardening and how to enjoy what you produce — how to cook or preserve it, how to serve it to friends. It talks about canning, pickling, drying, and wine-making.

You'll find history here, philosophy, entomology, and a generous measure of just plain old-fashioned horse sense. You'll find things to think about and, perhaps, some things to question and try for yourself.

Most of what you find has been adapted from material originally written by the authors for the Minneapolis Tribune and published in their Sunday columns. Much of this has been brought up to date and enhanced for this book.

William L. Nunn is your guide to vegetable gardening. The phrase "avid gardener" falls short when applied to him.

Bill Nunn's career in higher education began in Japan and ended in Minnesota. During these years, he collected titles: professor, chairman, arbitrator, director, author, Lt. Cdr., mayor, husband and father—and gardener.

He first napped in his father's 1902 garden in Loachapoka, Ala., and later pulled weeds in the Buford, Ga., garden.

His own gardens were in tubs, window boxes and garden rows—and now in raised beds and permanent trellises. Their produce—liquefied, frozen, dried, canned—lasts the whole year.

William L. Nunn

He's still an educator, he tells us how.

Nunn and his wife, Jo, raised their family and still raise their bountiful gardens on an acreage near Elm Creek in Champlin, Minn.

The chapters about fruit-growing are by Leon C. Snyder, a respected authority on the growing of food who retired in 1976 as director of the Minnesota Landscape Arboretum.

The questions following the chapters came from readers of Snyder's columns whose contributions have enriched this book.

A native of Michigan, Snyder joined the faculty of the University of Minnesota after teaching in South Dakota and Wyoming.

He was head of the university's department of horticultural science from 1953 to 1970, when he relinquished that post to devote full time to the Arboretum. He is a veteran gardener and an accomplished one; in 1963 he re-

A Minnesota Gardener's Companion

A Minnesota Gardener's Companion

How to grow and enjoy vegetables and fruits

By William L. Nunn and Leon C. Snyder
With George Luxton's Grandma anecdotes

Published by the Minneapolis Tribune
Minneapolis Star and Tribune Company
425 Portland Av./Minneapolis/Minn./55488

First Printing

Library of Congress Cataloging in Publication Data

Nunn, William L.
  A Minnesota Gardener's Companion
1. Vegetable gardening — Minnesota. 2. Fruit-culture — Minnesota. I. Snyder,
Leon C. II. Luxton, George E. III. Title.
SB321.N82   635'.09776   81-2480
ISBN O-932272-05-3   AACR2

Leon C. Snyder

George Luxton

ceived the gold medal award of the Men's Garden Clubs of America, that organization's highest honor. He also holds the Liberty Hyde Bailey Award, the highest honor of the American Horticultural Society.

He and his wife, Vera, live on an acreage in Excelsior, Minn.

Old-time gardeners will recall the years when George Luxton was garden editor of the Minneapolis Tribune. His down-to-earth advice guided Upper Midwest gardeners from the late 1930s until his death in 1962.

Readers of the column chuckled over his anecdotes about Grandma and Uncle Jerry as Luxton recalled their adventures in gardening at their Canadian home. Many of the anecdotes are included in this book.

Earlier in his career Luxton earned fame as a photographer for Twin Cities newspapers. His newspaper work spanned 64 years. His book, "Flower Growing in the North", was published in 1956 by the University of Minnesota Press.

This book was compiled and edited by Wallace Allen, associate editor of the Tribune, and Richard C. Reid, assistant to the editor. It was designed by Michael Carroll, Tribune design director, and illustrated by Nancy Entwistle of the Tribune's design staff.

Finally, we appreciate the contributions of the many Upper Midwest gardeners whose interest in and love for nature's wonders led to the publication of this book. May their soil be warm and easily workable, may their plants be bountiful and their fruits unblemished.

To them this book is dedicated.

Contents

Vegetables you can grow in Minnesota

William L. Nunn

Fruit you can grow in Minnesota

Leon C. Snyder

Vegetables you can grow in Minnesota

By William L. Nunn

1/In the winter, thoughts of spring

Chapter 1/A northern gardener's dream

It is March. Several hours of bone-warming sunshine have cleared snow from the garden. Lying quietly before sleep, the gardener hears water dripping in a downspout by the bedroom window.

There may be more snow, maybe lots more. But it's time to think of fingers in the soil, it is time to dream of the garden to come.

Time to dream, to think, but not yet time to plant. What does the northern gardener need to think about as winter loosens its grip?

Choices, for one thing. Timing, for another.

Most seeds, cuttings, bulbs and sets offered for sale carry the legend "plant after the danger of frost has passed." In our northern area, Memorial Day traditionally is the gardener's "opening day." No damaging frosts are expected after this date, although twice in a memory of 30 years such frosts have killed garden plants and even oak leaves in June.

Some plants tolerate and a few others actually need the cold days and nights of early spring. Their seeds are apt to carry a different legend: "Plant as soon as the garden soil can be worked."

Sounds simple, but it's as complicated as gardeners themselves. Those who use only fresh produce and preserve little or nothing may rush the season. They have waited through a long and rough winter and are now paying high prices for the not-too-fresh offerings of the grocers. Already they have ordered or bought the seeds they will plant. They are antsy. The temptation to get going is overpowering.

However, those of us who preserve food from the garden will wait. Our shelves and freezers are comfortably full of jars and boxes and bags marked from earlier years. So we won't start most of our new garden until May 30 has passed.

If the weather turns and stays warm in early spring, all plants in the garden should do equally well. Similarly, if the antsy gardener knows what to plant before the season begins, all gardeners, again, should come out about even.

Let's see if my own garden can assist the gardener who risks everything with a complete early planting, and the one who wants to play it safe by putting out the things that can survive a weather relapse.

But first, what already is in my snow-covered garden waiting to come up — probably before May 30? These are the perennial and biennial vegetables such as New Zealand spinach, Egyptian onions, chives, plain and curly parsley, mint, sage, thyme, Russian tarragon, rhubarb and asparagus.

Included also are those planted last October and November: Cold-resistant Savoy spinach, turnips for greens, dill, edible chrysanthemums and, for chance, three loose-leaf lettuces.

Field mice permitting, these will arrive on their own schedules.

Now what about seeds that can be planted as soon as the ground can be worked? There are many. **Lincoln** peas, **Mammoth Melting Sugar** Chinese peas, **Sugar Snap** peas, lettuces and all greens, and **Fava** beans. All these and others may be planted early in northern gardens.

Red beets in my garden — just before Memorial Day — will be an old-time favorite, **Detroit Dark Red**; the yellow ones will be **Burpee's**

On the first warm day of spring — and if the brook was free of ice — Uncle Jerry would offer to cultivate the garden. However, Grandma would exclaim, "No. Be patient. It takes more than one swallow to make a summer."

I don't think Uncle's offer was inspired by horticultural enthusiasm — he wanted fishworms.

Golden. I'll plant no white beets, but those who do should order **Burpee's White**. The first beets harvested will be the small tender and sweet ones — to serve and to can whole.

The big and tough ones dug in September make the best beet-root wine. Those in between do well made into spicy pickled beets. Chopped beet greens should come to the dinner table as a special delicacy, especially if steamed — but only the tops of those that are pulled early.

Cold-weather **Burgundy** Swiss chard and Georgia collards also may be planted early, but I'll plant them late, just after the spinach has been harvested. The taste of Burgundy Swiss chard is unharmed by autumn frosts and that of collards is actually improved.

White, red and black radishes — any variety — will be planted frequently to provide fresh ones as long as possible. Wait until the middle of July to plant the first of the Black Spanish ones for they are winter keepers.

One of the huge Japanese white radishes — **Shogun** or **Daikon** — will be planted, but only twice. Peeled and cut into strips, they are tender and mild. They may be shredded as a cushion for meats and sliced raw vegetables with oil-and-vinegar dressing. The shreds may be frozen for wintertime use.

Three kinds of Irish potatoes will be in my garden before Memorial Day. One will be red **Norland** for eating at mid-season or later — even when only the size of center-ring marbles. The other two will be white **Cherokee** and **Kennebec** for baking and for storage.

Those who have never planted blue and yellow potatoes will find it fun to do so. Sets come from Gurney's Nurseries and are called **All Blue** and **Lady Finger**. Gurney's **Blue Visitor** has only a blue skin. Potato plants no longer are in rows, or even under the soil, in my garden.

Those for keeping will be whole certified seed potatoes. The cluster of eyes on each one will be discarded and the rest cut into pieces with one or two — never more — eyes on each piece.

These will be dusted with captan and left to dry for a couple of days. Then they will be placed, cut side down, in beds of rich and loose soil with no recent fertilizer, then covered with a mulch of old leaves that is never permitted to be less than a foot thick. To keep the leaves from blowing away, the beds are fenced with rabbit wire.

And there the seed potatoes grow, on the soil, under the mulch — shaping nicely for easy harvesting later.

What to plant? When to plant? Where to order seeds and materials? There in bed, sensing the changing seasons, the northern gardener dreams a little and thinks a lot. Nature is stirring. Something deep inside the gardener is stirring, too.

It's almost time.

Grandma had little trouble in persuading chronically-tired Uncle Jerry to spade the garden in the spring. He was as good as a robin at picking up worms and grubs. He would get enough in a couple of days to give him a summer's supply of fish bait. He stored them in an old horse trough filled with earth mixed with coffee grounds and bread crumbs. One day someone left the cover off the trough, the chickens discovered it, and "bang" went Uncle's supply of fish bait. My, but he was furious. He had to dig bait for the rest of the summer.

Chapter 2/Seed catalogs

Seed catalogs are excellent teachers. Just as some teachers are better than others, some catalogs are better than others. They can be had free — but requests for them should reach seed companies early — by the end of January, if possible. A postal card with your name and address will do.

A good seed catalog, like any good teacher, should answer questions in simple language — full of truth and honesty and without flamboyant words or color. The catalog's purpose is to teach, not to shock or subdue or misguide for the purpose of making a sale.

What do you want to ask? How deep and how thick to plant? What seeds should be soaked before they are planted and for how long? What fertilizer can be used — how much and when? What's the probable time between planting and harvesting? What's the effect on seeds and their plants of the sun, cool weather, frosts, strong winds, fertilizer, lots of water or not enough water?

Is the chosen variety resistant to one or more common diseases? Will the plants be bush or pole or spreading? If pole, how high? If spreading, how big is the spread?

What pests and what diseases may be expected, and what might be done for each? Have seeds been heated with a hot-water bath to check seed-borne diseases? May you ask for seeds that have not been bathed? Have the seeds been treated with an insecticide or a fungicide; if so, what? If male seeds are needed, as with some cucumbers, are they enclosed? Are they in separate packages from the female seeds? Have they been colored for easy identification?

These and many other questions should be answered in a seed catalog. Some gardeners, like some students, need more help than others. The question, "Which seeds will produce plants especially good for canning and freezing?" will be asked by those who preserve foods.

Organic and near-organic gardeners who use few or no commercial chemicals may have questions that good catalogs will answer.

A list of names and addresses of seed compa-nies that send free catalogs follows this chapter. Most of the seed companies will send a second copy if you order seeds from them.

Extra copies are handy if you keep record cards of each variety you plant. Information about each of your varieties may be cut from the spare catalog, pasted on cards, and consulted during the season and afterward, when you decide if you should plant the same varieties in succeeding years.

One of the many good catalog teachers is that of Stokes Seeds, Inc., in Buffalo, N.Y., and Stokes Seeds, Ltd., in St. Catherine's, Ontario, Canada. This catalog is rich in things experienced or novice gardeners need to know.

It's all in the language of a well-liked teacher. "Onions will withstand all kinds of abuse and bugs . . .most (bugs) . . .can be washed off with a hose . . .hairy-stunted carrots may be caused by irregular weather . . .or the improper use of weed control or fertilizer."

Stokes Seeds began in 1881 in Mooretown, N.J., when Walter P. Stokes joined the 3-year-old firm of Herbert W. Johnson Seed Co. In 1915, Johnson's name was dropped and the company became Stokes Seeds.

So 1981 is the company's centennial year and it was a banner year for us, too, because we discovered that prices of the 58 varieties from Stokes that we grow in our garden had increased by only .02 of a percent over the 1980 prices.

Another catalog teacher of note is Joseph Harris Seeds in Rochester, N.Y. Harris marked its 100th year in 1979.

In 1850, Joseph Harris left the Moreton Corbett area of Shropshire County, England, to see about settling in this country and his report soon brought the other Harrises to the Rochester area. Soon there was a Moreton farm (1863), a 44-page catalog under the name of Moreton Farm Seeds (1879) and a Moreton Farm postoffice in 1890.

The Joseph Harris Seed Co. is still at Moreton Farm, 3670 Buffalo Rd., Rochester, N.Y. 14624, and its president bears the name of his grandfather — Joseph Harris.

The third member of this good teaching trio is the George W. Park Seed Co., Greenwood, S.C. This Park started the firm in 1852. Four generations later, the president is William J. Park. The Park catalog contains five times as many pages devoted to flowers as to vegetables. But its listing of the latter is more than respectable; the teaching is thorough, complete and well stated.

My father, and perhaps his father, used Park seeds. Those planting such vegetables as sweet potatoes, okra, collards, speckled Lima beans, black-eyed peas, mustard and other greens should know that such seeds from Park do well in northern gardens. The Park offerings include an excellent selection of herbs and another of foreign vegetables and still another of miniature ones.

Another good catalog is from Burpee Seed Company, Warminster, Pa. As its ads claim, "For more than a century, Burpee has provided gardeners with the best seeds that grow." The Burpee line is also available on racks in most garden centers.

The catalog of Gurney Seeds and Nursery Co., Yankton, S.D., advertises "strawberries so big they are patented and may reach 2½ inches in diameter," or elephant garlic, blue potatoes, vegetable spaghetti, jumbo sunflowers, black corn and black radishes, purple beans (among the best, by the way), pink and golden as well as red tomatoes, 15-pound radishes (not freaks — they're sweet and wonderful for grating), yard-long beans (genuine, from China), white strawberries and yellow as well as red beets and radishes.

Gurney's is another of the "senior" seed companies. It claimed the newest and best back in 1866. Its 1981 catalog was a trip back in time and well worth perusal.

Johnny's Selected Seeds of Albion, Maine, is a newcomer to the business and will be interesting to all gardeners, but especially to devotees of organic methods.

Johnny's is not yet 10 years old and is reaching out to a larger market. It has no customs to grow out of, no barnacles of obsolescence to scrape away, no gaudy colors or extravagant language. And it is a good teacher. Minnesota gardeners should note that Maine's short growing season and harsh climate are much like ours.

Minnesota's two seed companies will soon mark centennials, Northrup King of Minneapolis in 1984 and Farmer Seeds of Faribault in 1988. Northrup King seeds are available at almost every garden center in the land.

Farmer is a catalog company with 12 Minnesota garden centers, in Rochester, St. Cloud, Fairmont, Mankato, Albert Lea, Newport, Bemidji, Windom, Forest Lake, Glencoe, Montevideo and Faribault.

Orders for seeds should be placed as soon as catalogs arrive. Even so, the seller needs your permission to make substitutions and it's a good idea to give it.

Of course you can buy seeds — good seeds — from farm cooperatives, from garden, yard and nursery stores and from the racks of seeds in all sorts of places. But clerks rarely are able to answer your questions, and the few who know are apt to be busy with customers who got there first.

If you need a packet of seeds to fill out a row, or if you didn't have the time or inclination to order from catalogs, then by all means go to the nearest nursery or garden center seed rack. You'll find seeds that will grow well for you.

A few seed companies, unfortunately not enough, state the approximate number of seeds in each packet they sell or the approximate number of plants that will be produced by these seeds. This key information, as well as price, will strongly influence your buying decisions.

If you don't know the number of seeds in a packet or the number of plants they will produce, you're almost buying a pig in a poke. Seed companies aren't really helping much when they say only that 3,000 cauliflower seeds weigh an ounce, or only that a quarter-ounce of cauliflower seeds will produce seedlings to fill a 100-foot row, or only that a gram of cauliflower seeds can be bought for 50 cents.

Soil testing

Now that you are on your way to a supply of seeds, let's turn to one more thing that should be handled early in the gardening year — telephoning the agricultural county agent in your county to arrange to have your soil tested.

When you reach the agent, you will be talking to one who represents, and is responsible to, the county in which both of you live, the Uni-

Grandma used to sit at the kitchen table, excitedly studying the new seed catalogs by the light of a kerosene lamp — she called it a coal-oil lamp. Uncle Jerry had brought them from the post office four miles away, for there was no rural delivery. The post office was in Johnstone's harness shop. Uncle was sure Johnstone held up the catalogs at least a week while he looked them over. These catalogs contained not more than twenty pages, each illustrated with a few woodcuts that were used year after year. Only one page was given to flower seeds and from it Grandma got her list.

versity of Minnesota and the federal government. Tell the agent you wish to have your garden soil tested and ask that instructions and a mailer box be sent to you.

After they arrive, fill the mailer box with soil samples from various areas in your garden. When you return this self-addressed box, you should enclose $4. To this, I suggest that you add $3 and request that a test be made for soluble salts, since Minnesota highways have been flooded year after year with such salts for snow removal purposes. Some may have been spilled or tracked into your garden.

Computer-run tests will be performed on your samples by the university's Soil Testing Laboratory. When you receive the results, you will know not only the existing levels, but the recommended additions, of lime, nitrogen, phosphate and potash. From the report the laboratory sends you, your fertilizer dealer will know what to sell you. If that dealer is confused, go to a larger or better store.

You might also consider adding trace minerals, especially if you have grown vegetables in the same place for many years. The trace mineral fertilizer I use — calcium, magnesium, sulfur, boron, iron, cobalt, molybdenum — could make your tomatoes redder and your spinach leaves greener, as I think it did in my own garden.

Directory of seed catalogs

Seeds — good seeds — are down the street or even around the corner in garden centers, nurseries, co-ops, even in drug and grocery stores. You may want to consult the yellow pages under "nurserymen."

Good seeds are also available by mail from companies that furnish catalogs free. Here are names and addresses of seed companies mentioned in this book or otherwise worth knowing about. A postal card will bring a catalog.

Stokes Seeds, Inc., 737 Main St., Buffalo, N.Y. 14240; Stokes Seeds Ltd., 37 James St., St. Catherines, Ontario 6R6, Canada.

Joseph Harris Co., Moreton Farm, Rochester, N.Y. 14624.

Burpee Seed Co., Warminster, Pa. 11891; Clinton, Iowa 52732; Riverside, Calif. 92502. The Midwest is served from Clinton.

Geo. W. Park Seed Co., Inc., Greenwood, S.C. 29647.

Johnny's Selected Seeds, Albion, Maine 64910 (especially for organic gardeners).

Gurney Seed and Nursery Co., Yankton, S.D. 57079.

Herbst Brothers Seedsmen, 1000 N. Main St., Brewster, N.Y. 10509.

J.W. Jung Seed Co., Randolph, Wis. 53956.

Farmer Seed and Nursery, Faribault, Minn. 55021.

Twilley Seed Co., P.O. Box 100, Farmington, N.J. 07727.

Henry Field Seed and Nursery Co., 5538 Oak St., Shenandoah, Iowa 51602.

Olds Seed Co., P.O. Box 1069, Madison, Wis. 53701.

Burgess Seed and Plant Co., 905 Four Seasons Rd., Bloomington, Ill. 61701.

Alberta Nurseries & Seeds Ltd., Bowden, Alberta, Canada, TOM OKO

Vermont Bean Seed Co., Garden Lane, Bomoseen, Vt. 05732 (for beans and corn and peas only).

Seeds from Europe may be bought from **Epicure Seeds**, Box 69, Avon, N.Y. 14414. **Le Jardin du Gourmet**, West Danville, Vt. 05873, specializes in herbs, including shallots and Egyptian onions.

Some oriental vegetable seeds may be ordered from the catalogs of **Park** or **Stokes** — or, if you wish, Japanese vegetable seeds from **Kitazawa Seeds**, 356 W. Taylor St., San Jose, Calif. 95110, and Chinese ones from **Tsang and Ma International**, 1306 Old County Rd., Belmont, Calif. 94002.

Grandma always bought the best seed obtainable. She used to say, "If ever the old adage, 'Penny wise and pound foolish' is timely, it is when a body is buying seed."

Chapter 3/Rows or beds?

During the winter, when nothing is growing outside except icicles and snowbanks, gardeners have time to sit with their seed catalogs and think about spring. They have some planning to do and some decisions to make.

One of the questions: Should you plant in rows or in beds?

Nowadays, most gardeners are row gardeners — just as their parents and grandparents probably were.

First you will need to mark the rows.

Nylon or cotton strings that curve and twist with the wind and sometimes cause trouble, or strands of thin wire that don't, are stretched taut to trace the rows and keep them straight. Crooked rows will hold more plants, but a garden of crooked rows will hold fewer, so good gardeners try for straight rows.

Before you dig the row, take a bucket with a hole in its side, fill it with commercial fertilizer and carry it along just above the string or wire. A stream of tiny balls of fertilizer (the number can be controlled by the tilt of the bucket) drops from the hole. You can then use a pointed hoe or push cultivator to make a straight row of any desired depth.

For some gardeners, this is the principal method of fertilizing most vegetables. The fertilizer pours out in a thick stream, so be sure to push the cultivator or pull the pointed hoe vigorously. The pellets of fertilizer must be scattered to the edges of the rows to keep them away from the soil that will receive the seeds. Some seeds — especially Lima beans — will be burned if "touching contact" is made.

Before you cover the seeds, mark the ends of a row with identification tags tied to stakes. Attach a tag with needed information to the stake nearest the garden entrance. Aluminum tags are best. You can mark them with a nail or the point of a dry ball pen. Rain or sun will not affect words written on these tags.

What words? Mark the English name of what's planted, even the Latin name if there is need for it. Date planted, date of expected harvest, source of seeds, possible diseases. If old seeds are used, this might be noted.

Although I like aluminum tags best, they are getting hard to find. And the narrow slivers or half-moons over sticks made of plastic or wood are too small, too breakable, and cost too much.

So I make my own labels from 24 x 36-inch sheets of hard plastic. I cut this with scissors into as many sizes as needed — my labels are usually 3 x 6 inches. Plastic sheets come in various colors and that's useful. In our garden, green is for annuals, red for perennials and white for plants that need special treatment.

A hole punched in one edge makes it easy to tie each label to a stake high enough to be read without stooping. Northrup King and Park seed companies sell pens with ink that won't fade from sun or rain. We use nail polish remover to make erasures. My plastic sheets come from the Eiler Plastic Company, 110 S. 2nd St., Minneapolis 55415.

How far apart should the rows be?

Some plants like the Buttercup squash, which spreads, need lots of space and rows should be 6 to 8 feet apart. Other plants — beets, for instance — need little space so the rows may be as close as 6 to 8 inches apart.

Some gardeners carefully rotate crops and keep cabbage, for instance, in areas in which no cole plant has grown for three years. They have some difficulty with row gardens because the rows made last year disappear as new ones are made this year. Still, they do their best with records and memory to rotate the vegetables they plant.

Once cultivation was done by a plow with changeable shares, a mule with small feet rather than a horse with big ones, and a gardener who guided the mule by voice (gee!=right; haw!=left) and the plow by strength. Once learned, it was not a difficult job — especially if the same mule and the same gardener always worked together.

Today's problems with gasoline cost and supply may bring the return of such practices. If so, tomorrow's teachers may be those young families who have withdrawn to some degree and seek a simpler lifestyle that fits their notion of what's right and what's wrong with today's world, as well as those who think the world is fine but life is more rewarding if lived on a few acres where plants and animals — and children — may be raised.

Today's row gardeners use hoes and rakes and shovels of varying styles and sizes. They either plow and cultiate with the long-used push cultivator that uses the energy of the gardener to move along the rows, and doesn't cost much, or else they use one of the many kinds of power-driven rototillers that cost a lot.

Gardeners who cultivate with rototillers have no problem with the distance between rows. The width of the tines on the tiller will define the space between rows. Such a garden can be a thing of great beauty and exactness, with aisles free of weeds. But much of it will be free of vegetables, too, for those aisles take up a lot of room.

Gardeners who use the push-plow or garden cultivator, or just a pointed hoe, can vary the width of the aisles depending on space needed for each vegetable. The result may be a more compact garden that produces more.

The two may look quite different. The gardener who likes abundance, even crowdedness, will be pleased. The one who likes open spaces and sharp lines may be displeased. Each kind of garden can be beautiful.

Some vegetable gardens have beds with no rows or both beds and rows. In earlier days, beds were common and still are in some parts of the world. Such beds are permanent, are never walked upon or in any way packed, are generally wide enough to permit one's arm to reach halfway across easily and are as long as desired.

Let me tell you about ours. There are 36, each 21 feet long (outside measurement) and 3½ feet wide (inside measurement). These occupy only a part of the garden. Small fruits, perennials and most of the climbing plants are elsewhere. And there are more permanent rows than permanent beds.

Grandma had no prepared peats and mosses for garden purposes, but she fully realized that a good mulch kept the soil cool and lessened the need for watering. So in the cool days of early summer, she had Uncle Jerry bring in wheelbarrow loads of loose-textured, dark brown mulch from under the big trees in the maple grove and the nearby forest. Here it had been forming from fallen leaves for hundreds of years. This leaf mulch was spread one to two inches deep on the garden. Uncle was delighted to do this chore because the mulch reduced his weeding to almost nothing.

The beds are made from rejected, warped and twisted 2-by-4s bought for little at a lumber discount house. Each piece was 7 feet long. I would have preferred 2 by 6s, but they were expensive. My youngest daughter has a garden of raised beds made with long tree trunks of uniform length and size. A friend's garden beds are made from old railroad ties.

Half of our beds are on each side of a center walkway or aisle wide enough for a pickup truck. All other aisles between beds are 3 feet wide. This is wide enough for the Garden Way cart and the seldom-used rototiller.

Soil from aisles was removed and used to fill the beds that were 4 inches high. Wood chips from the Elm Creek Park Reserve, made from diseased elm trees, took the place of the removed soil. These chips make great cushions on which to sit, slide along, and reach into the beds for weeds that go into the compost heap and for pods and leaves and bulbs and roots that go to the kitchen. If the chips reach the tops of the 2-by-4s, one has a level garden once more.

I think it better that they not be quite so high, for chips have no business drifting into the beds.

Seeds may be sown by scattering or placing them in furrows as long as the bed is wide. Compost and mulch can be best handled if the seeds are planted in such rows. And harvesting is easier from the short rows.

The bed gardener uses his hands more and tools less than does the row gardener. Both use sharp pointed hoes, but perhaps with handles of different lengths. Both will use the Garden Way cart with big wheels. The rototiller, principal tool of the row gardener, is not essential to the bed gardener.

If a rototiller or a spade is used at all in the beds, it will be to mix compost into the soil. Otherwise, a rake or a hoe, or even a hand trowel, is adequate. Because no one walks on the soil, it remains loose and easily worked. Fertilizer is not wasted in areas between furrows as in row gardens. Rotation of crops can be exact; one does not need to guess exactly where last year's rows of celery grew.

A word here about the Garden Way cart. And you'll find it mentioned again later. There are many carts on the market but none quite like the Garden Way. It is nicely balanced so the axle (not your back) carries the weight and, also important, the front of its box is exactly perpendicular to its floor, not slanted. This makes it easy to tip it up so the front is flat on the ground and to slide heavy materials (big rocks, stumps, sacks of fertilizer) onto it. Then you simply tip the cart back to put the weight on the axle for a trip to wherever. The Garden Way is my favorite tool. Information is available from Garden Way Research, Charlotte, Vt. 05445.

In contrast to the soil of the row gardener, that of the bed gardener is loose and crumbly, for it is never packed. Each guest who visits my garden is told that anyone putting a foot in a bed will be summarily shot! In truth, it does take willpower to keep feet out of beds.

Each bed has its number and its own 5-by-8 card on which is written, year after year, the name and exact place of each vegetable in each bed: north, south or middle. Thus it is easy to practice an exact plan of crop rotation. Tomatoes will never be planted where tomatoes or eggplant or peppers or potatoes have grown within the last three years (all are close relatives). Fertilizer is placed where plants are feeding and not wasted in aisles or other areas that have no plants.

Frost is less a threat in bed gardens than in row gardens. If irrigation is present, as in our garden, a strip of 16 beds in four rows may be sprayed with water all night with no injury to any plant — if the water keeps running until the ice that makes a fairyland has melted. Plants in beds out of range of the whirling water may be easily and quickly protected by a plastic cover.

A major advantage of permanent raised beds is that they take a lot of the stoop out of gardening. One sits more, crouches or bends less and, if sitting, can see closer to leaves, produce or bugs.

If a move to an all-bed garden is too much to do at once, gardeners may plan it on paper, and then do a bed or two each year.

Grandma discovered that a very small pinch of snuff, dropped in the center of tulips and other early spring plants, often would repel squirrels and rabbits — depending upon how hungry they were. She always had Uncle Jerry buy it and explain to Zeb Klinkhammer, the storekeeper, for what purpose it was to be used. She was in mortal terror that somebody might think she wanted it for her personal use.

Chapter 4/Climbers or non-climbers?

While its surface is still hard with ice, let's think some more about how we'll use the garden after the sun and rain have turned it into the soil that invites fresh seeds, sprouts and bulbs.

The question now is vegetables that climb vs. those that don't.

Climbers have tendrils that grasp and cling to whatever they touch as their slender stems wave in the breezes. Without supports placed by the gardener, they will clutch each other and end up in such a mess as to make orderly harvesting difficult or impossible.

So gardeners have long devised methods to guide and support climbing plants and their fruits. First they used any poles that could be picked up, bamboo and similar canes that could be had for the pulling, and brush and boughs that could be dragged to where they could be useful.

Slowly they learned that the way these supports were used was important.

If poles were propped straight up, plants with tendrils would do better.

Several poles tied together at their tops and spread at the bottom created a circle around which seeds of climbers could be planted. Poles

Grandma used the grayish-green warp or cord that she wove into her beautiful hand-loomed rugs for her annual vines to climb on and for tying plants to stakes. This warp was strong enough to last all summer and was not conspicuous. I have used it for years. It still is obtainable in the stores and is surprisingly low priced -- fifty cents for half a mile.

might be tied in pairs and spread to make a slatted tent-like construction for the same purpose.

Supports for climbers included growing stalks of green corn and food canes large enough to support plants with tendrils.

In many cases, the word *pole* was added to the names of food plants that climbed. Pole green beans, pole wax beans, pole purple beans, pole Italian beans, pole white Lima beans and pole speckled Christmas beans grow in my garden just about every year.

My grandfather grew some of these, and more were grown in my father's garden. Grandfather piled limbs from apple and peach trees over double rows of beans and peas.

An old gardening book advised that birch saplings might be used for this — they were "twiggy" and made excellent "pea-brush." The author advised that this brush be burned each year after use. I'm certain my grandfather didn't burn his; he used the branches until they were worn out.

My father's method was new in his day, and it is described and recommended in many books to this day.

His garden was about 75 feet wide, the length of all rows. He began by erecting a row of posts about 10 feet apart. These supported an intricate network of wire and string that supported the reaching vines of his climbing vegetables. We'll describe this later when we talk about climbing vegetables in detail.

My father, at first sight, would not like my system, though he would think it much easier to manage. His posts had to be erected and dismantled each year. Mine are never moved. He bought cord each year. My yearly money costs are zero, for I use old steel fence posts and banged-up wire fences of no value.

It would take my father a while, as it does my fellow gardeners, to accept the idea that these fences are as permanent as those that keep the deer from the Elm Creek Park Reserve out of my garden. Gardeners find it strange to see tomato plants growing beside, and tied to, a fence. They are shocked to see corn growing just as closely but not tied, but they accept the explanation as to why this is necessary.

Cucumber vines — as well as most pole beans and peas — have tendrils. But cucumbers have bigger and heavier stems that aren't waved about by breezes.

So gardeners must guide the stems and help the tendrils wrap around the fence wire. Without such help, the plants become spreaders, as in most gardens.

But helped at the start, cucumbers find their way along the fence. And what a lot of garden space the fence saves!

Poles and trellises are not just for beans, peas and cucumbers. Tomatoes — which have no tendrils — do well when staked or tied and made to grow upright. But if tied to stakes or trellises they need a lot of help all during their growth.

If a single pole is to be used for each plant, it should be "planted" when the seedling is put in the garden. As the seedling grows, the pole and the plant are tied together with strips of cloth or string that won't cut into stalks, stems or fruit.

Wire trellises may be preferred for tomatoes. Ours, made from old wire fences, run the length of each row and are permanent. Tomato seedlings are planted on each side and are kept close to the fence wire with binder twine woven from fence to plant to fence.

Because I tie most tomatoes in my garden to movable stakes or to fences in permanent rows, I am frequently asked which varieties can be staked. My unconventional reply is that any tomato can be staked to climb.

There are other, more modern and more costly ways for the home gardener to assist plants that climb naturally or are forced to climb. These have different names — arbors, tepees, pyramids, towers, cages, pens, rings and things sold as "Train-ettes," "Add-A-Fences," or "Gro-nets." They may be moved around the garden, season after season. They may be stored, folded, easily joined together and taken apart. They are usually light, with much aluminum tubing and plastic strings and netting. Many are made for designated plants, and not all are especially for climbers.

I had never used one of these until fellow Minnesota gardener and manufacturer Judd Ringer (the Ringer Corp., in Eden Prairie) gave me one to try. It was made of easily joined wire sections with instructions to fill the enclosure they made with any kind of mulch. I used leaves.

With the box of wire sections came two packages of plant food for use in the mulch and in the soil around its outer sides where indeterminate tomato plants of my choice were to go.

The **Big Boy** plants I used were the only ones I grew that year that I did not prune, as suggested by the booklet of instructions.

Visitors to the garden had fun comparing the plants tied with the soft yarn to the Ringer product to those tied with binder twine to my permanent fences.

The difference? Perhaps a draw. Both methods produced beautiful fruits — "show tomatoes," one guest said. Ringer and I would have been equally pleased — and proud.

What about non-climbing varieties of vegetables? Snap beans and Lima beans, for instance.

For snap beans, there are bush green beans, bush wax beans, bush purple beans and bush Italian beans. For Lima beans, there are bush white (large and small) and bush speckled varieties.

Most home gardeners plant only bush varieties and avoid the work of building supports for the climbers. Some gardeners, like myself, plant both climbers and non-climbers because bush beans generally are exhausted just as pole beans start producing. (One can, of course, have fresh bush beans in late autumn if seeds are planted in midseason.)

Bush beans make life easier for the gardener, who can sit down with a bucket and slide along the row — no contortions needed to get beans from plants that are six feet high.

So we agree that good gardens can be made without climbing plants. But many gardeners join me in believing that better gardens and better foods can be had if plants that climb naturally, or can be made to climb, are included.

Once, in defense of this, I would have begun with bold statements that green and other snap beans from climbing vines taste better than those from bushes, and that of all grean beans, pole **Blue Lakes** have the best taste.

In those years, doubting visitors would have

Grandma permitted Uncle Jerry to have full charge of the tomato garden. He really did grow amazingly large and fine-flavored fruit, but he was almost tiresomely proud of his method and results.

Usually on Sunday afternoons neighbors would drop in to inspect the little farm, and also to enjoy the cool apple cider and Grandma's doughnuts which were served under a tree near the tomato plots. There was a two-foot pile of old sod on which Jerry loved to stand while lecturing on his tomato culture. One Sunday he suddenly quit talking and commenced to slap his legs, then his body, then started yelling and running toward the barn, disrobing en route.

Unknown to Jerry, a colony of red ants had taken over this sod rostrum, and they were climbing up Jerry's person, biting like old fury.

been given a mess of these and asked to decide for themselves. I take a tiny credit for the increasing popularity of these beans, for many converts have been made.

But now I can do better by showing any recent Joseph Harris Co. seed catalog and pointing to the bush Blue Lake bean description: "Developed from the famous Blue Lake Pole bean, this variety nearly matches their wonderful quality . . . ." I mark the words *nearly matches*.

Besides taste, there are other benefits to the home gardener from plants that climb. First, if the garden has room for only a single row of green or any other beans, plants that grow six and more feet high will provide more beans than short ones that grow only a couple of feet high.

The Blue Lake pole variety produces beans until stopped by frost; the bush beans stop long before frost.

Most gardeners think they need more space. One of the best ways of getting it is to have many plants that climb, fewer that remain stubby and no plants that spread.

Taste, yes. Space, yes. Also, compost heaps need heavy vines rather than light bushes to satisfy their appetites for things that rot and restore humus and nutrients to the soil.

Still more: All beans, whether snap or Lima, bush or pole (and a few other garden plants, too) are legumes that can convert nitrogen from the air into nitrogen compounds that plants demand for growth. This nitrogen is stored in nodules on roots. Some is used by the plant, the rest remains.

So spent legumes in my garden are never yanked from the soil. The bushy tops are cut from the roots and end up in the compost heap. Roots remain where they grew — alongside a permanent fence or in a raised bed. Seeds that follow grow directly over the rotting nodules of free nitrogen. Just great!

For years I have toyed with a hypothesis that ought to be shared and checked with others. Big plants have big roots, and since pole plants are larger than bush plants, their roots must be bigger. Big roots have more space for more nitrogen compounds to be made and stored in more nodules.

If this is not a fantasy, a major advantage of pole plants over bush ones is that the pole plants leave the soil greater doses of nitrogen.

Chapter 5/Seedlings

Many gardeners raise seedlings from seeds of their own selection. The advantages are legion: knowledge gained; more and earlier recreation and exercise enjoyed; money saved; new friends made; new interests to talk about; different problems to be discovered, thought about and solved, and the joy of planting one's own selections rather than those made by the merchant.

The first step is to put sterile potting soil, which must be used to avoid dreaded damping-off, into sterilized clay or plastic pots or trays (low and squat ones with holes for drainage).

(Damping off is probably our most-feared disease for young plants. It infects seeds and seedlings, especially those grown inside. Sick plants topple, stems become hollow, plants die. Many organisms cause it. We must destroy the dead plants, remove soil where they grew, and sterilize the flat involved.

(How to prevent it? Don't crowd young plants in any way. Pray that damp and humid weather will go away. Above all, never grow seedlings in soil from the garden; use store-bought sterile potting soil. Unless you are an organic gardener, dust the seeds with captan and spray seedlings with a captan spray. If you are an organic gardener, say a fervent prayer.)

The seeds are spaced carefully on the surface of damp potting soil in those pots or trays, covered lightly and made moist again with slightly warm water. Each pot or tray is then slipped into a transparent plastic bag and tied with a twister. Now perfect hothouses, these should be put in a dark place and checked daily. It helps if they can be placed on heating pads or coils with medium setting. When seedlings appear, the first phase has ended.

Next step: The plastic bags are discarded and the tiny seedlings given light — much light. In our basement these trays with growing seedlings are placed under grow-lights kept on for 14 hours each day about six inches from the tops of the seedlings.

Gardeners without grow-lights may use windows with no curtains or shades. Trays should be turned daily to prevent bent plants. Ingenious ladder-like contraptions with reflector mirrors and heating coils have been built by gardeners with few windows and many trays. We are, indeed, a nation of inventors.

This step ends when the seedlings develop a couple of firm leaves.

Next step: Each seedling is moved to a peat pot of its own or to a cardboard or plastic flat that will hold several carefully placed ones. Again, pots or flats are filled with a sterile potting soil made damp with tepid water. Each plant is removed and replanted with fingers that touch only a leaf and never a stem. Later the seedling and its pot will be planted in the garden or divided and replanted if in a flat.

Why not plant seeds in these pots in the first place? Some seeds won't germinate so the pots with these seeds are wasted. But you could put several seeds in each pot, then throw out all but the strongest seedling. But seeds cost money and discarded seedlings are wasted.

In recent years, peat pellets called Jiffy 7s (large) and Jiffy 9s (small, and maybe too small for certain plants) have challenged the older pots. These come as flat and dry-looking quarter-inch "biscuits," made of pressed peat. When soaked in water these become wider and higher pellets of a complete growing medium

---

Grandma knew about soilless horticulture. On moist moss, cotton, or blotting paper in shallow plates placed in the window, she scattered seeds of garden cress, sometimes called peppergrass. In ten days the seedlings, hundreds of them, would be up four inches high and ready to be eaten in her dainty, thin sandwiches. It took four entire plants to make a sandwich, so she raised many crops each winter. For salads she grew a permanent crop in flats of earth. These were more vigorous plants and bore all winter. You can purchase this seed in seed stores.

enclosed in weak plastic netting. They are then seven or nine times the weight of the original biscuits.

Most are made in Norway and sold for either seeds or for seedlings. Clearly they are less messy than pots and more convenient. Try a few.

Some more points about seedlings:

One should not attempt to grow plants without the proper space and growing facilities. A lack of adequate light results in tall, spindly plants that do poorly when transplanted.

Poor plants may result if seeds are started too early. Six to eight weeks are adequate to grow good transplants of most annual vegetables. A few, such as celery or onions, may take 10 to 12 weeks.

Knowing the date when seeds can first be planted and when plants can be safely planted outdoors will help in knowing when to start the seeds. We know that tomatoes should not be transplanted in the garden much before Memorial Day and that it takes only six weeks to grow good plants. With this knowledge you would start tomato seeds about April 15.

Good seed catalogs can help here. The tables in the catalog from Johnny's Seeds are especially helpful; they give dates for the climate in Albion, Maine, which we've noted is about like ours.

Good seedlings require clean containers, sterile soil mixtures, adequate light and proper temperature. Use new plastic containers or wash used containers with a good detergent and disinfectant.

Late in March Grandma always started her flowers and late vegetable seeds in shallow boxes or trays in the deep, sunny kitchen windows. But first she sterilized the earth by baking it in the oven with a potato or an apple buried in it. When they were baked, the earth was sterilized.

2/It's planting time

Chapter 1/Getting the garden ready

They're off: Each one running at the pace thought best — some fast and "going for broke"; others moving slowly, but steadily; still others taking time out to stretch a muscle, to listen to the call of a bird, to admire a cloud, to count the spots on one of the beetles clustered about a tiny plant.

Counting spots? On a bug? Of course. Unless we count the spots, we can't identify the bug. For this the gardener carries a small magnifying glass in the pocket of an apron, a garment that ought to be more used.

Good! The count is 12 and not 16. So we know that it's a ladybug — one of the gardener's best friends which devours aphids and mealybugs. But all ladybugs do not have just 12

Every autumn, Grandma would collect about a dozen ladybugs and turn them loose in her indoor window garden, where they would do valiant work keeping the house plants free of plant lice, mealy bugs and other insects. One of Uncle Jerry's jokes was, "I don't understand this matter of ladybugs. There surely must be gentleman-bugs, or there would not be any ladybugs or children-bugs. But I have never met a gentleman-bug that I know of."

Last week a little old lady called about the ladybug's husband. She said Uncle Jerry couldn't have been very bright if he had never seen a gentleman-bug. She had seen lots of them. They are a little smaller, have darker red wings and are much handsomer than the ladybug. If Uncle Jerry could have heard her, he would have said, "Of course he is handsomer, he is the male, isn't he?" Grandma would have retorted, "Oh, fiddlesticks! The conceit of these men is beyond all understanding." She never seemed to realize that Uncle was only teasing her.

spots — they may have any number, even 16.

But the ladybug has a look-alike that always has 16. It's the Mexican beetle weevil, which feasts on leaves of bean plants and reduces plants to skeletons. To battle the weevil, gardeners run for rotenone, diazinon or malathion in a can with holes in its top. A sprayer does it better, though, because it's easier to get liquid on undersides of leaves where weevil eggs are apt to be.

Before going to war, better count spots on a few more of the bugs. If others don't have 16 spots, relax. If more bugs have 16, declare war.

Identification of a single insect can make a gardener's day. One of the pocket-sized guidebooks to insects can get one started.

Yes, indeed, gardeners are off and running. Inside and outside the house there is great activity.

Thirty-four jars of syrup from our six maples stand on shelves in the "playroom." Each year, maple syrup is our first homemade product. How smug we are: at Bob's Produce Ranch, a pint costs $3.69.

Seeds and sets and slips ordered from catalogs weeks ago have arrived. Tomatoes and cabbages and celery and eggplants and leeks and Brussels sprouts and onions and cauliflower and peppers and broccoli are now growing in peat pots and trays by windows and under growlights in the basement.

Catalogs battered from use — evidence of worry over what kind of vegetable seeds and how many to order — have been put aside until the time they're needed for planting instructions.

Seedlings now in peat pots will be planted outdoors, pots and all, just after Memorial Day.

There is much to be done in the garden to make ready for the seeds and seedlings. The tomato stakes that should have been pulled up last autumn must now be dipped in a solution of three parts of water and seven parts of denatured alcohol. Microorganisms cling to the stakes in the ground all winter and shouldn't be spread about the garden now.

The movable trellises on which Chinese and

Sugar Snap peas will climb must be moved to new beds. Or perhaps these will grow in the permanent rows and cucumbers moved from there to the movable ones.

Do we want compact tomato vines that reach their natural growth and stop? These are called bush, compact, or *determinate*. Or do we want vines that grow and produce until stopped by frost? These are called *indeterminate*.

We settle on indeterminate (**Ultra Boy VFN**) and semi-determinate (**Ultra Girl VFN**) tomatoes to grow alongside and climb on permanent trellises. Only one determinate variety (**Veeroma VF**, one of the Romas) will be allowed to spread — in a 75-square-foot bed. All three are from Stokes Seeds.

There is more, much more to be decided and done. Hand tools lost in leaves or snow should be picked up, cleaned and oiled. Tops of some perennial plants like New Zealand spinach that were left as a winter mulch must be removed to the compost heap. Other mulches must be moved about so that the sun can thaw and warm the topsoil.

The rest of those old tomato vines and cornstalks must be chopped with a hatchet and added to the compost heap.

And the frozen compost must be thawed, an exasperating job. The once-hot heap is now a pile of ice. Thawing is hastened if sides of the bin can be removed to expose the compost to warm spring air. A heavy pickaxe will break up big pieces for quicker thawing.

Many gardeners avoid this chore by working compost into their soil only in the fall. Others, like me, wait for it to thaw and use part for mulch between rows of growing plants.

It's time to be sure the rototiller is ready. Soon we'll need it to mix soil and manure and compost. The tiller will return in the late autumn to assist in putting the garden to bed for the winter. Other jobs for the tiller will have to do with the perennials in separate rows: rhubarb, asparagus, horseradish, grapes, strawberries, raspberries and comfrey. But there is no rush to get to these for they can wait a while.

All these chores can be done as seeds and seedlings are being planted to grow inside. Each one is a diversion, but an essential one, to the main business of gardening: sowing and harvesting.

Record cards, the 5 x 8 ones that carry notes on planting and rotation of crops, must be consulted to make sure, for instance, that cabbage-like plants will not be planted where any have grown in the last three years.

Most gardeners will plant one or more vegetables that they have never grown before. I beg my gardening friends to plant celery, Italian parsley, Savoy cabbage, New Zealand spinach, Oriental cucumbers, kohlrabi and Egyptian onions. Once these were new to me, but now they're standbys.

Planting new vegetables and watching them grow can be such an exciting experience that the gardener must remind himself of the real purpose of a garden — to produce food — and keep on that basic job.

Chapter 2/The early birds — a matter of timing

Early spring is not only in the garden, but also under grow-lights in the basement.

Seeds of onions (except green bunching ones), and of hot and sweet peppers, eggplant, Chinese chives, celery, leeks, peanuts, Savoy and red and green cabbage, broccoli, white and purple cauliflower, Brussels sprouts, and all tomato plants germinate and grow under those lights.

All these plants will end up in the food garden, but at different times. On their way, each will stop at the cold frame for a week or more to slowly get used to the rough world of wind and chill and rain.

Some, such as cabbages, will be the first to leave the basement, for they won't mind the frosty days of early spring. Gardeners say these can go into the ground "as soon as it can be worked."

(This date varies from year to year and may not be the same in your garden as in your neighbor's. The feel of the soil in the prongs of a fork or the tines of a tiller will let you know when it's ready.)

Other seedlings, like tomatoes, must stay under the grow-lights until all danger of frost has passed — again, usually any day after Memorial Day.

But most of the plants that go into the garden before Memorial Day will know nothing of the grow-lights that lengthen our northern garden year. They will go directly from seed packets into garden rows or beds.

This list includes Swiss chard, beets, carrots, almost all peas (including English, Chinese and the Sugar Snap, but not chickpeas or blackeyed peas or other cowpeas), radishes, greens of mustard and turnips and collards and kale, spinach, the Chinese cabbage called Michihli but not the kind called Wong Bok, kohlrabi, Bok Choy, parsnips, Irish potatoes and lettuce.

Now let's consider the possible varieties of these vegetables. And, where important, we'll note the number of days from seed to a plant ready for the dinner table or for the blancher used for freezing.

1. *Swiss chard.* One with white stalks and veins that mark wide green leaves: **White Rib, White King,** or **Fordhook Giant** (all in 60 days). One with red stalks and veins and wide green leaves: **Rhubarb** (60 days). Don't use the whole plant; use only the tender outer leaves and let the rest grow for future harvests. This will give leaves all summer for greens or for stir frying. We have washed, blanched, chopped and frozen chard with good results. Herb vinegar will sharpen its taste.

2. *Beets.* Most of ours are **Detroit Dark Red** (63 days). My grandfather planted this variety and it's still the most popular one. Detroit Dark Red beet roots do well canned, frozen, pickled or used for beet-root wine. Their leaves are adequate for beet greens, fresh or frozen. We will have a few of the yellow ones: **Burpee's Golden Beets** (50 days) for an interesting variation. I see only idle curiosity as a reason for growing **Albino White Beets** (50 days). If you must, plant three or four seeds and give the rest, if untreated with captan, to the chickens. Two different red beets from Stokes, **Winter Keeper** (78 days) and **Formonova** (58 days) may be added.

3. *Carrots.* Any one of the several **Nanteses** with their blunt ends are my choice. They can be eaten raw, baked or boiled. They may be fro-

Grandma used to place a mirror — she called it a looking-glass — in the bird bath. She said, "It reflects the sun's rays and warms the chilled water much quicker, and also it attracts the male birds because, man-like, they like to preen and admire themselves."

zen, canned or turned into an exciting folk wine. Cook with honey or with onions and vinegar to make sweet-and-sour dishes.

The Chinese outdo us with their slanting slices. The Europeans beat us, too, when they grow the carrots big and remove and discard the cores. Slanting slices look prettier.

When the core is removed and discarded the toughness and bitterness go too. The two methods can be combined if the center core is removed by slicing the carrot lengthwise and then slicing each half just as the Chinese do, but minus the core. A really new vegetable to most of us and just great!

Carrot seeds are hard to see and easily blown away. I use the **Pioneer** variety from Joseph Harris. Each of these seeds is coated to make a small white pellet that's easy to see and handle. Pioneer is one of the Nantes carrots.

4. *Peas.* For the home gardener: the **Lincoln** peas (65 days), once called **Homestead,** as they still are in Canada. It's the only variety left that hasn't been monkeyed with to produce peas that ship well, machine-harvest well, store well, commercially can well or commercially freeze well.

Seed companies such as Harris, Stokes, Gurney, Farmer, Northrup King and Vermont Bean and Seed not only sell these seeds, but most use extravagant language to explain why. This variety is disease-tolerant and does well even in July.

Sugar Snap (70 days). These are eaten pods and all, even when fat with seeds. The Sugar Snap is not yet five years old.

Chinese peas, sometimes called snow peas, edible podded peas, or gray peas. These, too, are eaten pods and all, but only when the seeds have just begun to form. We always have two varieties: **Mammoth Melting Sugar** (68 days) from Joseph Harris Seeds has climbing vines that are 4½ feet long and pods that are 4½ inches long. Pods of the spreading **Ho Lohn Dow** (60 days) from Stokes are as large as those of Mammoth Melting Sugar. Every three or four years we will also plant **Little Sweetie** (60 days), also from Stokes. These pods are only two inches long, about the size of the frozen Chinese peas from Taiwan found among supermarket frozen foods. The bush peas Ho Lohn Dow and Little Sweetie need no staking or trellises.

5. *Turnip and mustard greens.* Those who like greens at their best should plant turnips for their leaves rather than for their roots. I recommend one of the mustards with crinkly leaves because they are more pungent or "mustardy" than their smooth cousins. So I can harvest both at the same time, I plant **Southern Giant Curled Mustard** (50 days) and one week later the **Seven Top Turnip** (45 days). For cooking or freezing the two should be mixed equally.

6. *Collards.* Collards are at the top of the list of favorites. They're especially good cooked with bacon bits or grease. And collards get along fine in Minnesota's weather. Fresh for the table — or blanched, chopped and frozen — let them get touched with frost, even a freeze, before you harvest them. There are two varieties, **Georgia** and **Vates.** Either is good, but Vates may be a little sweeter.

7. *Kale.* Kale is a first cousin to collards. Try **Vates,** which, like Vates collards, was developed at the Virginia Truck Experimental Station (VATES). Kale has been called a Yankee collard; I've never seen kale in gardens or on menus in the South.

8. *Spinach.* For some time I have planted only two varieties of spinach, both from Stokes. **Cold Resistant Savoy** (45 days) is planted in both October and March for springtime harvest, and in August for late fall harvest. We freeze just about all our spinach for year-round use, but all green salads will have spinach leaves if fresh plants are available. The other variety is **Melody** (43 days), which has thick and plain leaves that are tolerant to most ills of spinach. Spinach is just about our favorite vegetable, so we use a lot of seeds.

Grandma always half filled the bird baths with fresh water when the river and the streams were frozen and there was no snow for the birds to eat. They would drink it all up before it froze. My robin won't take his morning bath unless the sun is shining and his bath is filled with warmed water. I think his wintering in Florida has made him a softie.

Chapter 3/Stagger your plantings

My Florida daughter continues to tell about her father's spinach. Her story is that once upon a spring visit she came downstairs in the morning just in time to open the front door, help her father spread a plastic sheet in front of the television set and watch him dump a Garden Way cart full of spinach. "Today we will freeze the spinach," she quotes her father as saying.

And the day was well spent. When it came time for a candlelight dinner in a clean living room that evening, 60-odd packages of spinach were in one of the two 30-cubic-foot freezers in the garage.

My daughter always tells a good story. If she had arrived from her Clearwater home one autumn, she would have had an even better story. For then we "did" the corn: 44 packages for the blancher and then for the freezer, plus 46 mason jars for the canner and then for the shelves, and, finally, nine pounds for the blancher and then for the dryer and then into an assortment of used glass jars with tops.

That sounds like a lot of corn for two people, but there is both good insurance and joy in such a large amount. It's insurance in case the next crop turns out badly.

Most gardeners don't want all their bush beans, or cabbages or tomatoes to be ready for the table at the same time. They'd surely get tired of wax beans twice a day. This predicament may be avoided in two ways:

• Use varieties that mature at different times: Cabbages, corn and tomatoes are available in early or late varieties, and even if planted at the same time will ripen at different times.

• If seeds of only one variety are to be planted, they need not be planted on the same day. Plant just part of a row every fortnight, and vegetables like carrots and beets and Chinese cabbage will reach the table as needed over a longer period of time.

We have now divided gardeners into two groups.

The first includes those who "eat from the garden" and glory in the freshness of what they eat.

The second is made up of those who "eat from the freezer" (and from the pressure canner and from the dryer with its circulating hot air). They glory all year in the cheapness of living. Probably most who eat from the garden preserve some food, just as those who eat from the freezer also eat some fresh vegetables from their gardens.

Now let's make another division, but this one in plants, not in gardeners. The vegetables we grow are either planted each year, the annuals, or they are planted only once and from then on spring from the ground in the same place year after year, the perennials.

If for no other reason than the differences in cultivating, annuals and perennials ought not to be planted in the same row or bed.

Only a few of our garden vegetables are perennials. Among them, rhubarb and asparagus are the best liked. But good gardeners who are good cooks plant sage, mint, parsley, horseradish, garlic, New Zealand spinach, chives and Egyptian onions.

Most gardeners have separate rows or beds for the asparagus, rhubarb and mint. They may plant garlic and onions and chives together. They may have a separate place for all the other herbs, which, except for horseradish, may grow together.

Horseradish is in a class by itself. This perennial, a spreader, should be planted only if a place can be found for it far, far, far away from everything else and if one does not mind grubbing out the little horseradishes that will appear and appear and appear over a wide area year after year after year.

But the horseradish plant is pretty enough to be admired as an ornamental, and horseradish is good to eat, as well as being useful if one needs to open the nasal passages. However, let's plant no more than one horseradish.

Those Egyptian onions are the priceless ones. We eat their white stems and bulbs that are underground, all of their green tops and the bulbils that grow on top of the green tops. Gardeners and frequent visitors never cease to enjoy watching the cluster of bulbils grow fat and heavy and fall to the ground, take root and grow big enough to produce bulbils that in time will get fat and fall to the ground, and on and on generation after generation.

With confidence, we can serve our Gibsons with slightly-sprouted bulbils instead of the anemic-looking pearl onions that are generally used.

And in the spring, when the stalks of the Egyptian onion are small and slender, they can be cut into one-inch lengths, and lightly cooked. Laced with bacon fat, Bacos (an imitation bacon product), thick cream, salt and pepper and well-covered with a thick sherry. Then we will have produced a dish that the old fashioned Southerner (with a capital S) will recognize as Sherried Southern Spring Onions. Wonderful, even as a dessert.

We should never forget that, once planted, the perennials can't readily be moved about. We would be wise to pick with great care the spots we want them to use in future years.

Chapter 4/Space for the garden

The lady said that she wanted a garden, but had no space for one. Her question was a good one. I assured her that she could still have a garden and that I would tell her how and where.

First of all, the entire yard should be re-examined. A garden does not have to be in just one certain place. Garden patches may be scattered here and there. Each should be reasonably level and fairly well drained, with lots of sun and with no roots from nearby trees.

If the soil is too sandy or too full of clay or just the kind that won't "grow plants," don't worry too much. These conditions can be changed. Your county agricultural extension agent will help you get your soil analyzed and will tell you what you should do about it. He will have the ideas and you will furnish the muscle power. And vegetables will grow.

Garden space may be borrowed from a friendly neighbor in return for a share of the products. If the lender is a watcher and you are a worker, both will enjoy the garden.

But if your neighbors are not friendly or have no space, just keep searching.

Visit the factory or the warehouse not too far away. The manager there may like the idea of turning over space to his neighbors for their gardens. Both he and they will gain.

The search for space could easily lead to the door of the place where you work. If approached by you and your fellow workers, the firm might donate garden spaces and thank you for the idea.

Enthusiasm is contagious. A locked shed for tools, seeds and fertilizers may appear, followed by electric power for seldom-used tools and frequently-used coffee pots; water and garden hose; indeed, an eight-horsepower rototiller with rear tines.

But why stop with these? Upon invitation, the agent in the county agricultural extension service or the principal of the nearest vocational school might arrange for "show-me" demonstrations and for question-and-answer sessions. If these are held on late Saturday afternoons, beer kegs and pop bottles and potluck suppers for the gardeners and their families might be organized.

And what about an FM radio with a loudspeaker? Community gardeners like to listen to music as much as gardeners who work alone in their own gardens.

The search for space may lead to the offices of the mayor and the school superintendent. A good many community gardens have been started as a result of such visits.

Tell the superintendent that one year 80,000 children in Cleveland's schools grew about a million dollars worth of garden produce on 350 acres of school land. The superintendent may quickly agree that the harvest was the least important product of the project. He may also agree that fairly orderly gardens kept by students may be prettier than manicured lawns and shrubbery.

Children may come to enjoy summer more when they no longer search for something to do. The garden "course" is never crowded. The students won't have to wait for a court or a putting green. The exercise is good, the young gardeners are waiting and willing to become friends, and the produce from the garden, especially if brought home without payment, makes the

Soon after celluloid was discovered, Uncle Jerry wanted to buy a celluloid collar that "did not have to be washed, just wiped off with a damp cloth". Grandma, who loved fine linens, said that if Uncle brought one into the house, she would put it in the stove. Uncle did and Grandma did and the collar promptly exploded. The stove lid hit the kitchen ceiling, the stovepipe was blown out of the chimney and soot was everywhere. Grandma was in a nervous "dither" for hours. The rascal, Uncle Jerry, chuckled for several days but never when Grandma was near.

young gardener a proud and admired participant in the life of the family.

Consider, too, the advantages of meeting with the mayor and the superintendent at the same time. If they work together, the city they represent may become not just a candidate for garden funds, but for international recognition as well.

But suppose all quests for land fail. You can still have a garden.

A young navy officer, Lt. Cdr. William L. Nunn if you must know the name, living in an apartment near a naval station during World War II, enjoyed a garden about 45 feet long and 18 inches wide. Strollers frequently came to ask questions and admire the plants he cultivated with only forks and spoons as tools, as he leaned over to work the soil in his garden of self-made window boxes.

Sister Nola filled wooden tubs with soil, lugged them to the roof of St. Mary's Hospital and grew tomatoes, using water that also had to be carried to the roof. This became her much-admired garden, continued after her departure by other sisters who shared her love for things that grow.

Perhaps you can put tubs, jars or boxes with soil and plants on your porch, at your gate or on the edge of your driveway.

Gardens may be productive even in the darkest corner of a cobwebby basement. However, grow-lights must be kept on for about 16 hours each day, about six inches above the tops of the growing plants.

All seeds and plants need warmth and light. Most rooms are warm, and if you remove the curtains and shades, you will get the light that growing plants need. Containers of any sort, with holes in their bottoms for drainage, will do nicely for the seeds you plant.

So you can have a garden — you really can!

Chapter 5/Architecture of the garden

Tools, boxes and bags shouldn't be scattered about and left where last used. They should be out of sight and out of the weather.

So why not a tool house? Perhaps the simplest to build is an A-frame of 2-by-4s, full sheets of plywood and rolls of roofing. It must be a walk-in, neither a stoop-in or a crawl-in. It should have a stout door and a strong lock — and a floor.

Each garden day at my house begins with a trip to the barn. A key opens a room that once housed Wanda, a Jersey cow and, later, Scarlet, a half-Arabian mare. It is light and airy with shelves, racks and bins made for garden purposes and no leftovers from Wanda and Scarlet.

Inside are the garden tools and supplies. The things that will be needed for the day are loaded in the Garden Way cart for a trip to the torii that stands at the head of the garden.

That torii is of special interest to my visitors. Veterans of the Pacific theater in World War II, and others who have lived in Japan, quickly recognize it for what it was intended to resemble — the entrance to a Shinto temple and its grounds.

For four years, long before World War II, I worked in the Kyushu city of Oita and lived in

the village of Beppu, a hot-spring resort at the foot of the Inland Sea. My house, alone on a cliff overlooking the city and bay, was Japanese, and strolling in the yards of temples and shrines was a relaxing after-dinner pleasure.

So why not let memories help design a roofed torii with nails and hooks on which to hang garden tools and make them easily retrievable without stooping? I hang most of the tools under the slanting roof of the torii, removing and returning them during the day as they are used. I put seeds or fertilizer on a table a few feet away. The cart and the remaining items go with me to where work will begin. At the end of the garden day everything will be returned to its place in the former home of Wanda and Scarlet.

All gardens need a table to help keep things organized and help the gardener avoid stooping. Mine is eight by eight feet, made from two sheets of outdoor plywood. Occasionally it seems too small for all its uses.

Its legs rest on sheets of plywood which keep down weeds and provide space for trash containers. The table is for washing vegetables, mending things and for note-taking. Always on it are a couple of dozen capped jars with a stapler, small knives, marking pencils, aluminum and plastic plant labels, cans of mosquito repellent, rodent bombs, matches, scissors, machine oil, nails, tacks, rolls of tape and on and on.

On the table, too, is a weatherproof box of 5-by-8-inch cards on which are pasted paragraphs cut from seed catalogs that tell all about each vegetable in the garden. On the margins of many are notes on the progress of a particular variety of a particular vegetable — handy when seeds for next year's garden are selected. Also likely to be on the table are gloves, sweaters, Band-aids and an FM radio.

Most gardens do not have fences and gates. But more and more they are needed to protect the garden from animals, including humans, that ought to be kept outside. Picket and rail fences are more attractive, but should give way to wire fences and gates of greater height.

If deer are problems, as they are in my gar-

Grandma always scattered three-inch pieces of soft cord around the garden in early spring. These were for the birds to use in tying together the twigs of their nests. She knew that longer pieces were dangerous, however — the birds would get them twisted around their necks and hang themselves. She also had little puddles of mud for them to use in plastering their nests.

den, the only fence of reasonable cost and acceptable appearance is one of chicken wire, six feet high, tightly strung.

Skunks and raccoons are problems too. So the bottom edge of the high chicken-wire fence will be tied to a strip of chicken wire two feet wide that is laid flat on the outer side of the fence. Varmints inclined to tunnel under the fence will find it tough going.

What about birds in the garden? Friends or enemies? The former, of course, for with a little assistance, birds and the garden and gardener can live together in peace.

In the spring a pair of elderly mallards will reappear at the foot of the bird feeder. Once satisfied, they will go to the vegetable garden to find a stack of 13 bales of fresh straw arranged for a nest. Under the top bale a clutch of 12 eggs will be laid. While setting, there will be only the mildest interest in the noise of the rototiller and the comings and goings of people — but people have a lot of interest in the nest.

And then there are the robins that build nests side by side in the lower frame of the torii — a rare sight of great interest to all who pass. They, too, are apart of the architecture of the garden, which can be enhanced with birdhouses made from milk cartons, birdbaths from large can covers and bird feeders of grains and suet — and, if orioles are about — of half oranges or grapefruit swaying on thin sticks.

About this time Grandma saw to it that Uncle Jerry took down the purple-martin house and gave it a thorough housecleaning before the martins returned. The martins arrived here from their winter vacation in Brazil almost on the same date every spring.

These birds are considered the farmer's friends because they gang up and drive away predatory birds that are hunting a chicken dinner in the poultry yard. Don't paint the martin house if you expect them to occupy it this year.

3/Vegetables for you to grow

The basic crops

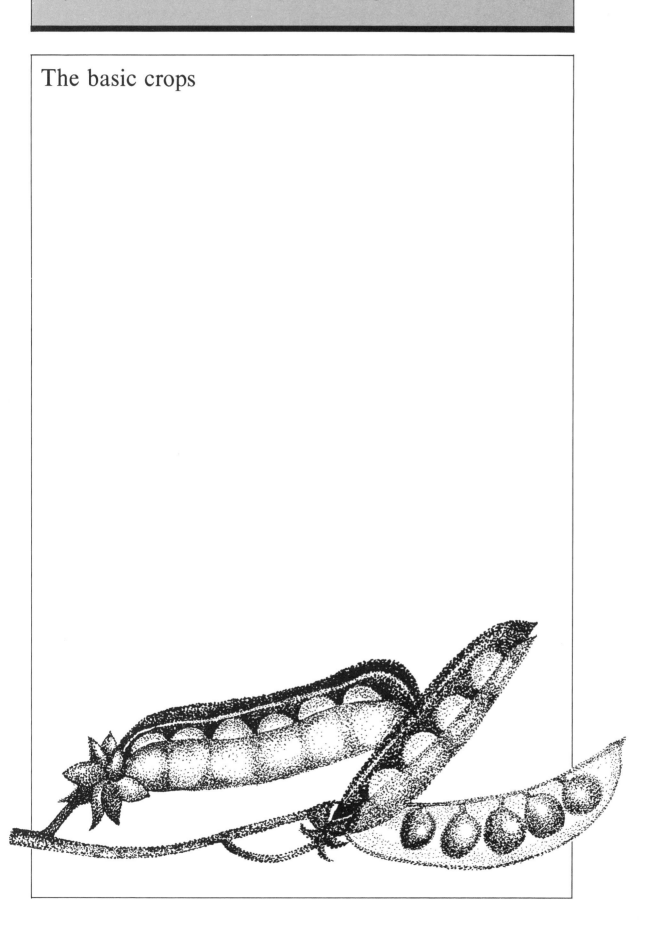

Peas

English peas and cousins such as **Novella** — and Chinese peas and their cousins like **Sugar Snap** — will be as disappointed as their growers if they are not planted early enough to germinate in the cool soil of spring.

But that does not apply to the peas called cowpeas or Crowder peas, most of which are known by the color of their eyes: black, purple or brown. Those peas are closer to beans than to peas and need the warm soil that beans require.

In early America, black-eyed peas were grown in corn patches, and peas and their vines and cornstalks and their ears were for animal food — though young ears and tender peas were avidly picked for fresh vegetables for the table.

Later in the year, to get dried peas for the table, pods were put in sacks that were beaten and bounced. When the peas were winnowed, chaff was blown away and the peas were put in clean flour sacks with a few slices of unchewed tobacco to keep weevils away. The sacks were then hung out of the reach of mice and rats. There the peas awaited washing and overnight soaking and then boiling with fresh hog jowl, salted fatback, smoked hocks or strips of rind.

Until a few decades ago in our country, English peas were grown in all home gardens and were one of the first vegetables to reach the dinner table in early spring.

Then, shelling fresh peas to get seeds to eat was a time-consuming and tiring matter, as it still is — but only for home gardeners who depend on their hands, as I do.

Early peas were so good to eat that shelling moved from kitchens, porches and living rooms to huge food factories. Most peas now come from cans and not from home gardens. But let's look back a bit.

Grandma's garden at this time of year was seldom injured by frost. She used to say, and Uncle Jerry agreed with her, "When the wind has been blowing strongly all day from the north, and then drops to calm just as the sun sets and the thermometer is 35 to 40, watch out for a frost. If you have some delicate flowers and new transplants in your garden, give them some protection."

I have pleasant memories of my mother in a starched apron shelling peas while sitting in a rocking chair on the shaded porch near her ferns, sometimes visiting with a friend who, on occasion, shared the shelling.

Gardeners in those years wanted their peas to be one of the varieties that were shriveled when shelled, for those were sweeter. They were the "variable-seeded" peas in catalogs. Vines were shorter in length and in growing season. They were susceptible to rot of one kind or another. And they couldn't be planted quite as early as could the other peas. They were just good to eat.

The "other" peas at that time were the round, even, smooth-seeded peas. They could be planted earlier. They were more resistant to disease. But taste? Such peas were not often planted in home gardens, and when they were it was chiefly to have garden peas earlier while waiting for the better-tasting wrinkled ones.

Then came the big farm and food-factory machines to serve growers and canners. Which peas won? Nowadays peas are sown by machine and, since World War II, frozen by machine. And the search has been for those varieties that can best withstand the rigors of the machine, the cans and the frozen packages. Sellers of seeds for home gardeners ought to offer wrinkled peas. Perhaps they think that the word *wrinkled* repels, while the words *smooth* and *round* attract. Perhaps they believe that only the peas that look like those from cans are the ones we want.

The fact is that I have found only one seller, the Vermont Bean Seed Co., that lists a variety, **Perfection Dark Green** (70 days), described as "...dark green wrinkled, and each 4-inch pod produces eight to nine honey-sweet peas."

It's nice to know that there is one advertised pea that shows its wrinkles with pride — a pea, I'm sure, that, like **Lincoln** (67 days), has not been changed by those seeking a pea for our machine age.

It was the late Ruth Stout who found and popularized the Lincoln, once called the **Homestead,** as it still is in western Canada. Ruth was a devoted organic gardener and writer. Last year, at 96, she was still working in her garden. (Her brother, Rex, was the writer who gave us detective Nero Wolfe.)

The Lincoln is the least monkeyed with by scientists in their search of new varieties to meet new needs. Slowly this pea caught on. Now it is sold by Stokes, Harris, Farmer, Gurney, Vermont Bean Seed and others and is offered in glowing terms: wonderful, best tasting, exceptional quality — to which I'll add the greatest in taste, garden habits and disposition.

Lincoln should be given low trellises on which to climb. Seeds may be planted on each side, and when plants are about six inches high they should be leaned toward the trellises and soil pushed against them. They will climb.

A variety called **Alderman** (70 days), also called **Tall Telephone,** has vines that come close to reaching the top of a 4-foot trellis. A variety called **Improved Thomas Laxton** (55 days) can get along with a trellis 1½ feet high. A second crop of peas can be ready for harvest just before the autumn freeze if planted in late July, for cool soil will then be in the garden again.

A new garden pea may turn out to be more exciting, but in different ways, than was the Sugar Snap. In America, this one goes by the name of Novella (57 days). The word *novella* is for students of literature. Novella is a short novel or tale of the type developed by Giovanni Boccaccio in the 14th century, characterized by epigrammatic terseness, devoid of embellishments. The name of Boccaccio's book is Decameron. It is a naughty one. Why call a garden pea Novella?

I talked to Chuck Green of the Rogers Seed Co. in Idaho Falls, Idaho, where this new pea was discovered, developed and named. There just had to be a student of literature at the seed company — someone who knew the meaning of novella.

"Probably so," laughed Chuck "let me just say that we liked the appropriateness of the name to the new pea plant so much that we tried to register it in Europe. But we failed, so we did the best we could. In Europe, Novella is sold as **Bikini!**"

Plant Novella seeds and grow naked plants that are without, or almost without, leaves. Instead of many leaves, these plants have many tendrils. The tendrils clasp together and cause the vines to grow upright without a trellis for support. Pods are not lost in the bush: they are in pairs, sticking out from the tip of each vine.

After shelling, peas are easily blanched, chilled and frozen. If boiling bags are to be used rather than freezer boxes, put a small amount of a sauce of melted butter or margarine, sliced mushrooms, with a little salt and pepper, and monosodium glutamate (if you use it), in each package before sealing.

Months later the frozen bags can be tossed into a pot of boiling water just before serving. And the cook can go to the head of the class.

But wait. Isn't there some sort of machine that home gardeners can use to shell peas? Yes indeed.

One, with a small motor, will do three bushels of peas per hour. It will also make French beans out of big pods. It's called Mr. Pea Sheller and sells for $159.

Then there is Magic Fingers, which will use the power of any mixer or like machine and will do two bushels an hour. It costs $18.50 if you get one that also makes French beans, $11.50 if it only shells peas.

Finally there is the Clamp-on Metal Sheller, which operates on the power of your wrist. With the other hand you feed in the peas one by one. The sheller clamps on the side or corner of a table. It costs $17.95.

The machines can be bought from Garden Way (Charlotte, Vt. 05445).

Another quite different pea to consider is the black-eyed pea, which climbs, though there is a bush variety. It ought to be more appreciated above the Mason-Dixon Line. Down south it is known as the cornfield pea. Planted together, peas and field corn assist each other. Peas give nitrogen to the corn, and the corn provides the poles on which peas can climb, or at least lean.

There are two kinds of black-eyed peas. **California Blackeye** grows on a bush or dwarf plant and has a large, creamy pea. It sometimes appears in Minnesota supermarkets shelled and in plastic bags.

It will do, but only if fresh or dried **Magnolia Blackeyed** peas—even the dried ones canned by

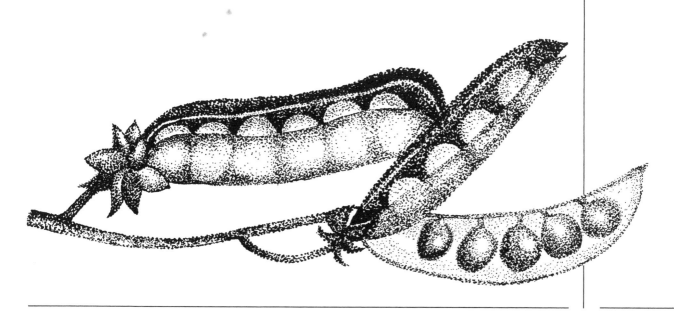

the Stokes Canning Co.—are unavailable. Magnolia Blackeyed peas are smaller and better for eating fresh, frozen or dried.

Pole blackeyed peas must be given supports for climbing or they'll climb on themselves and create a jungle. We shell our peas when they are green, but others let the pods dry on trellises, when peas and pods can be separated with ease.

Dried shelled peas are easy to store, but only after they have been heated for 30 minutes at 140 to 150 degrees F. in the oven. A a glass jar with a tight lid is needed. The fresh ones should be blanched and kept in the freezer.

I never miss the chance to urge gardeners who plant any legume, such as garden or field peas, not to pull spent plants by the roots. Instead cut the vines at ground level and leave behind the valuable nodules of nitrogen. They enrich the soil—thank-you gifts from the harvested legumes.

Beans

Most garden beans come in both bush and pole varieties, so what should your choice be? There are lots of reasons for either choice.

The late gardener/TV teacher/writer James Underwood Crockett urged his listeners and readers to plant only the bush varieties — they were simpler to grow, he said.

My father's garden had only pole beans that climbed on trellises. He thought pole beans tasted better and produced longer. Some kinds of beans in my own garden are only bush, others are only pole, and some are both pole and bush.

The choice involves more than just the taste you prefer or the amount of time and energy you must spend arranging the pole-like supports climbers need.

You must consider the space in your garden, too. Plants that grow straight up are ideal for the small garden. They save space because rows don't have to be more than three or four inches from each side of a fence that might support the beans.

Now and then a gardener reports success in planting a climbing bean seed next to a high stalk of garden corn, but I suspect that neither the bean vine nor the cornstalk is happy with this arrangement.

Consider, too, how hungry the family may be for fresh garden beans after a long winter of store-bought ones. Bush beans will deliver much sooner than will pole beans.

A fellow planter of pole beans likes to remind me that folks today know only the taste of bush beans. Most, perhaps all, canned and frozen beans are the bush variety.

If your appetite is jaded, maybe you'd like to grow your own pole beans. My friend says home gardens and roadside stands are about the only places where you can get them any more.

But places where you can pick your own fruits and vegetables are becoming more numerous. Some roadside farmer or gardener is sure to be trying pole beans of different varieties: green, wax, purple, Italian, both speckled and white Limas, and even ornamentals. You might ask the grower if he has pole beans you can pick. But they will cost more than the bush ones.

Southerners have yet to agree that the speckled butter bean is superior to the white butter bean. Both will grow in Minnesota, but we call them Lima beans.

Most seed companies offer edible soybeans. If kept on the plant to dry, the beans are easily shelled, but then they must be used either as dry beans are used or turned into bean sprouts. If you want beans earlier, pods should be picked and dipped into boiling water to make shelling easier. A pair of scissors can be used to open the pods to get the beans.

A delightful member of the soybean family is the small red-brown **Azuki** bean that, too, is best cooked as a dry bean. It comes from Hokkaido, Japan's northernmost big island. Azuki beans may be bought at the International House of Foods on Nicollet Island in Minneapolis.

There, too, one can buy mung beans, which grow well in Minnesota. We know these as bean sprouts. Like other soybeans, they may replace beef in diets and can be fixed many ways.

What about varieties?

For many years I could point with great pride to the **Kentucky Wonder Green** pole beans (once called the **Homestead** bean and later the **Old Homestead** bean), in my Champlin garden — one of only three varieties of vegetables that were favorites in the gardens of at least three generations of Nunns.

The late George Luxton, popular garden writer for the Minneapolis Tribune, one day told me about the newer **Blue Lake** pole beans (55 days).

I switched, but I'm pleased that the old and steady Kentucky Wonder Green pole beans (58 days) are still offered in just about all seed catalogs — Stokes, Gurney, Park, Jung, Twilley, Farmer, Herbst, Burpee, The Vermont Bean Seed Company, and perhaps others too — and in both Northrup King and Burpee racks.

Kentucky Wonder Green is still the most popular pole green bean.

Blue Lake pole and Blue Lake bush beans are neither tolerant nor resistant, but we put the Blue Lake pole beans atop all others for taste. Its vines grow in our garden year after year. We try to keep people and animals from touching any leaf, pod or stem when the slightest bit of water or dampness is about because this spreads the dreaded mosaic disease.

We freeze most of the Blue Lake pole beans. We pick pods of them when they are just long enough to fit whole into a pint freezer box.

Blue Lake beans, though wonderful to eat, don't tolerate any of the ills of beans. So the second green bean in my garden is the **Provider** (50 days), a bush variety tolerant to mildew and mosaic. And, of special importance, it thrives in weather that's too hot, too cold or too wet.

I plant the Blue Lake pole and the Provider bush at the same time. Providers will be ready for harvest first, and we allow their pods to grow to full size. A few go on the table. The rest are snapped, packed in jars and canned.

The larger ones, with vinegar, dill and onions, can be made into bean pickles. If by chance some pods get too big for pickles, but not too big and tough for eating, they can be sliced lengthwise like French beans — still good to eat and not wasted. If there are many of these, a French Bean Slicer may be bought from the Garden Way catalog (Charlotte, Vt. 05445).

Green beans are our favorite vegetable — indeed the first or second favorite of most Americans. The Blue Lake beans I plant are from the Geo. W. Park Seed Co. The Providers are from Stokes seeds.

First cousins to the green snap beans are yellow snap beans. Until recent years, my garden produced a pole yellow wax bean for freezing — **Kentucky Wonder Wax** (61 days) — and a bush yellow wax bean for canning — **Sungold** (56 days). Seeds for both were from Stokes.

Now our garden has only the bush Sungold.

That's because more space on the trellises was needed for cucumbers, fast becoming one of our favorite baked vegetables. Then, too, wax beans seem to be cooked and eaten more from duty than desire at our house these days.

We grow, can and freeze the Sungolds. The bean is tolerant to mosaic, and pods are round and straight. The younger the pods when harvested, the better they taste. If you grow both the yellow Sungold and the green Provider, consider mixing them for canning, freezing or serving. The combination looks attractive and the taste of the wax ones is improved when the beans are mixed.

We grow two other snap beans: the Italian and the Purple. The Italian variety is **Green Ruler** (51 days) from Joseph Harris. Italian bean pods grow six inches long and a half inch wide. When cooked, fresh or frozen or canned, with Roma tomatoes, sweet pepper strips, Parmesan cheese and a sprinkling of oregano, we have a perfect meal made better with spaghetti and cheap Chianti.

The other snap bean is **Royal Burgundy** (51 days). Only the pods of these green plants are purple. They are excellent for eating and canning, and, I think, of a somewhat firmer texture than other beans. Our purple bush bean is a good dry-weather plant and its foliage provides ample cover for the pods, which will appear until autumn frosts.

With a needle and thread make long strings of Royal Burgundies and hang them to dry. When dry, they can then be stored in any tight jar. Months later, soak them in water, cook and eat.

You will be eating "leather britches" just as our great grandparents did. This is a good way to teach today's children something about the history of our country. Any green or yellow bean can be used if you don't have purple ones.

Italian and Purple beans come in climbing varieties. Once we planted climbers but now we think the bush varieties are about as good, and they, too, will produce up to frost time.

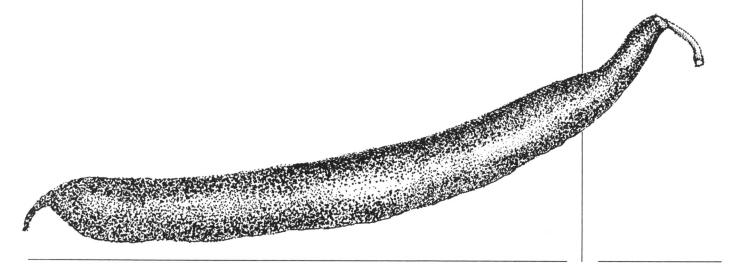

The last of the beans on my garden list are white Limas — pole and bush. **King of the Garden** (68 days) is fat and big. Its vines love to climb and are quite capable of moving in midair to trellises up to three feet away. We also plant **Fordhook 242** bush white Limas. Both are from Harris.

Fordhook produces the large white Lima beans that will be ready three weeks before the pole Limas. At our house, first pickings are used fresh or frozen; later ones are left to dry on the plants and reappear some cold Sunday evening in a single-dish supper as Lima Bean-Ripe Olive Casserole.

Some years we have grown the pole **Large Speckled Christmas** which provides big, flat beans with deep crimson blotches. Though not often planted in northern gardens, the speckled Lima bean does well here.

Among beans I grow every year is the **Fava,** also called the **English Broad** and sometimes the "Horse Bean." For centuries, until those from South America arrived, it was the only bean in Europe. It has the thickest round pods and seeds of any bean. The bush is slender, not leafy. Use shelled beans either fresh or frozen or, better, give them to garden guests.

And then there are the edible soybeans — one, **Frickley V.,** was developed in Sweden; the other, **Azuki,** from northern Japan. If it's too difficult to shell when dry, even with scissors and boiling water, let the pods dry on the vine. At our house these go into Bill's Thick Soup.

Speckled Lima beans are rarely seen in northern gardens or in the bins of dried beans and peas in northern supermarkets, which is a pity.

There is a bush speckled Lima bean called **Jackson Winter** (65 days) and a pole speckled Lima bean called **Large Speckled Christmas Bean** (88 days). There is a close speckled-bean relative that is mistakenly called **Dixie Butterpea Speckled** (75 days), a bush variety that we have enjoyed eating, but not shelling, in past years.

Corn

Sweet corn will grow in almost every home garden — if permitted by raccoons, skunks, woodchucks and squirrels (which like the whole ears) and crows, grackles and starlings (which like only the kernels).

The careful cook/gardener will make sure sweet corn is served when picked less than an hour (15 minutes would be better) before it reaches the dinner table. Once there, corn-on-the-cob needs only melted butter and real or artificial salt to bring smiles of delight.

Older gardeners can remember when kernels from the same sack were planted in the kitchen garden, just to be near the house for roasting and boiling ears, and in the distant fields to feed farm animals. Since then, research has changed just about every aspect of life, including sweet corn.

Sweet-corn varieties are almost without number, and that makes choices difficult. Stokes offered 49 varieties in its 1981 catalog. Gurney Seed and Nursery had corn offerings scattered over five of its 1981 pages.

Some cornstalks grow tall, others short. Ears may be slender or fat, long or stubby. Kernels may be white or of different shades of yellow, black, purple, red or mixed in every combination. Some varieties are early-bearing, others late-bearing, and many are in between. Kernels may be in orderly rows on the cobs or in a complete jumble.

The gardener with little space must suppress the temptation to plant mixed varieties and, even worse, to include popcorn for winter snacks and Indian corn for door decorations. Otherwise the harvested ears may be identified merely as corn, so illegitimate as to defy identification of parentage.

Each variety should be planted away from others in side-by-side rows of short length because pollination of corn in long single rows is chancy. Corn patch is a term of real meaning.

The taste? Varieties are as different as people. Gardeners have preferences and prejudices and can argue in defense of their favorites or in hope of gaining converts. Corn is the only vegetable that inspires such behavior, most gardeners will agree.

I'll tell you which varieties I plant, but will make no recommendations, for I want no con-

When wind and rain storms laid the sweet corn flat, Grandma would shout the clarion call. Everybody, headed by her, would rush into the fields, raise the fallen corn and firm the earth around the roots with their feet. Next day, the corn was as good as ever. Whenever Grandma said "come", everybody "came".

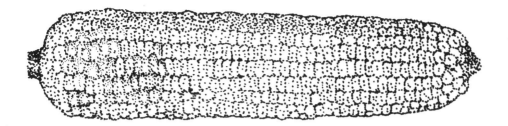

troversy with fellow gardeners who have their favorites.

Also, I think any ear of corn in its milky stage is wonderful. And I'll tolerate watery and doughy ears, for I like corn — on the cob if fresh, in kernels if frozen, canned or dried, alone or in soup, or in stew or pudding.

I buy my seed corn from the Hennepin Cooperative Seed Exchange in Golden Valley, Minn. I get Northrup King's **Sugar Loaf** (83 days), **Sugar King** (77 days) and **Earliking** (66 days). I buy them by the pound, in paper bags. Because I plant corn before the middle of June in a northern garden, I buy only seeds that have been treated with captan, a mild fungicide.

Gardeners should know that all corn seeds from Joseph Harris Seeds have been treated with captan, that seeds from Johnny's Selected Seeds of Organic Seed and Crop Research and from the Burpee Company have had no chemical contacts, that Stokes offers some corn varieties marked "UT" (untreated) especially for organic gardeners, but that all other seeds have been dusted with captan. Other seed suppliers should be asked if their products are treated.

If you want prime-tasting sweet corn for the dinner table most of the summer, you may plant early, midseason and late varieties at the same time. A better way is to plant two or three feet of each side-by-side row each fortnight and harvest the corn when it's ready.

When is ready? Harvest sweet corn when the kernels are in the milky stage; that's just after the water stage and just before the dough stage. It's a pity that the tips of so many ears in markets and in home gardens have been pulled back and so many kernels have been gouged by fingernails to be sure the milky stage is present.

Gardeners would do better to watch the color and texture of the silks and firmly feel the ears when the silks are brown and soon to turn almost black. Soon gardeners become experts with each of their varieties.

Plant kernels just after the last killing frost has passed — one inch deep if planted early and two inches deep if planted later. I plant kernels of one variety not more than three inches apart (to be thinned later) in four rows that are only six inches apart. Then I skip a two-foot strip to make an aisle for weeding while sitting. Then comes the first of the next four rows.

Remember: Even one dropped and uncovered kernel invites birds to find and scratch up the rest.

Most northern gardeners plant sweet corn the last two weeks in June. Corn borers do less damage if seed is not planted earlier. If seeds are planted earlier, they should be treated with captan and diazinon, an insecticide, as aids against rot and maggots.

Pests and diseases may appear after the corn is planted. Sevin, which is carbaryl, sprinkled or sprayed as soon as "silks" appear, will control ear worms. A squirt of mineral oil into the silks will do as well. Black puffy balls of smut should be cut off and burned, or they will burst and spread spores.

Scatter a band of fertilizer (as strong as is recommended by a soil test) — one pound for 20 feet of row — when the plants are two or three inches high and again when they are about a foot high. Plants may be mulched for better weed control. Otherwise weeds should be

---

One morning Uncle Jerry said, "Do you know you can hear corn growing at night?" Grandfather replied, "What nonsense! Are you loony?" Jerry quickly replied, "I'll bet you a dollar I am right. We will go to the corn field if the night is not cold or windy." Grandmother said, "I'm not a betting man, but I'll take the bet just to teach you a lesson."

That night with Grandma they stood facing the corn field, and sure enough, from it came a faint rising and falling, sizzling sound with some crackling.

At length, Grandfather said, "Jerry, you win. Here is your dollar. Where have I been all these years?"

Then Grandmother proudly exlaimed, "Jerry, where did you hear of it?"

Jerry said, "I read about it, and I have been here several nights to listen. When it is windy or cold you can't hear it. I figured such information was valuable, and it was. It just got me a dollar."

Grandfather snorted and Grandma chuckled.

pulled or scraped away — corn roots are close to the surface.

A question: Should gardeners pull and destroy the corn suckers? Once it was thought yes, but now it is thought best not to; they help support the stalks.

Another question: Can gardeners wait to remove stalks until late fall and clear the area completely all at once? They can, but it's better for the compost heap if stalks and their suckers are removed as ears are harvested. Chopped when green, or almost so, stalks and suckers make better compost. For this I use a hatchet and a block of wood; I don't have a grinder/shredder machine.

Raising corn for eating makes demands on the gardener. Remember these tips:

Pollination is enhanced if rows are short and bunched together. Be careful not to damage roots: When weeding, use only hoes that just scrape the ground. Provide water when the plants show any wilt and as the tassels appear and develop.

If you're a really dedicated gardener, you may carefully put two or three drops of a vegetable oil on the silks of each ear as it appears.

With great pride you can explain to guests why you did this when you serve them ears without a sign of insect or other blemish.

Corn-on-the-cob is as American as hamburgers. And eating corn with two hands is an approved table manner, even if finger bowls and extra napkins become necessary.

The old-fashioned corn roast for a host of eaters is giving way to something better and simpler. The corn is shucked and the silks removed, but never washed. All are taken, by appointment, to the nearest creamery to be cooked in boiling water and then packed in large metal milk containers.

Back at the party, the ears, too hot to be handled without gloves, are dipped in hot melted butter, sprinkled with salt and eaten — and eat-

en — and eaten. Slowly the mound of cobs grows as relaxed guests eat corn and drink a barrel or two of malt beer. There is no dessert!

With care, corn kernels, not corn-on-the-cob, may be frozen, canned or dried. If corn is mixed with Lima beans and pepper strips to make succotash, we enjoy a dish taught to our forefathers by the Narragansett Indians, one of the Algonquin tribes.

If you mix these three vegetables with chopped tomatoes and chicken, pork and beef (in colonial America, squirrels were used) and any other vegetables that are about, and if enough hot pepper is added, you'll have Southern Brunswick stew.

All of this is a far cry indeed from the time and customs when the colonists learned from the Indians how to plant corn.

The first Europeans to eat corn were those who manned the Nina, the Pinta and the Santa Maria. The place is now called San Salvador; the donors were American Indians. Later, Indians in Jamestown, Va., after 1607 and in Plymouth, Mass., after 1620 taught the first colonists from England to dig holes, bury fish and plant kernels of corn.

Let's consider the foods, like corn, that once grew only in the gardens of American Indians. Some of those gardens, far from San Salvador, Jamestown and Plymouth, would be the envy of most of us: terraces to level the ground, canals to bring water for irrigation, stone houses and clay pots for storage of crops. Discoveries of such things that bring awe and respect are still being made in the dense jungles of South and Central America.

A quick list of what was grown there centuries ago would include, in addition to corn, potatoes, strawberries, squash, sunflowers, peanuts, sweet and hot peppers, pumpkins, tomatoes, sweet potatoes, Lima and snap beans — even Jerusalem artichokes, which got misnamed as the new plants were moved about in Europe. In terms of what the home gardener now grows and what's important in feeding the modern world, the list is impressive.

From Cuba in 1492, Christopher Columbus described a flour made from a grain the Indians called maize. Soon, other explorers were to observe how widely used it was in both North and South America for grain, for sugar and for a kind of beer.

Times and customs have changed, but to the home gardener it's all for the best. Gardener James Underwood Crockett put it this way: ". . . Sweet corn is the supreme home-grown vegetable simply because growing it yourself is the only way to get corn fresh enough to have full flavor."

Grandma said, "The dark of the moon has nothing to do with planting seeds, just use common sense." But I noticed that when Uncle Jerry complained about his corns hurting, she would never plant corn. She said that a cold and rainy spell always followed, which was bad for freshly seeded corn.

Tomatoes

The tomato once was thought to be poisonous and was grown only for its beauty. Today it is the pride of almost every home gardener.

Some tomatoes are red, some yellow and some pink. Some are round and some are pear-shaped. But no matter what their color or shape, tomatoes are objects of admiration and appetite.

Let's start with the old question of stakes: Are they necessary or not? Some, but not all, tomatoes in the garden should be tied to stakes.

It's the indeterminate tomatoes — the ones that stop growing and producing only when killed by frosts of late autumn — that must be tied. The words "beefeater" or "boy" in their names will identify some of them.

Tie the plants to four-foot stakes with thick cords or cloth strips as they grow. Remove each sucker as it appears in the crotch where a branch joins the stem. It's better to bend the sucker and snap it off than to use a knife.

Plants that are staked and pruned will produce larger and prettier, but fewer, tomatoes than those permitted to sprawl. But because they grow in the air and not on the ground, plants staked close together may produce more tomatoes than a like area of sprawling plants.

Determinate tomato plants are shorter and blockier. They stop producing when they have reached their growth. They need more space than staked plants. If possible, the entire area should be mulched with straw or leaves to prevent weeds and keep the fruit clean.

Tomatoes are not just to be eaten raw, mixed into salads, made into sandwiches, or combined with onions and peppers and leaves of parsley, basil or dill and "blenderized" to make a fresh tomato juice. Tomatoes from a summer garden are meant to be used each month of the year.

No vegetable is easier to store, and the rows of canned tomatoes can never be too long. We can never have too many tomato plants in our gardens.

With the simple, world-famous, Minnesota-made Foley food mill and a little muscle power, any cooked, skin-on, ripe tomato can be reduced to juice. Elaborate juicers that substitute electricity for muscle power have entered the market, but they are costly.

A pressure canner is not needed, but can be used, for canning tomatoes, whether they are whole, crushed or reduced to juice. When the skins are removed after a quick dip in boiling water and then a plunge into ice water, the raw tomatoes may be pushed into any pint or quart mason jar.

The capped jars are placed in a large metal pot with a bottom rack to prevent bouncing jars that might break, covered with two inches of water and boiled for 35 minutes for pints and

45 minutes for quarts.

Salt is used only for flavor. No water should ever be added, for tomatoes are canned in their own juices.

For reasons that escape me, tomato breeders have introduced an acid-free tomato that, like many things these days, has been featured and ballyhooed.

If these are to be canned in a boiling water bath, add a spoonful of vinegar to each jar. But then, of course, the tomatoes will no longer be acid-free.

Those who need the low-acid tomato for reasons of health, or just because they prefer it, should plant **Starshot, Golden Delight, Orange Queen** or **Caro Rich.**

There is disagreement and confusion about these varieties. I join those who hope they will just go away, except for the fact that low-acid red tomatoes make a better wine than others.

When selecting tomatoes, consider the small red and yellow, round and the pear-shaped ones

Grandma showed great bravery by eating tomatoes in an age when many people considered them deadly poisonous. Some people still called them "love apples". They were smaller than ours today and usually grown only for ornament. But Grandma knew they were not poisonous, and she would eat them calmly while her neighbor children stood around watching in horror.

that add zest to salads and appetizers. A few kept in the freezer make startling substitutes for the clear ice cubes generally used in bloody marys.

Grandmother used green tomatoes in many ways, and we should too. Sliced and fried, they make any breakfast or lunch memorable. Green tomatoes, and ripe ones, too, may be made into jams, relishes, conserves, chutneys and pickles (even dills). They add piquancy to green salads.

All tomatoes may be made even prettier if removed from the plants to spend their last two or three days under grow-lights.

Now then, what kinds of tomatoes should we plant? The questions are many.

Red, yellow, pink, creamy, white, green or golden ones? Tomatoes with a lot of meat and little liquid or with little meat and a lot of liquid?

Determinate tomatoes — those that are compact and stop growing when they reach their natural growth — or indeterminate ones that grow until killed by frost?

For canning, freezing or drying or only for raw use?

Big ones as round as baseballs or little ones the size of marbles? Those with natural acid that make canning safe or those that must have vinegar added to each jar?

Tomatoes with an inborn resistance to verticillium, fusarium wilts and nematodes (the ones with VFN in their names) or those that are friendly hosts to such diseases and pests?

Tomatoes are wonderful for those who like to make decisions. Here's the way I feel:

I plant to get green and red and yellow tomatoes. The green are the young ones that have not turned their final color. They are great when sliced and fried for breakfast or made into jam and pickles and relishes, especially when picked just before the first freeze in late autumn. But only those that are completely green

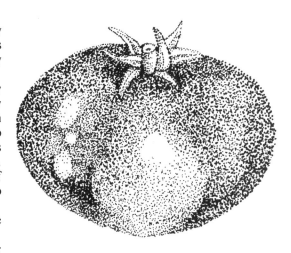

at first frost are used this way at our house.

Those with a touch or more of color are put under grow-lights until they turn their expected color. Gardeners without grow-lights can wrap them in newspapers, being careful to let no light enter the wrappings. In darkness as intense as the grow-lights are bright, the half-ripe tomatoes will ripen, too, if kept warm.

The yellow tomatoes in my garden are from two of the small fruiting varieties, **Yellow Pear** and **Yellow Plum.** They are planted beside two red varieties of the same size, **Small Fry** and **Red Pear.** These little tomatoes go well in salads. They are good to munch in the garden when you're thirsty. But more: These red and yellow ones are frozen as they come from the garden to be used, for months to come, as ice cubes in drinks.

Here are other red varieties likely to be in our garden:

Ultra Boy VFN, an indeterminate, is tied to five-foot stakes or trellises and pruned as it grows.

Ultra Girl VFN, an All-American winner, and **Wonder Boy VF** hybrid, are semideterminates that can be either staked or left to spread.

Ultra Girl has done well in our garden staked and not pruned. The fruit will be in the seven-to nine-ounce class. Gardeners with problems of nematodes or some ill-defined root illness should consider this variety. All hybrid seeds are expensive, but if extra seeds are kept in the package, stapled shut, and stored in a tight jar in a cool place, they can be saved for use in later years.

Ultra Boy VFN is a late hybrid (72 days) that may be staked and pruned or used inside or just outside tomato cages of wire and wood. Fruits may be well over a pound. This hybrid is resistant to wilts and blight and little things that crawl — not just resistant, but extraordinarily so and extra worthy of the VFN in its name. This one and **Roma VF** are the two best tomatoes in our garden.

In Grandma's day there were few remedies for tomato trouble.

Grandma had her own formula for tomato pests which sounded like a spice cake recipe. She mixed a cupful of baking soda and wood ashes, half a teaspoonful each of powdered cinnamon, cloves, ginger, mustard, sulphur and red and black pepper.

As I remember, all self-respecting pests beat a hasty retreat from the tomato patch, including Grandma's grandchildren.

Most gardener friends are surprised that more than half of our tomato plants are one of the determinate Romas because this variety is usually used commercially for tomato paste and ketchup — neither of which we make at our home.

Roma tomatoes can be planted close together — eight inches or so apart. Leaves are somewhat scant and stems crawl over each other without apparent damage to plants or fruits. A thick mulch will keep the tomatoes clean and off the soil, where microorganisms are apt to flourish.

Varieties in addition to those already mentioned are:

Veeroma VF (73 days), a better-yielding and crack-resistant Roma type, which is taking the place of Roma VF.

Sub Arctic Maxi (48 days). Canadian plant scientists have done wonders in decreasing the growing time that tomatoes need — this is their earliest, I think. As with the Veeroma VF, I grow only a few — perhaps in a flower bed outside the vegetable garden — because they are not tolerant and are very susceptible to early blight. I don't want them close by.

Gardeners who wish short-season plants should ask for the catalog of Alberta Nurseries and Seeds, Ltd., Bowden, Alberta, Canada, as well as the Stokes catalog.

Floramerica VFN (75 days). This is a determinate hybrid. Leafy and short, it is called the most tolerant to more tomato diseases than any other variety. Most gardeners will not stake this plant, but provide mulch to keep fruits clean and off the soil. In our garden Floramericas will be tied to one of the permanent trellises. Fruits may be big — 12 ounces or so.

Cutworms are one of the tomato's worst enemies. For generations they have been thwarted by a collar of plastic or strong paper pushed an inch into the ground around each seedling. Now chemicals can be bought at garden centers that, if carefully worked into the soil around each plant, will kill the cutworms. I still prefer homemade collars that can be sterilized and used each year.

The gardener who ties a string of cans above the tomato row or drives nails close to the plants and then escapes damage should simply be thankful the worms were elsewhere. The cans and nails had nothing to do with it.

Moles and shrews eat insects and cutworms, which is good, but unfortunately they eat both good and bad insects and earthworms, too. But let's leave them alone.

And here's a final tip — but for dog owners only: If dogs haven't yet learned to avoid skunks, the gardener should have a few quarts of good red tomato juice on hand. The veterinarian is sure to suggest that the dog be bathed in it.

For years Uncle Jerry blamed the squirrels for eating holes in the ripening tomatoes, but he could never catch them at it. He also was puzzled because the holes were so small. Then Grandma discovered that it was birds that did it, so she placed a few pans of water on boxes out of reach of cats, near her tomato plants, and saved the fruit from being punctured by birds. The birds drank the water instead of the tomato juice.

4/Their leaves are good to eat

Lettuce

Lettuce leaves provide a cushion of beauty on which salads, cold meats and cheeses rest. Too many of these leaves for too many years have gone back to the kitchens and their garbage disposals after the meats and cheeses have been eaten.

Lettuce is a food, and not merely decoration. It is not just for salads but ought to be on the table as a cooked vegetable for dinner, lunch, even breakfast.

Lettuce joins bean sprouts, parsley and green onions as a desirable addition to beaten eggs about to be scrambled and served with toast and coffee for breakfast. Interestingly, cookbooks call this "scrambled lettuce." Almost everyone likes wilted lettuce for lunch and dinner but few cook it. It's our favorite.

You start it when bacon is fried crisp and readily crumbles. Into the pan with the crumblings and hot juice go small doses of vinegar, sweetening and water and large amounts of lettuce leaves. Quick stirring will produce just the right degree of wilt, but with some crispness.

Any lettuce may be used for this and for most cooked lettuce dishes, but the pleasantly pungent taste of romaine lettuce is preferred.

Good cookbooks have recipes for braising, browning, boiling, frying, simmering, pureeing, stuffing and "souffleing" lettuce. Other ingredients used include chopped boiled eggs, onions or chives, apples, butter or margarine or cooking oil or bacon grease, lemon juice or vinegar, cheese or cheese spread, gravies, clear soup, beef marrow, cream, croutons, white sauce, ground meat, fried parsley, bread crumbs and fried bread.

One recipe is for "lettuce stumps." These are the lower sections of tall stems of lettuce that has bolted.

Bolting is a well-known word to gardeners.

When Grandma was a little girl, there was a real tomato vine with oval leaves that was used to cover small buildings up to 10 feet high, and unsightly objects. The fruit grew in grape-like clusters. It was not considered edible, but a few years later some brave souls discovered that it was not poisonous, and soon it was used extensively in home-made pickles and preserves.

A plant bolts to produce seeds — and gets fat and tough in the process — usually ready for the compost heap. But, in some cases, recipes for special dishes made with bolting plants are eagerly sought and prepared by gardener/cooks. The Larousse Gastronomique (American edition) includes one for lettuce stumps.

Cos (romaine) lettuce has especially big stumps after bolting. These are trimmed and cooked like asparagus. Just let a few of these popular plants bolt and be surprised at their tall and stout size. Cut and discard the outer rind and braise what's inside.

So we have the fun of using these exactly as asparagus is used, and learning something new about the unlimited capabilities of the food garden.

Lettuce is probably the easiest vegetable for the home gardener to raise. It's a cold-weather plant started as soon as the ground can be worked and before the last spring frost is expected. Wise gardeners will plant lettuce at least once more during summer, for it likes the coolness of autumn as well as of spring.

Since so many varieties of lettuce are offered, it might help to know that lettuce can be divided into four categories: head, looseleaf, butterhead and romaine.

Head lettuce. We buy this one in the food markets. It is the only lettuce that ships and keeps well. It is grown in a section of California that is warm in the winter and in areas of the Great Lakes states where summer is cool. Gardeners in Minnesota can plant head lettuce seeds inside in early spring and transplant seedlings outside in the garden when they are sturdy.

Varieties include **Great Lakes** (94 days), **Ithaca** (85 days), and **Pennlake** (82 days). **Ithaca,** developed at Cornell University, is recommended for the home garden. It is resistant to tip-burn and brown rib; it is slow to bolt. If the sun is a bother, shade the plants with raised covers of wooden slats or of cheesecloth. If slugs are a bother, saucers of beer should be placed among the rows.

Looseleaf lettuce. Varieties are legion and all are good. We plant **Black Seeded Simpson, Oak Leaf, Salad Bowl** and **Ruby.** All are green, except Ruby, which is reddish.

Those wanting more colorful leaves than Ruby might try a French lettuce, **Merveille des Quatre Saisons — Laitue Pommee,** sold by Epicure Seeds. Visiting gardeners and friends can't resist picking a leaf from my Laitue Pommee.

Looseleaf lettuce should be pulled early in the day it is to be used, washed and placed without crushing in a dark, cool place free from circulating air. If space permits, the refrigerator is ideal if the door is rarely opened. If placed in a tightly closed can, this lettuce may be kept for a week or so. **Black-seeded Simpson**

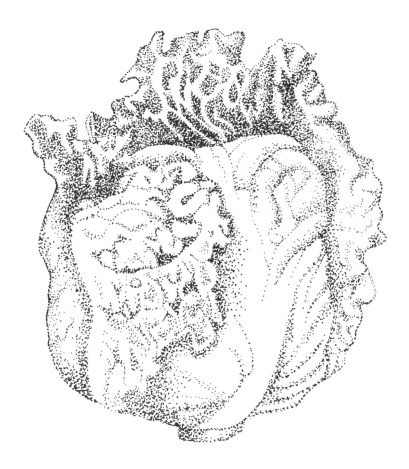

(44 days) is the earliest; for this reason it is always in our spring and late-fall gardens.

Butterhead lettuce. To my family, this lettuce is the great one. Types include the older **Bibb** and the newer and slower-bolting **Summer Bibb; Buttercrunch,** which is another Cornell University product and, to us, just about the perfect lettuce — slow in bolting, slow to become bitter, and always thick, crisp, sweet and crunchy; **Butter King,** an improved Boston variety developed in Canada that is twice as large as its forebears, and **Tania,** developed in England and now exclusively distributed in America by Harris Seeds. It's the only lettuce to produce sweet leaves even after bolting.

Romaine (Cos) lettuce. For good reasons, no lettuce patch is complete without romaine or Cos lettuce, originally from the island of Cos. The best is **Parris Island Cos** or its cousin, **Valmaine Cos,** which is tolerant to mildew — important to gardeners who irrigate, as I do. It's so slow to bolt that it has been called the summertime lettuce.

Leaves are upright in fairly firm heads that may become 10 inches high before the plants bolt. The outer leaves are green and the inner leaves are almost white if natural blanching is encouraged by pushing outer leaves together with mulch or even tying their tops with string, as with cauliflower.

But don't forget, blanching lessens nutritive value. This is the price we pay for the whitish colors we like. Above all, either variety is delicious green or white. It should find its way into vegetable markets for it ships and keeps tolerably well.

Lettuce, too, has "come a long way." The Persians ate it as a dessert. The Romans, who

---

Squirrels enjoy ripe or green tomatoes. Although Uncle Jerry was a kindly fellow, it always made him furious when he found a partly-eaten tomato that a squirrel had pulled off the vine.

Jerry would explode vociferously at all squirrels in general and throw the tomato as far as he could into the woods.

But when Grandma found a partly-eaten tomato, she wouldn't touch it. Sometime after, she explained to Jerry that a squirrel would return to the partly-eaten tomato before starting on another one. Often one tomato would last a squirrel several days to a week.

But it did NO good, until one day Uncle Jerry threw a rather soft one that hit Grandfather in the face, and then Grandfather exploded at Uncle, and Jerry ceased throwing tomatoes.

gave it its present name, changed it to an hors d'oeuvre. Americans created the salad bowl as a complete meal with strips of meat and cheese and pieces of fruit — and of course lots of lettuce leaves in bite-size pieces.

Once doctors recommended lettuce for stomach troubles and insomnia; now they recommend lettuce to overweight patients.

Once, too, lettuce was a sacred plant that grew wild, as it still does in India and the Caucasus areas of Russia. It is included in the Seder feasts on the first and second days of Passover, which commemorate the exodus of the Israelites from Egypt.

The symbolism is perfect. The Israelites' first days in Egypt had been sweet ones, as with young lettuce leaves. As time passed, their days turned bitter, as do the leaves of old lettuce plants. Over the centuries of Passover, a plate of lettuce has reminded descendants of those who walked through the Red Sea.

Spinach

The spinach in my Minnesota garden is far from its native land. The name is Arabic. The Moors left it here and there along their route to Spain. Monks planted much spinach; it was a fast-day food of note.

It was grown in America and written about as the 1800s began a new century. Even then it was no stranger, since colonial America was full of kitchen gardens; seeds and recipes were swapped and tried out by all.

Today spinach is a potherb in most northern gardens and a major commercial product. It is frequently included in menus offering good-tasting foods to hungry people who seek vitamins A, B1, C and G, and minerals such as iron, rather than calories.

For many years, restaurant owners sought the variety called **Viking.** They still do, but many are now using a recent All-American selection called **Melody** (43 days) which is almost as satisfactory to them.

Why these two? Simple: They have smooth leaves and are easier, therefore cheaper, to wash. Those who sell cooked spinach must get rid of sand on leaves.

But home gardeners who have time to clear the leaves of garden soil are apt to plant one of the varieties with crinkled (savoyed) leaves. They include one of the **Longstanding Bloomsdales** (48 days**)**, or **America** (50 days), or my favorite **Cold Resistant Savoy** (45 days). The last resists blight and withstands hot weather a bit easier than its rivals. But better, it winters over. I buy the seeds from Stokes.

At our house, we have finished, in one June day, freezing and canning the spinach from three 75-square-foot beds. One bed was planted the previous September and two the previous October. Seeds planted in September were intended for use 45 days later. Those planted during the last week of October were expected to lie dormant and sprout as soon as winter snows and thawing garden soil permitted.

But it didn't work that way. An early winter caught the September-planted spinach a couple of inches high, so it was not harvested, but left to battle the winter, not as seeds under the soil but as growing plants on top of it.

The interesting result: The three beds of spinach were harvested on the same day in June, each an excellent crop. There seemed to be no differences among them.

This first harvest made 29 packages of spinach for the freezer and 31 pint jars for the pressure canner. And we still had fresh spinach from these beds for green salads and for a few jars and packages to can and freeze.

Only the leaves — no stems and certainly no stalks — are frozen. But these leaves must be washed and washed and washed for they are heavily savoyed with lots of tiny places for soil to hide. At our house, this washing is done outdoors near the hydrant of unlimited cold, cold water from a very deep well.

Once washed, the leaves go into the kitchen for blanching. This stops a ripening process, which must be done if foods are to be frozen. After a minute in boiling water, the leaves are chilled in cold running water and then added to a large vessel with ice cubes and water.

When all leaves have been blanched, they are chopped with a wide knife on a board, then packaged in plastic bags, labeled and deposited into one of the large freezers in the garage. When frozen, these are stored in the nearby locker plant and returned as the home supply dwindles.

Stems and stalks are washed, easily because these are not leaves, and then cooked in very little water. When done, the soft stems and stalks go into the blender set to liquefy, or into the food processor with the knife blade, then into the Foley food mill to remove any tiny pieces that might have been missed.

Finally, season it to taste: salt or salt substitute, black pepper, butter or margarine, garlic and onion powder, pepper sauce — whatever you like. But don't add any liquid, only the small amount of water used while cooking. Now you have a thick spinach puree that can be packed in freezer boxes, or, preferably, in boiling bags and frozen for future use.

When spinach soup is needed, the contents of either box or bag may be cooked with added

stock or milk, sprinkled with chopped wide-leafed chives, Bacos or homemade croutons sauted with an herb.

We need more lunches waiting in the freezer that can be fixed in a dozen minutes. Spinach stems go better here than in the compost heap.

Normally we try for a somewhat smaller crop of late spinach, to be ready just before the ground is expected to freeze. If Oct. 25 is the selected date for the big freeze, we'll plant seeds Sept. 10.

The "big freeze" in our vocabulary is the day that water can no longer be pumped from the creek to sprinkle the garden and cover it all with a protective coat of sparkling ice that will slowly dissolve as the creek water from the sprinklers melts it all — without any damage even to ice-coated tomatoes.

I can't agree with those who say spinach is a single-harvest plant and that it is best to cut it close to the ground. If cut a bit higher, thus leaving a couple or so bottom leaves (the yellowing and weather-beaten ones will do), the plant will start to grow all over again if the weather is cool.

There are two other kinds of spinach. A wild spinach plant, **Good King Henry,** is picked along stone walls and fence rows in England. It is so spinach-strong that it is cooked in two waters, the first one discarded.

A better known and widely planted spinach is called **New Zealand.** This one is not a true spinach in any way other than taste. It has a fondness for our kind of heat and our summer sun will cause no problems. In the Middle South where it is warmer, the plant will be smaller, and in the Deep South it just will not grow.

The most important advice is to harvest and use only the top three inches of each sprig; to harvest more leaves is to have a tough vegetable to serve.

The seeds of New Zealand spinach are slow to germinate. If not carefully marked, they may be lost in the garden. There is a quicker way: Before planting, soak the seeds in warm water for 24 hours.

To Stokes Seeds, New Zealand spinach "is a

perennial spinach suitable for home gardens only." The Park company says it "often survives cold winters to grow again next season." Gardener/writers Ann Roe Robbins and Leon C. Snyder believe it to be an annual. All others I know avoid the issue.

In my own Minnesota garden, last year's New Zealand spinach came from a bed that is three years old, which would indicate Stokes is correct. But there have been years when what was there did not come up, which supports the Park belief. So plant your seeds and let me know what happens to your spinach.

Raw spinach leaves of any kind will improve a tossed salad. Spinach is cooked briefly with little water and salt, or it can be steamed and salted — an adage says that the only water needed can be shaken from freshly washed leaves. It is then chopped or minced, and stirred while butter melts to make a great and simple dish.

Colonial America ate "Spinach Timbales" and "Shaker Spinach with Rosemary," which featured onion, parsley, nutmeg and rosemary. Recipes abound.

My favorite book of vegetable recipes is volume 5, "Vegetables," in the "Favorite Recipes of America" series (Favorite Recipes Press, Louisville, Ky.). This has 28 recipes for spinach — all good, but, sorry to say, neither of the ones from colonial America is included.

Helen Belinkie has four good recipes in her "The New Gourmet in the Low Calorie Kitchen Cookbook" (David McKay, New York). James Beard and Sam Aaron in "How to Eat Better for Less Money" (Simon and Schuster, New York) have more than a couple of dozen that will make a dedicated cook out of any gardener.

One of the world's best-known teacher/cooks, Julia Child, in her "Mastering the Art of French Cooking" (Alfred A. Knopf, New York) has wonderful things to say to spinach eaters tired of the methods of cooks with little imagination or adventurous spirit who just clean and boil and serve.

All one needs to cook spinach well (or anything else) is a good book and a closed door into the kitchen. Painting, writing, gardening and cooking are best done in solitude. If a teacher is needed, let it be the pages of a book. They can't chatter or drop things.

If the "teachers," above aren't adequate, try the English edition of "Larousse Gastronomique" (Crown Publishers, New York) with its 1,100 large pages, 8,500 recipes, and 1,000 illustrations. Spinach is on pages 926, 927 and 928.

But nowhere in all the above will you find the first and true recipe for what I believe is the greatest spinach dish of them all.

It seems reasonable to me that, when chefs at

Antoine's in New Orleans, one of the nation's finest restaurants, decided to feature oysters in shells baked on hot rock-salt and covered with a special spinach mixture of good things, they needed a name for such a special treat.

I suspect that, to them, one of our nation's greatest leaders was the elder Rockefeller, not because he passed out dimes and smiles to friends and strangers, not because he was then the world's richest man, but because to those chefs he was the epitome of the best there was.

So they introduced Oysters Rockefeller, to the delight of their patrons. A half century and more ago, I found those oysters and over the years they and the fast Crescent Limited express train have been the magnets that have pulled me back.

But time marches on and now the spinach dish tied to the Rockefeller name has been pushed several notches lower. Let's look at the victor and new champion.

The first great cookbook since "Larousse Gastronomique" was published in France is the many-volume one published by Time-Life. It is still appearing, book by book, with the name "The Good Cook."

The last volume to arrive, the 12th in the series, was opened with a frown because its title, Pies and Pastries, is not for me. I had my last sugar years ago.

I scanned and admired the copy and wonderful picture in the introduction and then came to Chapter 1. Its frontispiece is a full-page color picture of an unusual Provencal tart — "a sweet spinach custard enlivened by pine nuts."

Elsewhere the recipe begins with "a handful of raisins macerated in brandy" and includes, among other items, nutmeg, allspice, cream lemon peel, sugar, butter, eggs and, you guessed it — "2 pounds of spinach, stemmed and washed. . . ." Though never to be tasted by me, for now, I'll place The Good Cook's Spinach Tart ahead of Oysters Rockefeller. Surely there are sweet-toothed spinach growers who will make a spinach tart and let me know more about it.

Dandelions

Spinach leaves are not the only ones ones for "boiling greens" or for a tossed salad, and thus the only such vegetable for gardeners. Let's consider others.

Most any list of greens would include collards, kale, Swiss and rhubarb chard, beet and turnip tops, endive, escarole, parsley, lettuce, mustard, Tex-sel (a cabbage-kale development from Texas A&M University), French or Belgian endive (which ought to be called witloof chicory), comfrey, bok choy, celtuce (which combines uses of both celery and lettuce but is not a cross), corn salad (not well known), watercress, edible chrysanthemums (which the Japanese call shungiku), New Zealand spinach, dandelion and lamb's quarters.

Some would add Chinese and Savoy cabbages to the list, as I do.

Of these, only lamb's quarters has not been domesticated and garden grown. But it does grow in most northern gardens as a persistent but attractive weed. This is a pity, for it ought to be at the top of the list.

All greens are rich in vitamins and low in calories. Some are rich in folklore and history. We feel better when we eat greens and not cathartics. Our children grow stronger and become brighter if junk food loaded with sugar can be exchanged for raw and cooked greens.

Children ought to have equal opportunities, not just to eat better things, but to grow and harvest and preserve them. To dig and weed and water and sweat and get dirty is to enjoy the acts that follow: an absolutely necessary hot bath, the clean and sweet-smelling clothes that are exchanged for the ones that go directly into the washing machine.

An even greater gain is the sense of accomplishment of being part of a team, not just a part of a family.

One of the most neglected greens in America is called dent-de-lion in France; its leaves are shaped like lions' teeth. The English had a problem with this name and somehow it came to be called dandelion.

(The English had the same difficulty with a valuable garden product grown for centuries by American Aztec Indians. This vegetable reached England from Spain via Italy with the name "girasole," which the English converted into Jerusalem artichoke. Quite a feat.)

Grandma expected Uncle Jerry to keep the front lawn clear of dandelions. Jerry said they were "a pain in the neck" to him and also a pain in the back, from bending over to knife them out. One spring when Grandma went visiting he got a brilliant idea. He turned a herd of twenty sheep on the lawn for two days. Results: no dandelions for several years; also no lawn to speak of for most of the summer.

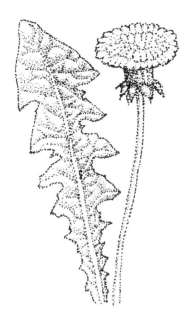

In Biblical times dandelions were one of the bitter herbs used by the Israelites. Their native country is Eurasia. In North America, and far above the Arctic Circle, they are immigrants that behave as if they owned the turf they have settled.

Most of us think dandelions are evil weeds to be fought and destroyed. Digging them is difficult, for even a part of their long taproots will produce new green leaves and yellow flowers with the arrival of spring. So chemicals are sprayed on leaves and reach root ends. Not only will the plant die, but so will the bees that come for pollen and nectar needed to make honey unless the spraying is done in late evening.

One result of the widespread use of such destructive herbicides is the decline in America's honey production. Another is the danger of contaminating garden soil, especially if "weed-and-feed" products remain on grass clippings that become garden mulch or compost.

Leaves of young dandelions are used as salads when raw, or cooked or steamed to make "boiling greens." Flowers have other purposes: necklaces and finger rings and bouquets for little girls.

Once, in Switzerland, shepherds depended on these flowers to indicate when it was time to turn sheep out, or bed them down for the night because dandelions nod and sleep as the land darkens and then slowly wake up to a rising sun.

The yellow flowers go to seed and become blowballs — the curse of those who mow and manicure their lawns. With annoying success they refuse to be cut by whirling blades of the mower and stand up again after it has passed.

For centuries these blowballs have been used to foretell events. The number of "blows" it takes to blow the blowball away is the number of years or days before something happens: the

swain proposes, the baby is born, the son returns, the delayed rain falls. One can cheat, since hard blows hasten and weak ones extend the arrival time.

A fellow winemaker tells me that more people make more folk wine from flowers and heads of dandelions than from any other flower, herb, vegetable or fruit. Some use only the yellow petals and nothing of the green cups that hold them, others use all of the flower head (which is easier).

Recipes may be found in any book on winemaking; even small public libraries probably have one or more such books. Of all, I suggest that "Folkwines" by M. A. Jagendorf (The Vanguard Press, New York) be your choice if it is available.

Dandelions should have an honored place in American home gardens as they have in Europe. There new varieties have been developed; all have thicker and larger leaves, some curly.

Gardening and cooking of most anything go together — or ought to. In the kitchen and on the dinner table we discover that the older dandelion leaves are bitter. Some people like the taste, but many don't.

Blanching while plants are growing will remove this bitterness. One way: On dandelions headed for the kitchen, tie the outer leaves together as with cauliflower. Another way: Place pots over plants or cover, but don't bury, them with sand (as with endive or escarole).

If the leaves are not blanched before harvesting, the bitterness may be removed by boiling in two waters, discarding the first. Those who freeze and store dandelion greens should do so each spring when the leaves are not bitter. Dandelion wine should be made from flowers, not leaves.

Dandelion roots are good to eat, too. Use a vegetable peeler to remove the outer coating. Then boil the roots in salted water until tender; they'll taste sweet when they reach the table.

Grandma did admire the golden dandelions as harbingers of spring, but in reasonable quantities. It was up to Uncle Jerry to keep the big front lawn free of them. This lawn extended from the old farmhouse to the Windsor-London highway, in plain sight of passersby, and year after year the dandelions kept getting worse, hence Grandma's phobia.

There were no chemical dandelion killers in those days, only Uncle's big jackknife, and it was tedious work. Uncle pondered — result, a 6-by-10 foot piece of big mesh chicken wire was dragged over the lawn every few days, and off came the yellow heads. In two years the dandelions were practically gone.

The roots also may be baked or roasted. If roasted, the peelings may be retained and the entire root ground and used in coffee like chicory. And wonder of wonders! The roots may be dug in the late fall, removed to the root cellar and covered with damp, not wet, sand. From these, almost exactly as with witloof chicory, small heads of tightly bound white leaves will grow along the roots to make a wonderful winter salad.

But where does the home gardener find seeds of dandelion plants that have been domesticated and improved? At least two American seed companies with catalogs offer them: Burpee and Stokes.

Dandelions are perennials. Seeds planted one spring will produce plants that should be harvested after their second year begins. Plants should be thinned to stand a foot apart, but mine do nicely with only four inches between them.

Remember that seeds of the wild dandelion are not covered because light is necessary for germination. So, in rows you prepare for seeds, just scatter them and press them down so they don't blow away.

Cabbages

Of all cole plants, cabbages probably are grown in more Western and Oriental gardens than all their relatives together. It has been so since early Egyptians considered the cabbage to be an article of worship. Later, Romans used it to prevent drunkenness. Still later, eastern Europeans were picking it wild.

Where salt, once usually made from sea water and moved by caravans to faraway markets, could be had, cabbage became a year-round food in Europe and Asia. Cooked sauerkraut (to make it milder) was served to those who built the Great Wall of China, around 200 B.C.

This use of salt as a major way of preserving foods continued until the revolution in transportation, shipping and controlled storage climate placed many vegetables, cabbage included, in fresh-food markets most of the year.

But home gardeners will continue to plant cabbages for fresh-from-the-garden use and less fresh from storage, and to fill sauerkraut jars and crocks.

And also for their home freezers. Not even the giants of the food industry have discovered the wonders of frozen shredded cabbage. But home gardeners can enjoy in March cabbage that has spent months in their freezers.

Let's select varieties of cabbage seeds for our garden. The choices are many; Stokes alone offers 49. Some gardeners plant seeds inside to grow either by the side of a window without curtains or shades or under grow-lights.

Others buy their plants from nurseries, and their choices will be few — mostly early, mid-season or late. They will be good plants and will grow to make good cabbages.

The Savoy cabbages are the most important at our house. They are not likely to be sold in markets, for they ship and store badly. It is hoped that the Savoy will never be converted to such purposes, for they are now superior, tastewise. At our house, these are used raw in salads and slaw; they are steamed, boiled, baked, pickled or stuffed; they are shredded or used as wrap-arounds and frozen for year-round use.

Savoy cabbages must be cleaned more carefully than the tight-leaved green or red cabbages because loose leaves make it easy for worms to wander about, leaving spotted areas along the trails they make between the leaves.

The inspected and cleaned cabbage goes into the food processor for shredding. This shredded cabbage can be made into coleslaw and frozen, or it can be blanched and then cooled and packed in freezer boxes or bags for future use in cabbage soup, in salads and in various casserole dishes. Or it may be proudly brought to the dinner table as a dish in its own right.

Here are the varieties we plant:

Savoy King (82 days). These are big and flavorful hybrid cabbages (five pounds) with moderately crinkled leaves that can withstand summer heat. This variety is not yellows-tolerant; I know of no Savoy cabbage that is. From Joseph Harris, Inc.

Savoy Ace (85 days) is considered better than Savoy King, but is hard to find. The George W. Park Seed Co. offers both Savoy King and Savoy Ace. I know of no other that does.

Red cabbages are our second choice. At our

Grandma's remedy for cabbage heads that were beginning to split open (usually caused by too-rapid growth) was to bend them over sharply one way and far enough to break half the roots.

This treatment slowed the growth to normal. This was one job Uncle Jerry delighted to do. He named the big-headed cabbages after local politicians he didn't like. And how happy he was to crack their necks!

Grandma approved of the method, but not Uncle's motive.

house these have just two uses. In large amounts they are made into the dish the Germans call *Rotkohl mit Apfeln* and we call red cabbage with apples. By either name it is a great food frozen for future use. The red-cabbage variety we use is:

Red Acre (88 days). A yellows-resistant cabbage that can withstand splitting. It is rich blood-red, just right for our purpose. Stokes Seeds.

We have a few green cabbages, for Jo Nunn has a fine hand with sauerkraut that has so little salt that it is easy to wash away. But green cabbage makes for wonderful slaw, especially when mixed with shredded sweet peppers, red cabbages (their second use), chopped green onions and herb vinegar and then frozen. We also have a single variety of green cabbage in our garden:

Harris Resistant Danish (95 days). So yellows-resistant that seeds can be planted in infected soil. The heads are round and firm. (Harris Seeds)

But let's talk more about what to do with these denizens of the cabbage patch.

Gardeners who preserve food by blanching, then by drying and pasteurizing it, and then by packing the brittle or leathery results are apt to include cabbages of any type.

Brittle cabbage pieces may be packed in ordinary glass or plastic jars with tight lids and stored away from light. When moisture is restored, dried cabbage is apt to find its way into soups and casserole dishes.

Gardeners have learned that Savoy cabbage (good) and Chinese cabbage (best) can be shredded, blanched and frozen with much better results. And surely all gardeners know how to turn cabbage shreds into kraut with the aid of canning salt.

Now let's find out how cabbage can be preserved, even better, in other ways. We will use the kitchen stove and the freezer, but "boiling bags" are the key.

We first stumbled onto these bags while poking about in the frozen-food section of a food market. Something new: contents of frozen-food packages were to be cooked in the bags in which they were packed. These new bags were air-tight, vaporproof and waterproof, and could withstand boiling. Frozen foods in these packages were to be cooked by tossing their sealed boiling bags in an uncovered pot of boiling water and boiling each one for 15 minutes.

The older way was to remove the frozen food from its plastic bag or box and cook it, always in water and unthawed, just as if it came fresh from the garden. Fine for frozen green beans or carrots or Chinese cabbage or cut corn or kohlrabi; terrible for such foods as frozen applesauce or baked cucumbers or corned beef and cabbage or foods that have sauces or similar liquid.

Clearly the boiling bag was, or could be, revolutionary in the kitchen if used to preserve all leftovers that suffer from having water added before they make their second table appearance.

So, again, hail to the boiling bag! But where can we get them and how do we use them?

Not as easy as you may think. It's surprising how many obvious sources of supply had none. The manager of an outlet of the largest such chain had never heard of them. And they have different names in different stores!

At K mart they are "Seal-a-Meal Bags;" at Sears, Roebuck they are "Seal-n-Save/Boilable Cooking Pouches." Prices are about the same. Each bag is 8 by 9 inches, holding 1½ pints. They can be washed and reused.

Sealing? Yes, first you look for an oblong plastic box, just called "the sealer," with an electric cord to be plugged into an outlet. These are sold by those who sell the bags. Raise the lid for four minutes and a single protected wire turns red hot. Close the lid on the two edges of a boiling bag, count to four and the bag is sealed.

The bags are apt to be in perforated rolls or in single units of pint, pint and a half, or quart bags. Along the sides of each bag are small punched holes. The holes can be used to hold and stretch the bags for the hot wire to make its seal. At our house this almost became a two-person operation — a most exasperating one, for the holes of the pint bags we first used and the pegs on which they are placed became wet, which made slipping and spilling inevitable.

The third time I began, reluctantly, to fill and seal bags (this time they were the 1½-pint size), I saw what had been wrong the first time. Then I had been using the 1-pint bags, now with the bigger ones I did not have to use either the side holes on the bags or the pegs on which to hang them. With each larger bag filled with

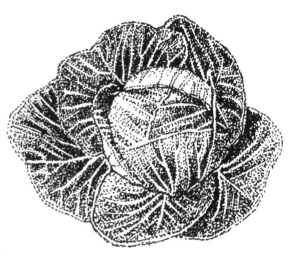

only a pint, I had no problem. In no time I had 30-some bags of chilled baked cucumbers on their way to the freezer. So I learned that it's necessary to pack pints of food in larger-sized bags.

A day or so after publication of my Sunday Minneapolis Tribune article on boiling bags, I answered the phone to be greeted by a friendly voice who understood my problem of the too-small bag and the unneeded pegs. Now, she said, "Let a competitor tell you about another sealer and different plastic bags that will give you no problems."

A few hours later, I sat and learned about a company that has long supplied plastic sealing bags for laboratory specimens and for evidence to be presented to courts.

Kapak Industries, 9809 Logan Av. S., Bloomington, Minn., operates under agreement with 3M Co. Kapak supplies bags in many sizes but, as this is written, it plans a special package of a few sizes especially for home gardener/cooks.

The Scotchpak sealer used for these bags uses a narrow band heater for sealing. It's better than the single-wire types.

Filled boiling bags from any source can be placed in the freezer without any shifting about but the bags will stick together unless separated by a double sheet of freezer paper.

Even when drained, most cooked cabbage that reaches our dinner table comes with dripping juice — a perfect candidate for the boiling bag. Recipes for such dishes are in every cookbook. May I add four especially useful ones that are not apt to be found easily?

Frozen or canned borscht: This famous Russian soup is made with any kind of thick or thin (generally thin) meat stock; lots of any shredded or chopped cabbage for taste; sliced, minced or whole red beets for color; maybe leeks or onions or garlic for extra flavor; and mashed potatoes for filler; always water and salt and pepper, sometimes sherry, even vodka.

At our home, if borscht is to be frozen for future use and space is at a premium, we'll use as little water as possible. One simple way is first to cook each ingredient separately in the same liquid, beginning with the cabbage.

After everything is cooked, put it all back into the liquid to mix and meld the flavors in a final brief period on the burner. Extra water can be added after boiling bags have been opened for use. And remember the great advantage of soups: they can be stretched!

When the borscht is removed from plastic freezer boxes, boiling bags or glass canning jars, and made ready to serve, its appearance and taste will be improved if a blob of sour cream, a tablespoon or two of thick chives and bits of fried bacon can float on top. This is a great meal by itself, especially if served with hot yellow corn sticks and ice-cold buttermilk, or the traditional black bread.

Makers of borscht have their own individual methods and even these change as hot weather turns to cold, and vegetables come and go in gardens and markets. If more cold borscht is used than hot it merely means that the area has more summer than winter. Jo Nunn's parents were born in Russia. She can make wonderful borscht that fits the seasons — it always is unmistakably borscht — especially as a winter dish as natural in cold Minnesota as in the cold Ukraine.

Corned beef and cabbage. Easily made with chopped or shredded cabbage, lots of catsup, and shredded corned beef from cans filled in Brazil or Argentina by American meat packers. Be sure all liquid used in cooking gets into the boiling bags.

Rotkohl mit Apfeln that melds red cabbage, sliced apples, vinegar, bacon grease, bacon bits, onions and sweetening into "Red Cabbage with Apples." Toss a boiling bag of this cooked and frozen mixture into boiling water in January and enjoy one of the greatest German dishes.

Leaf-wrapped cabbage rolls. These start with cabbage leaves made soft by blanching and by reducing the thickness of the center stem with a sharp and serrated knife. Large amounts of cooked chopped cabbage leaves and lesser amounts of chopped cooked meat (any kind), other vegetables such as onions, carrots and sweet peppers, or with such fruits as chopped apples, raisins, cherries and pears, or with cereals like rice, grits, hominy or croutons.

Consider adding a dried or fresh herb like basil or dill or a spice like ginger or cloves. A single toothpick will hold each roll together. These will stick together when frozen but will be separated when the boiling bag is opened.

Mashed potatoes made better: Chopped or shredded, even blenderized, cabbage may be mixed into mashed potatoes to make a favorite dish often served by the late Tom Moore when he owned the Radisson Hotel in Minneapolis. Delicious! And it freezes easily at home in boiling bags.

Now for a word about Chinese cabbage. There are two kinds well-known in America.

Michihli (78 days) is the variety frequently seen at better greengrocers in larger cities. Slender and tall, with green outer leaves and white inner ones, it is used raw in salads and cooked as a boiling green. It is sometimes called celery cabbage because of its spicy taste.

It freezes well, but doesn't keep well. It is a fickle plant in fickle weather. It may bolt to seed if planted before the middle of July. To avoid the risk, use the late date or divide the seeds for two plantings — one now, one then.

The second Chinese cabbage is **Wong Bok** (50-60 days), which will be found in Oriental restaurants and in the chilled bins of Oriental stores.

Wong Bok is the shorter and thicker variety that keeps and freezes well, is less fickle and thus can be planted as soon as the soil can be worked.

Michihli seed comes from Joseph Harris Seeds; Wong Bok is called **Early Hybrid G** by the Harris Co.

If you are more adventurous, there is more. Under the name of **Siew Choy,** (50 days), packets of Chinese cabbage can be had from Tsang and Ma International Seeds.

They also offer **Choy Sum** (60 days), a flowering white cabbage; **Bok Choy** (45 days), a white Chineselike cabbage that is in my own garden and frequently can be bought at large supermarkets in the Twin Cities; **Gai Lohn** (70 days), Chinese kale; **Heung Kunn** (65 days), Chinese celery; **Cee Gwon** (90 days), called Chinese okra because of looks rather than taste, and **Yuen Sai** (50 days), Chinese parsley.

Don't fail to include **Sow Choy** (90 days), Chinese chives. These perennials have wide, flat leaves 12-plus inches tall with a garlic taste.

Collards

Collards, sometimes called cabbage trees, are in a class by themselves. In much of the South their leaves are brought from the garden all winter. Even thin ice is no problem: leaves are simply knocked together to jar the ice loose.

Minnesota ice gets thicker and lasts longer and always wins, but the collard is the last fresh vegetable taken each year from the northern garden. It freezes well.

Georgia collards grow as well in Minnesota as in Georgia. **Vates** collards will, too. These are the two varieties most often planted. Georgia collards may be stronger in taste and Vates milder, as some believe, but those of us with ordinary taste buds won't notice a difference.

Each has a main rib in the center of large, fully grown leaves. It's best to discard these ribs unless you are the kind of cook who puts the leaves on the stove after breakfast to be ready in time for evening dinner, as most Southerners did in the old days.

These collards were never boiled without a piece of pork — a ham bone or fatback. Nowadays, all lovers of collards will use less pork — a smidgen will provide the flavor — and the collards, without the midribs, will go into the boiling water only after the meat is about done.

The result is few calories without too much damage to the amounts of vitamins A and C, which are greater than those in cabbage.

The leaves of collards taste better if hit by frost, or even by winter rain that covers every inch with ice. Pick the leaves, knock them together and the ice will shatter. Don't ever do this to leaves that remain on the plants, because you'll break the plants and bruise stalks and leaves. Let late autumn sun do this deicing.

Garden enemies may make holes in leaves, but they won't rot as cabbage will.

Collards, like most all plants that grow in unfriendly places, quickly respond to fertilizer scattered in foot-wide bands on each side of the row, lightly worked into the topsoil. Ten ounces for each 10 feet of row is about right.

Seeds may be sown in rows or beds and the plants may be thinned anytime and eaten or frozen. Take care that collards, and all other cole plants, are never planted where they or their relatives have grown during the last three years.

Only the mature collard leaves — not the young sprouts — are the delight of the gour-

Grandma had no rubber or plastic treated gloves for gardening. But she had a home-made lotion which she used before going out into the garden. She washed it off when she came in and used it after her hands had been in hot water. It also acted as a mosquito repellent. Her formula was four ounces each of glycerine and rose water and one drop of carbolic acid. Any druggist can make it up. Grandma also rubbed a thick lather of soap around and under her fingernails before working in the earth. This kept her nails free from stain. In spite of hard work she had beautiful hands, and she was proud of them.

met, who may insist on buttered cornbread and a soup spoon for the pot liquor. Collards should be in every northern garden. For too long only southerners have enjoyed this vegetable, which has become a mainstay in a regional cuisine.

Boiling Greens

"Boiling greens" have made history all over the world. Primitive people began gardens by moving wild plants, or seeds, to locations near their dwellings.

Tender in the spring, greens became one of the purges of winter, a universal spring tonic.

During the winter of 1612, colonists in Virginia suffered from scurvy while waiting for the turnips they had planted in the fall to produce leaves for boiling. Even tougher leaves in late summer were used. One, two or three times these could be brought to boiling point and the waters that were poured out carried bitterness away and left a tolerable dish rich in vitamins.

Greens and their roots were the salvation of the poor and of those who wandered or moved long distances. Seeds could be planted as soon as ground thawed. Plantings made after the heat of summer could produce food until the ground froze again. Then roots could be pulled and kept for the winter.

Those tiny mustard and turnip seeds are rich in the lore of people. They were illustrations often used by great teachers and Biblical prophets.

But boiling greens in our kitchens are not just mustard or turnip leaves. We use leaves of other domesticated plants and many still are wild. The latter may be poke *(Phytolacca Americana)* leaves.

This word, poke, comes from the Algonquin-speaking Indians of Virginia who used the leaves and stems, but not the poisonous roots, of the plant they called "pakon." Pakon also was used by the Indians for painting their bodies.

In early Virginia, to Indians and colonists alike, poke was pokeweed, pokeberry, poke root and inkberry. In the Piedmont and in the Appalachian valleys, poke became the leaves of any edible wild plant, and poke greens included the leaves of once-domesticated plants growing wild.

High on the list of such plants are turnips and mustard, for, if once planted and not harvested, they will come up year after year, spreading as the wind distributes their seeds.

I have a list of wild plants (and their Latin names) used as food and I am delighted when friends and strangers tell me why, when, how and where they came to be so used. The largest number, 18, are boiling greens.

In at least three definable periods in our history, the eating of wild plants has been significant: The movement of both cotton and people from Virginia to the Carolinas, then to Georgia

and Alabama, then to Mississippi and finally into Texas is one such time.

The other two are the Reconstruction period in the South, especially in areas of Sherman's march, that followed the Civil War, and the years during the great drought and Depression of the 1930s.

Most pickers knew the local names, or gave names of their own, to greens they picked. They knew a surprising number of things about each — what it went well with, how it could be cooked, when it was best and so on. They learned these things from their mothers, neighbors and from visitors.

In front of me as I write is the cookbook of the Progressive Farmer, a magazine with a large southern circulation. Some of the recipes are Sauteed Fresh Turnip Greens, Greens Gumbo (Louisiana), Greens and Eggs, Southern-Style Greens with Salt Pork, Poke Greens or Sallet, Cornmeal Dumplings with Turnip Greens, and Southern Gumbo. No doubt about it, this cookbook is Southern; it comes from Birmingham. And it is used today.

Americans may eat more turnip greens than any of the other "boiling greens," except spinach. There are several reasons. One is the good taste. More important, turnips are easy to grow and cook.

All one needs for cooking is a pot of water, a hot stove, salt and pepper (preferably red), and a piece of pork or some bacon grease. The elegant, who also like good food, can just cook the leaves, chop them finely and douse them with salted butter.

Growing turnip greens is as simple as cooking them: All one needs are seeds and space in the garden.

Turnips are not just for leaves, but for roots,

too. The roots, yellow or white or white with a purple top, are in great demand. These can be peeled, then sliced thinly and eaten raw, or peeled and cooked in boiling salted water to be chopped or mashed for another simple dish. Leaves and roots may be preserved together by canning or freezing, but separately is better. Only the roots, not the leaves, can be kept in root cellars, buried in moist sand.

Selection of seeds and times for planting ought to be made only after the gardener decides what to do with the crop.

If greens are preferred over roots, the seeds should be planted as soon as the garden soil can be worked. Spring frosts will not be a bother because turnips are a cold-weather crop. Although any turnip seed will produce a plant with leaves that can be made into delicious dishes, some varieties have better leaves than others.

One such is **Just Right Hybrid.** Another choice is **Tokyo Cross Hybrid,** which has even larger leaves. These will produce acceptable roots, too. Another variety, popular in the South, is **Seven Top,** grown principally for leaves.

If turnip roots are preferred over leaves, the seeds should be planted in late summer for harvesting before the soil freezes. **Purple Top White Glove** is just about best for acceptable leaves and sweet and tender roots. But turnip leaves left on roots held for late harvesting may be too strong and bitter.

Turnip greens mix well with other things, chiefly the leaves of mustard plants. Mustard seeds can be sown the same day as turnips and the leaves of both will be ready to harvest at about the same time.

Three varieties of mustard have been in my garden: **Green Wave** with curled leaves, **Florida Broadleaf** with flat ones, and an Oriental mustard sometimes called Chinese and sometimes Indian. Leaves of the Oriental ones taste and smell strong. Any will add pungency to cooked greens.

There are those who cook mustard leaves alone and then enjoy the sting of a special dish not apt to be served to company.

Turnip greens also may be mixed with bits of dry bacon, chopped onions, hot and sweet pepper strips, or seeds of dill or celery. If a family cannot agree on what's to be added, ingredients can be chosen individually at the table.

Hot biscuits or toast go well with dishes of any poke greens — wild or tame — and their liquor, but with results not nearly as good as with corn bread. A good corn bread can be made with 3 cups of meal, a little more than half as much of flour, 4 teaspoons of sugar and 2 of baking powder and one of salt, 6 tablespoons of butter, 4 egg yolks blended with a pint of milk and a half cup of heavy cream. When all has been mixed, the beaten whites of the eggs can be folded in, the whole poured into hot and well-buttered muffin cups or a pan, and baked for a half hour in a hot oven.

Parsley

Parsley still grows wild in the Middle East, its native region. But it has moved about.

The Greeks fed it to their horses before races and made crowns of it to mark victories. The Romans found it during their eastern campaigns and carried it west to England. The English took it everywhere.

It's my candidate for the plant that has been used to cure and prevent the most ills and injuries of mankind — even wounds, foul breath and to make drunk men sober.

The Greeks gave parsley its name — stone breaker (in Greek) — which may be related to kidney stones, and not their famous sculpted marble. Its use in diseases of the kidneys is of ancient lineage — parsley is a diuretic.

Medicinal or not, parsley is so rich in vitamins and minerals that it should be eaten or drunk as tea rather than just admired for the grace it gives a plate of food. Parsley has more vitamin C than oranges.

There are several kinds. The flat leaves of **Hamberg** parsley have little flavor; the roots have more. Dug in the fall, the roots can be

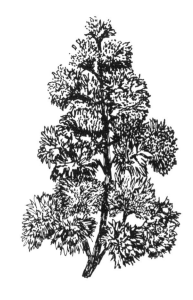

stored, cooked and served like carrots, parsnips or potatoes.

Gardeners who want to add this root crop can get seeds from Park Seed Co., Gurney Nurseries, Stokes Seeds, or Joseph Harris Seeds. Seeds may also be found in Northrup King seed racks in garden centers.

Little parsley is grown just for its roots. Most of it is destined for use as garnishes and in soups, salads, sandwiches and even mashed vegetables.

Parsley may be dried by hanging it on strings in a darkened, ventilated room. When it's dry, rub it between the palms to get bits and pieces of leaves — but not stems — for packaging in plastic or glass jars, wrapped to exclude light and to preserve color and flavor.

Sprigs may be frozen by loosely standing them in freezer boxes or by chopping them and packing with little water in ice cube trays.

Parsley plants resent transplanting; so if plants are needed indoors, plant seeds in pots — unless you can devise a way of moving plants into pots without disturbing the soil around them. Difficult, but possible.

The variety planted for garnishing — fresh or frozen — is **Curly** or **Curled** parsley. The variety we ought to know more about and plant more often is the **Plain Leafed** (like the leaves of celery), often called **Italian** parsley. Those who want exceptional taste and only moderate beauty should go for this variety. It's a larger plant, especially good for fresh and dried leaves, that grows with gusto. Makers of especially good wine know much about this variety.

If a table centerpiece is needed and no flowers are available, cut a few handfuls of this parsley at least a foot high and use it instead. Dinner guests will love it.

If Italian parsley seeds are not readily available, never mind. Just look for chervil, which, though not parsley, is so much alike in taste, in appearance and in habits of growth that it is an ideal substitute. Indeed, it may be superior.

Not strange at all, it is called French parsley and is more used in France than the true parsley. Its flavor is somewhat subdued, which, to many is a great asset.

Before they are planted, parsley seeds should be soaked in room-temperature water for a couple of days. Just before planting, they can be dried on paper towels to make handling easier. If this soaking is not done, up to six weeks may pass before the tiny plants appear.

If chervil is used, soaking is not so necessary. Only one or two weeks are needed for these seeds to sprout. If you can't wait this long, soak the seeds. Chervil is an annual; parsley is a biennial, though most gardeners treat it as an annual.

If left alone, parsley will get through Minnesota winters in good shape. Until the plants

flower and go to seed, its leaves may be used in the first year. But don't make folk wine from parsley heavy with seeds. Even isinglass (which isn't glass at all, but the bladder of fish), which can clear most any wine, left mine too cloudy to serve. If parsley wine is to be made, the celery-leafed variety should be planted and used in its first year.

Parsley, like most herbs, may be started inside and moved to the outside garden when seeds become seedlings.

Parsley seedlings, especially curly parsley, can be bought in peat pots from most seed and garden stores. They are planted, pot and all, directly in the garden. Each pot contains a single plant. If a large number of plants is needed, seeds, not seedlings, will start the frugal gardener's parsley bed.

5/They grow beneath the ground

Potatoes

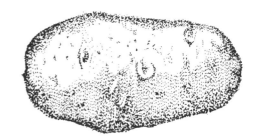

Minnesota shares with Idaho, Wisconsin and Maine the soil, the cool weather and the number of daylight hours that make northern-grown potatoes the best. They are firm, dry and excellent keepers.

Large-scale growers plant potatoes by machine, cultivate by machine, harvest by machine, grade and sack by machine and deliver to buyers by machine.

And they sell potatoes for less than the home gardener spends to grow the same sackful. Their potatoes are available all year — fresh from storage in rooms with controlled temperature and humidity and with chemicals to delay sprouting.

Minnesota gardeners who don't grow potatoes can choose among those bought at roadside stands or in stores, among fresh, canned, frozen and dried potatoes, between cooked and uncooked ones, even between powdered and flaked ones, and finally among the myriad packages of food that contain potatoes and other things.

Small wonder that almost all who write about gardening recommend that the home gardener forget about planting potatoes.

I am the exception: Not only does my garden produce potatoes used each month of the year, but I encourage other gardeners to follow my example.

Let's see about this — and at the same time explain why a few boxes of instant potatoes find their way to our kitchen.

Stored in our root cellar, our potatoes, we know, will begin to soften and crinkle by the first of the year. But by then there aren't many left; we've stored them in a different way.

Before the aging process begins, we take large potatoes from the root cellar to the kitchen, where each one is scrubbed, greased and baked.

Grandma, who was over eighty, always considered folks who had weeds growing around their houses "mighty shiftless". If a neighbor neglected his cutting, Grandma would take her sickle and go forth like a valiant soldier and cut the weeds herself. This seldom happened more than once to the same person. Sometimes a crowd would gather and cheer her on. There was a slogan in the village, "You had better cut your weeds or Grandma will do it for you." The whole village loved her in spite of her presumptuousness.

When done, they are halved lengthwise, the contents are scooped out, mashed and mixed with warm milk, melted margarine, salt and pepper and dried celery leaves.

This mixture, still warm, is stuffed into the potato shells. Each half is topped with strips of cheese spread or sweet red peppers or sometimes sprinkled with cut-up chives. The chives and pepper strips are stored in the freezer for just this purpose.

The ready-to-eat halves are put on trays and frozen. Each half is then wrapped in foil — tightly. Until next year's potato supply is harvested, we eat those baked potato halves from the freezer — resorting only now and then to the store-bought boxes.

At that same time, small potatoes are removed from the root cellar and peeled, boiled and mashed with margarine, milk, salt, pepper and dried celery leaves as if they are to be served for today's dinner. Instead they are packed in boiling bags and frozen.

Home gardeners should plant only potatoes certified as seed potatoes — not those bought for cooking and eating. Seed potatoes probably have been dusted with a chemical that retards sprouting.

Just as important, no part of the seed potatoes marked "certified" should reach the dinner table, for they have been dusted with chemicals that prevent illnesses of growing potatoes.

Many varieties of certified potatoes are for sale, but they are only a fraction of the total number of varieties. In fact, the potato has become the most common food of three continents.

Potatoes caught on slowly, however, after they were introduced in Europe and upper North America from Central and South America, where they were cultivated by the Incas and the Aztecs. Some considered them poisonous or carriers of leprosy; others thought of them as ornamental plants. Eventually their use became a veritable explosion: A rich man's luxury had indeed become a poor man's bread.

The potato provided a large crop with little attention. Introduced into Ireland in the 17th century, it is given credit for a population growth that had reached eight million when, in 1845, a blight almost destroyed the potato and brought on the famine of 1846-48.

Millions emigrated and millions who stayed in Ireland died. Rural population in Ireland dropped from seven million to three million by the turn of the century.

Present-day resources and knowledge will probably prevent recurrence of such a disaster, but areas favorable to potatoes do shift. Only recently have potatoes returned to one Minnesota area where a disease once eliminated them. Resistant varieties are available for both commercial growers and home gardeners.

We have grown several varieties of Irish potatoes in our garden. Those with blue skins and blue flesh and with yellow skins and yellow flesh were there just for fun. They were bought as sets from Gurney Nursery.

Others were main-crop varieties crowded into two 75-square-foot beds. We depend on these to supply our table needs for a full year. **Red Norland** is an early one, and **Kennebec** is late. Both tolerate diseases. **Cherokee** is probably the most resistant of all, and we think it's the prettiest. We could have just as well selected **Irish Cobbler** and **Russet Burbank,** which many people call Idaho; these are good, too.

If we couldn't find the Cherokee, we would probably switch to the white **Anoka,** derived from several varieties, one of them Cherokee. It, too, is resistant.

All these varieties once could have been selected from seed catalogs. But times change, and few catalogs offer any today.

Gurney offers sets made from certified potatoes — each a small cone with a single eye and adequate flesh. Those who buy from catalogs ought to know the time of arrival so the sets can go in the garden without too much delay. If not removed from packages on arrival, the sets may mold or dry out.

A few days before we plant potatoes in our garden, we select whole seed potatoes from bins that are increasingly present in garden centers and nurseries. Using a sharp knife and lots of time, we can make seeds (sets) if reasonably careful.

First, we slice off and discard the clusters of eyes at an end — the compost heap is a good place for these because they only waste garden space. We cut the rest of the potato into pieces — each with one or two (no more) eyes and as much of the potato flesh as can be attached to these, no matter what odd shapes result.

When finished, we dust the pieces with captan to prevent disease and rotting. This is easy if you shake a few sets at a time in a paper bag with a tablespoon or two of the powder.

The sets then should be placed in a warm room to dry for two or three days. Living rooms and empty bedrooms of gardeners get used for many strange purposes. The space between a kidney-shaped table and a wall of books in our living room just holds a plastic tarpaulin and two wire shelves brought from the root cellar. On these, dusted seeds are exposed to the air. Scarred sides crust over in two or three days and sets are ready for the garden.

Those dusted potato sets may be planted underground (four or so inches deep) or on top (if covered with mulch) but always with cut sides down and eyes looking up.

We put seed potatoes on the ground about four to six inches apart and cover them with mulch. We don't use commercial fertilizer or fresh manure because we want large potatoes, not lush foliage. A scant scattering of trace mineral fertilizer and homemade compost is worked into the soil.

Each of the two beds used for potatoes is fenced with 12-inch rabbit wire, which prevents the mulch from being blown away. We use leaves (any leaves) for mulch — older leaves, battered and worn ones resting on the potatoes and fresh ones to fill the enclosure. As rain packs these down, we add more. The enclosures may be filled three times before sprouts burst into the sunshine and clean air of the garden.

Harvesting is easy — potatoes are lifted as the mulch is moved about. If any part of a potato has been exposed to sun and air, it will be green. These green parts, along with any white sprouts, must be discarded. They are poisonous.

Skillful hands can wiggle in and out of the roots of the early potato plant, whether in beds or in rows, and bring up marble-shooter-sized

One midsummer Uncle Jerry discovered that on 10 hills of potatoes growing a few feet away from a row of tomatoes, green balls had formed on top of the plants. They looked somewhat like tomato fruit.

He casually mentioned it to just a few folks in the village, but cautioned them to keep it a secret, thinking that perhaps his fortune was made. Of course, the story got around that Jerry or the bees had crossed tomatoes with potatoes and he had some 12 plants that grew potatoes on their roots and tomatoes on the top of the plants.

A group came up from the village and offered him $20 for the crop. Jerry was to permit the plants to grow in his garden until they were ripe. He professed ignorance of the process of nature and told them they were buying them at their own risk. They paid cash then and there.

Grandma heard about it and told Jerry to return the $20 and call the deal off, but the villagers refused. The following spring, they planted the seed and got a few, rather poor quality potatoes, but no tomatoes. Of course, it was just a case of some potatoes growing seed balls. They occasionally do.

potatoes that are early garden delights. This will not hurt the plants, especially if the hands are those of a small child. We call these potatoes "grovelies."

Sweet potatoes

The sweet potatoes we eat in the north are usually shipped from southern states, but they can be grown in Minnesota gardens. They grow from slips, not sets.

Because the potatoes have vines that spread, slips are best planted in raised beds or in patches that can be covered by a mulch to prevent weeds from sprouting. This mulch is laid when slips are planted and then added to as the plants grow and spread.

The sweet potatoes should be dug after the vines are dry and just before the arrival of winter weather. The potato stores well.

Sweet potatoes can be baked or fried, mashed or sliced, even made into a delicious sweet-potato pie. When baked, cut open and smothered with butter, they are delicious. And sweet-potato pie, with or without a favorite spice, is a delicacy.

Slips of a near-bush sweet potato (the ones that spread need too much room) called **Vineless Puerto Rico** will do well in home gardens. A bundle of 25 may be bought from Park. If garden space and money are limited, several neighbors with gardens may share a bundle and its cost.

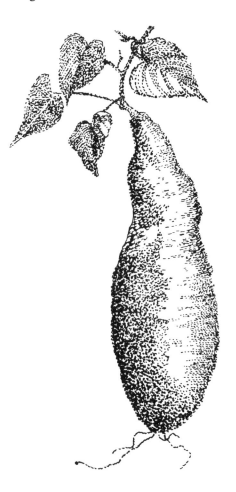

Onions

Now let's look at onions: Not Egyptian onions or shallots or close relatives such as leeks and garlic and chives, but the two known as ordinary onions and as bunching onions — the two found in most food gardens.

Bunching onions — so called because they are sold in bunches — have many names and different varieties. They may be called green onions, scallions or spring onions. Once I knew them as fresh onions, a better name than bunching.

Probably most home gardeners don't plant true scallions or spring onions, but use young ordinary onions instead.

Use the old gardening custom of thinning by pulling every other plant to let the remaining uncrowded onions grow big. Only the first one or two thinnings of onions will give you the small scallion-like ones.

Every cook, gardener or not, uses scallions or other bunching onions. They may be eaten whole and raw — better with salt and still better when right out of the garden, but chilled.

Nowadays we use scallions mostly chopped for salads, soups, casserole dishes and hamburgers. They may be boiled or baked to make "poor man's asparagus." When swimming in salted butter, they are fit for a queen and her king.

At our house, new scallions are chopped in the food processor, packed in plastic boxes and stored in the freezer for year-round use. Their green tops, like the tops of Egyptian onions, should never be thrown away. The joys of both go to their tips.

The true scallions in our garden have been **Stokes Hardy White Bunching,** a strain of the Japanese bunching onion that some catalogs call **Heshiko** and others, to help with the pronunciation, I suppose, call **He-shi-ko.** This variety produces no bulbs — not even tiny ones.

Their stems are long, slim and mostly white. Each plant will multiply into several stalks if spaced and not crowded in the row. They will winter over in our climate as will Egyptian onions.

Heshiko is disease-tolerant and I assume its descendant, Stokes Hardy White Bunching, is

also tolerant; ours seem to be. No true scallion, including this one, is a good keeper; each must be used when fresh — or frozen or dried for future use.

A packet of seeds from Stokes will contain about 600 seeds; an ounce, about 6,000. Because the plants will winter over and their seeds will keep for a year, we bought a whole ounce for at least an early and a late planting in both 1980 and 1981.

Now for ordinary onions.

Like most gardeners, we've jumped from one variety to another, always avoiding the sweet ones and those with thick necks, for they are poor keepers. We've tried for onions with a strong, pungent taste that doubles the tears when they are being chopped. Such qualities portend the best keepers.

Finally we decided that the **Stuttgarter** onions were best for strong taste, copious tears and long life in the unheated storage room.

For years we've planted these Stuttgarters — always with sets, never with seeds — somewhat uneasily. Stuttgarters are neither tolerant nor resistant to the ills of onions. However, I've had no difficulties — no pink root, no smut, no fusarium, not even a single hint of disease. Perhaps this has been by luck, perhaps by careful rotation, perhaps by tender loving cultivation and mulching — one will never know.

But luck and uncertainty do not make a strong garden. So when catalog and rack companies began to offer fewer and fewer varieties to be grown from sets and young plants, and more to be grown from seeds, we began to think of planting only seeds.

Decreasing dollars and increasing prices accelerated this thinking. There were obstacles to using seeds, but obstacles are for overcoming.

One obstacle: the worst onion disease is smut, more frequent in northern than in southern gardens, more frequent if seeds rather than sets

and young plants are used. Reason enough for tolerant varieties to be sought.

Another obstacle: decision-making. Stokes Seeds offered 38 varieties of onion seeds. A rack company offered 32, but its individual racks offered far fewer.

A much more formidable obstacle to using seeds rather than sets and young plants is the length of growing time: Seeds need 150 days to become onions, and where in Minnesota can a gardener find that many days for gardening? Grow-lights can be the answer, and I have grow-lights.

Seeds under grow-lights, turned on for a bit more than half of each day, germinate in sterile potting soil, each a quarter of an inch from other seeds. After sprouting, they are transplanted into twice this space. Even a third transplanting for more space may be needed. The tops of some spindly plants should be snipped off if more than four inches high.

All our plants are in garden beds in April or early May — just as soon as the ground can be worked. Beds have compost, 20-10-10 fertilizer, sifted wood ashes for lime, a scattering of trace minerals and an ample mulch of leaves.

At the plants' mid-growth, we'll add a side dressing of 5-10-5 fertilizer.

What about my selections of seeds? These are the ones I grow:

Storage King. An improvement of **Trapps,** which was a resident in our garden long ago. It is like Trapps in size and in color but has smaller neck and an extra heavy skin. "The smaller the neck, the better the keeper," and "The thicker and darker the skin, the greater resistance to fusarium diseases" are truisms that made Storage King an early first choice. It was developed by Stokes for use in Ontario and Wisconsin.

Canada Maple. An extra-good keeper and yielder, also with small neck and also developed by Stokes — from an onion called **Spice.** Canada Maple will do well in heavy soil, even in soil infected with fusarium.

Northern Oak. Developed from one of the several called **Elite,** but with smaller necks. Tolerant to fusarium and pink root and heart rot and likes hot August weather. Very popular in our area.

Stokes Exporter. Widely used, this one was developed by Stokes for our northern area. Fast grower, even in hot weather. A good keeper with thick skins and small necks. Tolerant to fusarium.

Spartan Sleeper. Developed by researchers at Michigan State University. Can be stored in bulk. Good tolerance to fusarium. If properly cured, these can be kept a year or more before sprouting — a boost to gardeners without a cold room.

Super Elite. Another Stokes introduction tolerant to fusarium and other ills. Small necks on large bodies with thick skins.

We hope the above six varieties of ordinary onions grown from seeds will provide worthy successors to the long-keeping and pungent Stuttgarters.

But there is one more quite different but still ordinary onion to consider — a sweet or Spanish or Bermuda onion — the big and juicy one that is copper-colored, white, red or yellow.

The **Riverside Sweet Spanish** onion is our choice. Like all such onions, this one is a poor keeper — no more than one or two months at best. But when chopped for salads or thinly sliced on hamburgers in buns, any Spanish or Bermuda onion will be at the head of the class.

These onions also can be frozen or dried for future use. Riverside Sweet Spanish onions are tolerant, even resistant to thrips and blight.

With all varieties of onions and onion-related plants, as with other garden vegetables, there are special problems in the patches of closely planted sets, seedlings bulbils and cloves.

Weeding is one problem. Young weeds look like young onions, plants may be too close together to hoe, and shallow roots are easily disturbed as neighboring weeds are pulled.

So let's plant so as not to have weeds. Here's how:

First drench the soil where plants are to grow. Then take a large container of water and a big batch of old newspapers to the garden.

Wet sheets of the paper, one at a time, and cover the area to be planted — four or more sheets thick.

Then with a tool or sharp stick (better than a forefinger), punch a hole through the paper into the soil. This can be done with one hand as the other pushes the seedling or the set into the soil.

After planting, spray the bed again — and later again, and again. The paper must be held down to prevent blowing. We cover the bed with old wire fence strips held down by carefully placed rocks.

If all goes well, paper and wire can be removed at harvest. There should be few weeds.

Note: Tears from onions may be lessened if you drop each onion in boiling water for a few seconds before it is peeled or chopped. If your hands smell oniony, wash them with salt, baking soda or borax and then soap and water. If you have a food processor and use rubber gloves you can avoid all of this, of course.

Beets

Gardeners who plant beets start with something that most people think of as seeds. But they really are pods, each containing from three to eight seeds.

This is why sprouting garden beets are in tiny clumps as they emerge from the soil. After planting, these pods swell and look something like the second letter in the Greek alphabet, beta, B, from which came the name *beet*.

Beets we plant are descendants of once-wild ones found along the Mediterranean as far east as the Caspian Sea. They have been a popular garden product in many parts of the world for generations and are grown commercially where soil and weather permit.

Beets may be bought in most groceries all year — sometimes tied in bunches, sometimes packed in cans and glass jars as whole or sliced vegetables or as pickles. Increasingly, they are

found in bins of frozen foods.

Beets are a cold-weather crop, not bothered by late-spring or early-autumn frosts. They become tough and stringy if planted during the hot days between July 15 and Aug. 15. My experience is that beets will sprout best when the soil becomes warm, which in my garden is not until the middle of June.

Gardeners can plant early or late varieties or some of each. **Little Egypt** (34 days) and **Early Wonder** (40 days) are early ones widely planted.

The long-standing favorite of most gardeners is probably **Detroit Dark Red,** either short or long top, (65-60 days). It's a good keeper for winter use. It's my favorite.

Like most food-garden beets, those we've named are red. Two others are worth your attention: Burpee's **Golden** (50 days) and **Albino**

White beets (50 days). Of these two, I plant only the gold-yellow ones.

I also plant **Winter Keeper** (78 days) and **Formanova** (58 days); a few, not many. The former, said to be better keepers and even redder and sweeter than Detroit Dark Reds, are huge. The latter are red, but carrot-size, ideal for slicing since all slices are the same size. Formanova is a beet much used in Europe for commercial and home production. Seeds for both may be bought from Stokes.

Most gardeners spend hours thinning their crops — especially beets, carrots, radishes and the like. To skip this is to risk being called lazy. Once, since I didn't thin much of anything, or thinned only in emergencies, I was overjoyed to discover that the late gardener/author Ruth Stout didn't either. She often said that plants know best and will do their own thinning if needed. I agree, but with some limitations.

Beets have few enemies and usually need no protection. Once in a great while a gardener may find beets with splotches on their roots. A spoonful of borax in a large trash can of water should be sprinkled about the beets, for the soil needs boron.

What if the beets you dig are hairy? Ah, now you know you shouldn't use fresh manure as fertilizer for beets or any root crop.

Gardeners who don't can, freeze or dry may still preserve their beets (or carrots, turnips or any root crop) for a considerable time. What is needed is moist, but not wet, sand and receptacles of wood or metal. Beets with an inch or two of stems and entire roots may be placed upright, side by side but not touching, and covered with the sand. The moisture will prevent the beets from shriveling.

We think Golden beets are sweeter than the red ones and we freeze most of them. Red beets are at their best when only an inch or so wide. With an inch of tops and all roots left on the beets to prevent bleeding, they may be cooked whole and plunged into cold water for easy removal of skins.

Then they're packed in pint mason jars with boiling water in which they were cooked added to within a half inch of the jar tops. Jars are sealed and processed in the pressure canner (20 minutes at 10 pounds of pressure).

When the beets become twice as large, their skins should be removed as above and the beets sliced with a corrugated cutter for attractiveness. The slices, with some of the cooking liquid, white vinegar, sweetening, salt, cloves, cinnamon and sliced onions, may be packed in pint jars and processed in a boiling-water bath (212 degrees F.) for 30 minutes. Serve these beet pickles with pride.

The juice of those big, tough, last-of-the-garden, beets finds its way into wine bottles at our house and ultimately into guests finishing Sun-

day night supper.

Little cans and jars of strained beets are always on the shopping list of mothers with babies and toddlers. If they are gardeners, they can make their own strained beets with the help of a Foley food mill.

The red color of beets gets used in the kitchen in many ways. Rice and potatoes, for example, may be made red and used in cold and warm salads and mixtures with appealing results. Peeled hard-boiled eggs, covered with beet juice and stored in the refrigerator for several days, can be used imaginatively.

Most all books with recipes have at least one for beet relish. Hot beets are chopped in the food processor along with cabbage leaves, onions, sweet peppers, ground cinnamon and cloves — and mustard, if needed.

Sweetening may be any kind: sugar, honey or a no-calorie powder or liquid, and a few drops of red food coloring if much natural color has been lost.

Thus far we have ignored the best eating and most nutritious part of the beets: the leaves. We know that far too many gardeners discard leaves loaded with vitamins A (a mixture) and G (riboflavin) and iron.

When young beets are dug — not pulled — their leaves are fresh and undamaged and ready to be washed and steamed, or cooked in a small amount of salted water, then chopped, buttered and brought to the dinner table.

They may be blanched, chopped and frozen for future use.

A Japanese cook who learned how to make borscht in Vladivostok, Soviet Union, taught me to like this great beet soup. Then my wife, Jo Nunn, of Russian parentage, taught me to cook it while we were on a Navy honeymoon. You use chunks of beef, pork or chicken and its stock, and red beets for color, then green, white or even red cabbage for bulk, tomatoes for taste, and then carrots, potatoes, onions, parsnips, celery (anything that's around), bay leaves, and vinegar of any kind.

As with the recipes of all borscht makers, Jo's recipe today will not be her recipe tomorrow. Even amounts of the indispensables — cabbage, beets and stock — will shift about.

Her borscht is salted and peppered and sweetened to taste, sprinkled with chopped chives or green dill, on which is floated a blob of sour cream, and eaten with croutons fried in butter.

With two exceptions — red beets and any kind of cabbage — any or all ingredients may be omitted and others may be added, which gives us incredible variations of borscht. — As many recipes as there are Russians, the saying goes.

This is a dish, especially if thick, that can be made in large quantities, then half-cooked, packed in plastic boiling bags and frozen for future cooking and eating.

Carrots

In the months before Pearl Harbor, civilians who wanted free flying lessons and those who enlisted in the armed forces with dreams of flight training knew a lot about carrots.

Twenty-twenty vision was a must. If their eyesight tested badly on the first try, applicants to the Civilian Pilot Training Program could apply again. Radio and newspapers taught listeners and readers eye exercises and advised eating carrots, lots and lots of carrots — cooked or raw.

Large amounts of vitamin A, as well as vitamins B1 and G, and calcium were there just for the swallowing.

It wasn't the first time carrots had been related to physical well-being. Pliny of Rome wrote that the Syrians cultivated "... a plant like the wild carrot ... which is eaten cooked, or raw" for stomach problems. Wild carrots once grew on every continent except Antarctica and Australia.

The wild flower we know as Queen Anne's lace, once confined to Eurasia, is still called wild carrot. This is a recent ancestor of those in our gardens, for the present-day carrot is not an old vegetable. Stokes Seeds tells us that ours started in the 1870s, when a French gardener was working with Queen Anne's lace, which has orange roots. He came across a mutation, the beginning of the carrots we know.

Seed catalogs offer many varieties of carrot — both early and late, round and cylindrical, with ends that taper and ends that are blunt. Colors range from pale yellow to golden yellow to reddish yellow. Some have inner cores with off-colors.

For years my garden had **Scarlet Nantes,** a thick, cylindrical carrot of a uniform color with a blunt end. Then I planted seeds of a new Nantes hybrid called **Pioneer,** from the Joseph Harris Seed Co. I still do.

My preference for the Nantes — any Nantes — runs deep. Its blunt ends make slicing, crosswise or lengthwise, easier. For just chopping or making puree, the other carrots with the long, tapered ends are no problem. But I don't make puree.

Gardeners who have had trouble with blight and rusty roots should plant seeds that are tolerant or resistant to these ills. One such carrot is the Nantes hybrid called **Klondike,** from Stokes.

Home gardeners probably never have seen carrots with stalks three feet high that have pretty little white flowers. These flowers produce the seeds that gardeners buy and plant.

The carrot is a biennial that produces seeds in its second year — as all carrots would if left in the ground in a warm and friendly climate. A few seeds planted in flower pots one year might become interesting house plants in Minnesota the next year.

But now let's get some carrot seeds planted in the garden. Buy more seeds than you think you will need, for germination rates are low. Many gardeners broaden the bottoms of their furrows to a width of two or three inches and scatter seeds in a band to cover.

The seeds should be covered with about half an inch of soil, better done by hand than hoe. I use peat for this; even a small amount is good for the soil. At the end of the season peat may be bought cheaply and stored to await spring planting.

Incidentally, I make sure that the peat I buy is from Minnesota, which has more peat than all other states together. Its infant industry needs support.

When planting carrots, I think it's wise to include a few radish seeds to mark the row so the carrots can be cultivated before they mark their own spot. The radishes will be harvested before carrots need their space, for carrots are slow to germinate and slow to grow.

Those radish seeds have another mission. The plants they become are tough — much tougher than those from carrot seeds — and can break through most crusted soil. Carrots follow with ease. Some soil easily becomes crusted, so the radish seeds may be useful.

Gardeners who use seed catalogs know about pelleted seeds — the Harris company leads the way. Because tiny carrot seeds can be easily lost, blown away or piled on top of each other and wasted in planting, Pioneer seeds from Harris are coated with a hard white substance that dissolves in the soil when planted. What a blessing! These heavier seeds are easy to see, easy to space in the row, and they stay put.

Too much fertilizer means large stems and leaves rather than large carrots. Fresh manure makes carrots hairy and unappealing. Only compost and wood ashes go into beds where my carrots grow — but this soil is loose and full of humus. Carrots get along well in it.

Growing carrots need protection from weeds, as do most vegetables. At our house we welcome these weeds. They are removed when half grown, more or less, and packed into the compost heap. After weeds are pulled, spaces between rows are heavily mulched — sometimes with compost, not always from choice, but from lack of good mulching materials. Once mulched, the plants are free to grow with little bother to themselves or to me.

I do not thin carrots that grow in our sandy loam. But we carefully select those for table use from here and there, never in one place. Small stones cause far more crooked carrots than mere crowding, I think, especially if the soil is loose and easily makes room for growing carrots. If my soil were a clay type, I would thin carrots and other root vegetables.

Carrots may be harvested when they are large enough to use. "The smaller the carrot the better it tastes" is a familiar adage. But the word *small* ought to be changed to *young,* for we have miniature varieties that are full-grown when only three inches long.

One of these is called **Baby-Finger Nantes** and the other **Baby Orange.** A round baby carrot, **Planet,** when grown, is 1½ inches in diameter. They can become as tough as leather and still be small and cute.

Regular carrots, when quite small and tender, don't have to be peeled — just washed, better with a cloth — and cooked in any way for table use or for freezing or canning whole.

Older carrots must be peeled, and for this a vegetable peeler is superior to a knife because only the thin covering needs to be removed. Large carrots may be sliced crossways, lengthways or, better still for most purposes, sliced diagonally, as the Chinese are apt to do. Certainly slanted ones are eye-catching and better-looking.

Chinese think they have a better taste. I agree — only because taste is a matter of individual choice that relates to appearance.

Huge carrots can be made to become a new and tender vegetable much in demand at our house — fresh or canned. Those big and tough

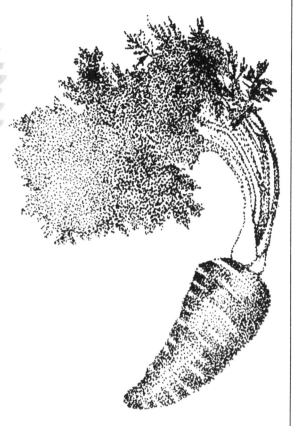

carrots are peeled and halved lengthwise. Center cores are removed with a sharp, narrow blade and discarded. Each half is then sliced into bite-size pieces. To us, there is no better carrot — not even the tender small ones.

Carrots may be preserved in many ways. Unwashed, whole and with at least an inch of top stems and all roots intact, they may be packed in moist, never wet, sand and kept in a metal or wooden container in a root cellar or similar place.

Even in Minnesota, carrots may be left in the garden if covered with baled straw or closely packed hay placed crossways over each row. In the spring, when the snow begins to melt and ground begins to thaw, you may harvest your first fresh vegetable — if field mice don't think you did it all for them.

There are less-risky ways to preserve carrots. They may be dried, canned or frozen. If dried, they are best when peeled, sliced and then blanched and oven-dried with the oven door open and an electric fan moving air over the baking slices.

For less than $200 you can buy an electric food dehydrator with its own heat and blower. This is clearly the easiest and least expensive way to preserve foods — and, with corn, one of the best.

If a pressure canner is available, whole or sliced carrots may be carefully arranged in mason jars and canned to become things of beauty — especially if a sprig or two of Russian tarragon is included. For freezing, carrots may be peeled, sliced, blanched and frozen.

So it's possible for home gardeners to eat their carrots every week of the year, as health services suggest. Carrots also may be used in liquid form, called whiskeywine by the English. (See H.E. Bravery, "Successful Winemaking at Home," Arc Books, New York, N.Y.) For another carrot wine, follow the first of the two recipes on pages 222 and 223 of M.A. Jagendorf's book "Folk Wines".

It seems every country — indeed every gardener-cook — has a favorite dish of carrots to serve to guests. Mine begins with carrots and onions cooked separately, but left firm. (To make onions stay firm, run a skewer through each.) Looks are improved if all pieces are about the same size. How many? Enough to be completely coated or covered with the following. Try a quart of each.

Three tablespoons each of melted butter or margarine, flour, sugar and vinegar; one teaspoon of paprika, and salt to taste; two cups of the liquid left by the carrots. When all are mixed with constant stirring, the drained carrots and onions may be added to simmer on a low burner until served.

Parsnips

The parsnips gardeners know best are in grocery stores, covered with white wax. What a pity they are not in every garden!

Even when seeds are soaked for a couple of days before planting, germination seems to take forever. As with carrots, a few radish seeds planted in the same row will keep the soil from hardening over and help the tender seedlings break through.

If you have never interplanted, you might move lettuce or other plants into or close alongside the parsnips' row. Radishes and lettuce will be out of the way when parsnips need the room.

Two popular parsnip varieties are **Harris' Model** and **Hollow Crown** (both 120 days). The longer and slimmer roots of Harris' Model are preferred.

Freezing weather and soil do no harm to growing parsnips. Gardeners who leave parsnips in the ground during winter say they are sweeter when dug in the spring.

I always pack mulch over our plants as winter approaches, for I fear that authors and professors of horticulture just don't realize how cold it really is when Minnesota temperatures drop to 20 and 30 degrees below zero.

In our garden, parsnips and carrots do well under their mulches. But they attract field mice happy to find a winter's supply of warmth, shelter and food waiting for them — until they find Warfarin, a rat/mouse poison developed by the University of Wisconsin and now sold in every garden center.

A superior wine may be made from the roots of parsnips dug after a few days of frost. Addition of a few parsnips to other roots used in making wine gives a pleasant piquancy to the drink.

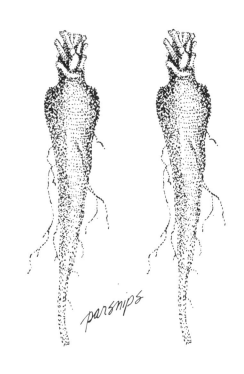

parsnips

Horseradish

Greeks called it wild radish. We call it horseradish, perhaps because of its strength, perhaps because the plant is so graceful and moves about so readily.

Home gardeners will find horseradish the easiest of plants to grow. Once planted, it needs no further help. It searches for and finds its own food and it battles weeds and survives, although it appreciates mulch.

The strength and aggressiveness of horseradish give it a trait that may cause trouble — it likes to wander.

So, plant horseradish in a corner as far as possible from everything else. Even then, for years afterward someone may have to dig it up from, say, the middle of the strawberry patch where a wandering root has popped up to start a new plant.

That's no great problem for me since I moved the strawberry bed. Other food plants now in the area — such as the **Concord, Beta** and **Niagara** grapes that grow on strings of wire, the **Latham** and **September** raspberries tied to stakes, the **Haralson** apples and the **Toka** plums — don't seem to mind those horseradish roots.

The **Martha Washington** asparagus bed, also there, has its own special root structure that seems impenetrable even to those horseradish roots.

If the location of horseradish is to be changed, every inch of the roots must be dug up and removed. Or you might douse the leaves with the new and expensive herbicide, Roundup, which travels to the very ends of the roots and destroys them — without affecting the soil.

Don't look for horseradish seeds, for there are none. Instead, ask for crowns or root cuttings. Those of the variety called **Bohemian** can be bought from Gurney Nursery.

Plant the root cuttings in good rich soil, big ends up — not quite vertically, but slightly slanted — with the tops three or four inches below the soil's surface. Plants should be a couple of feet apart. If the root sticks you buy have buds, fine; if not, buds will appear when planted.

Harvest horseradish by digging the roots, It's best in the fall. The roots may be used fresh or frozen. Always be careful that they are not exposed to air, but carefully wrapped to preserve both taste and color.

The dark skin may be removed with a vegetable peeler and the snow-white core can be grated. Run this core through the blender with a bit of water or vinegar or maybe with ketchup, mustard, mayonnaise or even with cream, depending on your wishes. What's grated is used — strong or weak — for sauces and salads, always raw and never boiled, wherever its flavor is wanted.

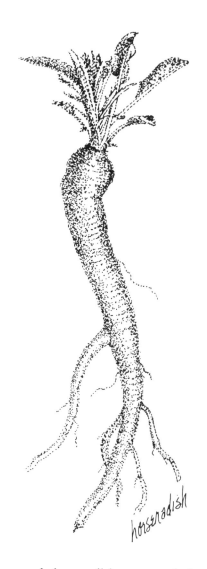

horseradish

Homemade horseradish sauce made just with vinegar and grated horseradish will keep for a long time in the refrigerator.

Whole pieces of horseradish roots may be packed loosely in jars, covered with vinegar, closed tightly and kept in a cool place until needed. We wrap them in foil and store them in the freezer.

For a rare treat in early spring, pull the first horseradish leaves soon after they appear and cook them with any boiling greens, or chop them fine for use in any salad.

No American needs to be told how to use horseradish as a condiment with food, but he or she may not know that it works wonders if a bad cold makes breathing difficult and the nasal passages need clearing. Only ground red-hot pepper does as well.

At our home, horseradish finds it way not only into the sick room, but into sauces and salads and stews — even into mashed potatoes and applesauce.

6/They spread out on the ground

Cucumbers

In Biblical Palestine, lush vegetable gardens were guarded by owners who sat in raised lodges made of climbing cucumbers and their trellises. This was undoubtedly so they could see and not be seen, and so they could be protected from the sun of the Near East.

At the end of the garden year these lodges crumbled as did a tortured civilization, Bible students will remember.

On their way from Egypt, the Israelites included cucumbers among vegetables they missed and lamented. Their references could be to two varieties: the cylindrical green ones that make good shade and good pickles and the rounder, sweeter ones with greenish flesh that we now call Lemon. Both are grown in Minnesota.

Today's cucumbers include not only those fresh from the garden that we slice and sprinkle with sweetened herb vinegar. Nor are they only those that go to the pickling crock to become dills and sweet pickles.

Today's cucumbers may go from the garden to the oven and then to the freezer or to the freezer without a stop to the oven — either for use all year.

There is much to know about the plant before seeds are bought and planted. Progress has been made in developing a bush cucumber, but most grow on vines that either spread and take up a lot of space or climb trellises and use much less.

The spreaders will do better and be cleaner if their areas are mulched with straw, leaves or hay. Pickers must have sharp eyes, for cucumbers have a way of hiding their fruit. Female blossoms are apt to be shielded by leaves of the plant and the cucumbers they produce are found under those very leaves.

If all of them, even misshapen ones, are not picked, production will slow or even stop.

In Grandma's day, cucumbers were thought to be poisonous unless peeled, sliced and soaked in strong salt water until they were limp and watery.

However, Uncle Jerry knew differently and he used to sit on the garden fence eating fresh cucumbers on which he had sprinkled a little horse salt.

We children would gather around him in horrified expectation, but nothing happened. Uncle Jerry often disappointed us.

The picker finds it easier if vines are on trellises (an old wire fence, for example). For then the cucumbers hang down, making them easier to find. Most garden plants on trellises have large slender tendrils that sway in the wind and easily catch the strands, twist and move upward.

Cucumber tendrils are heavier and don't sway about, so they may well need helping hands to find the spot where climbing will begin.

Some gardeners plant many varieties from a dozen or so packets; others plant only a few — one or two, or sometimes three if the garden is large. Only the latter gardeners can be the masters of what's growing.

For example, cross-fertilization can be managed more easily. If plants tolerant to the same diseases are together in the garden it will be better for the gardener and the garden. Similarly, plants that need more water or more fertilizer or both, or plants that can get along without much of either, can be grouped as to these needs.

This is one reason the better seed catalogs are so valuable. Free information about such matters is included.

Tolerant? To diseases? Which ones? Downy and powdery mildew, anthracnose, cucumber mosaic, scab, angular leaf and target and black spot — are all common to cucumbers. To avoid the time-consuming selection and use of chemicals, and their cost, look for tolerant varieties that can stand on their own. That frees our own energy to battle the beetles that like cucumbers as much as we do.

Before choosing tolerant cucumbers, we ought to decide whether we'll use them fresh for the table, made into pickles or baked in the oven.

If for eating fresh, we should plant the ones called slicing; if for pickling, those called pickling.

Pickling cucumbers may be eaten raw; slicing cucumbers can't be made into pickles. Consider planting only the pickling ones, and none or just a few of the slicing ones.

Every canning book has recipes for dill and bread-and-butter pickles made from the pickling varieties. It may be debatable, but we think that half-dills with lots of garlic are far superior to others even though they must be refrigerated and won't keep long. All season these can be served with pride, eaten with gusto, and remembered during the winter.

Cucumbers made with lime, as done in the deep South, are even better than the good bread-and-butter types we enjoy for summer picnics.

To make them, one needs only a pound bag of Mrs. Wage's pickling lime, a plastic container like a clean wastebasket and a pair of rubber

gloves. The lime comes from Tupelo, Miss., and the directions are on the package. But here's how it goes:

Begin by soaking seven pounds of sliced cucumbers (or sliced green tomatoes if it's this pickle you want) and two cups of pickling lime in two gallons of water in a plastic wastepaper basket for 24 hours. The slices will become almost white and very brittle. They should be rinsed several times in cold water to remove all traces of the lime.

Soak the slices overnight in a solution of two quarts of vinegar, eight cups of water, a tablespoon of salt and green coloring to suit your fancy.

Next day add pickling spices and whole cloves to suit your taste, and boil the mixture in a metal, preferably enamel, pot for 35 minutes. Pack while boiling hot in mason jars and seal.

Any cucumber can be baked. The bigger they are the better they will taste. The test of readiness is not the outer color (green or yellow or white will do) or the condition of the seeds, but the firmness of the inside flesh.

Firm, solid cucumbers should be peeled, sliced lengthwise into halves, seeds removed with a big spoon and discarded. Slice each half into long strips 3/8-inch or so wide and cut these slices into two- or three-inch lengths.

From these short lengths we must remove excess water or we will end up with a mush, not firm and crisp slices.

Our grandmothers removed excess water by first dissolving in a potful of water enough salt to float a fresh egg. When the egg floated, the water was salty enough to draw water from cucumber pieces — or from any other vegetable.

(Why only a fresh egg? Fresh eggs have no empty space to fill with air. An old egg with lots of air under the shell will float in water with less salt.)

But there's a better way.

Let's say we have five or six gallons of cucumbers from which water must be removed. Put a cup — maybe two — of canning salt in a bowl, enough to half fill it. Slowly add water, just enough to reduce the salt to a mush. This will remove all excess water and much of the flavor of the cucumbers, so add four tablespoons of vinegar to the mush to retain the cucumbers' flavor.

Wear rubber gloves if your hands are tender. Double handful by double handful, move the cucumbers to the bowl, slosh them around just long enough to get every stick covered with the salt-vinegar solution, then very quickly fill a plastic container with the sticks. Don't add any liquid to this container; we want to be sure that all water present is from the cucumbers.

Slowly the cucumber water will rise in the container. Just before the liquid covers the sticks, they should be drained and rinsed repeatedly until, by taste, the sticks are salt-free.

Now we are ready to bake the sticks for dinner or for thirty-odd other future dinners.

We begin by adding whatever you have and like: chopped green or Egyptian onions (with tips, if tender) or chopped chives (if they are the wide, flat ones), chopped green peppers if you have them, and chopped herbs such as basil or celery leaves or parsley (fresh or dried), melted butter to lightly coat each stick, garlic powder and black pepper to taste.

When stirred to mix well, all can be poured into greased (Pam is better) baking dishes and baked at 350 degrees until, by taste, you guess that they are about half done — about 30 minutes.

When cooled they may be packed in plastic freeze boxes or, better, in plastic boiling bags that will be frozen with pieces of waxed paper between the bags when they are placed in the freezer.

Now let's consider how to freeze sliced new cucumbers. Here's our way:

Slice about 12 medium unpared cucumbers

In midsummer, when cucumbers and muskmelons were blooming close together, the question would arise among the farmers: "Will they cross?" Uncle Jerry usually settled the argument by declaring there was as much chance of that happening as there would be for a cow to have a calf smoking a corn cob pipe because she was pastured near a corn crib when it burned. Uncle was right. Cucumbers and muskmelons cannot cross-pollinate. If muskmelons have a poor taste, it probably is due to poor growing conditions or diseased vines.

(they will be more attractive if the tines of a fork are pressed the length of the cucumbers before slicing), mix with 4 medium onions sliced and 4 tablespoons of salt and let stand for about 2 hours. Drain well and put the mixture into plastic containers.

Take 2 cups of cider vinegar, 1 teaspoonful of celery seeds and either 2½ teaspoons of sugar or sugar substitute. Mix well, pour over the cucumbers to cover, and freeze. You can add green pepper pieces if you wish, or bits of grated carrot for color. For best taste and texture, serve while ice crystals are still present.

Perhaps it's wise to decide what kind of cucumbers we don't want to plant before deciding the ones we do want. The first one the home gardener doesn't want is the *European*. It's only for greenhouses of special construction and exacting requirements. The vines inside are self-pollinating and must be kept free of drifting or insect-carried pollen. If they aren't, the plants will have "gourds." Also, amounts, timing and composition of food for the cucumbers are exacting.

The fruits are seedless or almost so; they hang side by side, close together. They develop into the long, beautiful, costly cucumbers we buy with envy because we can't duplicate them in our gardens.

Special note: Some few of these, locally grown, are appearing from time to time in produce sections of the better supermarkets. Maybe the gas stations now being abandoned over the land could be converted to indoor gardens to house the growing vines of European cucumbers. The buildings have water, electricity for grow-lights, movement of air, a source of heat and a need to be used.

The true gherkin is considered a native of both North and South America, but it may be an early import into the West Indies from Africa that spread rapidly in the New World.

Packets of the **West Indian Gherkin** (60 days) can be bought from Burpee Seeds or the **True Gherkin** (60 days) from Gurney.

Like most gardeners, I've planted the seeds of Gurney's **Little Minnie,** Stokes' **Double Yield Pickling,** Farmer's and Park's **Tiny Dill,** Burpee's **Spacemaster** (one of the newer bush varieties). All produce a little cucumber that looks and tastes like we think a gherkin should and can be used the same way. They have been developed from the Asiatic originals by plant scientists.

Home gardeners have three choices: they can plant the real gherkin, the little ones that faintly resemble the real ones, or no gherkins.

Real gherkins look so unlike "real" cucumbers that I plant a few just so I can ask visitors if the two vines involved are of the same family. Only if you have lots of space and curiosity would I suggest gherkins.

We said goodbye to our long-time favorite cucumber, **Mariner,** for this variety has been dropped by the Joseph Harris Seed Co. This one was not a slicer but a canner. At our house it made half-dills and full dills and reached the dinner table sliced and sometimes floating in a mild herb vinegar solution with a touch of artificial sugar and mustard seeds. It was just this dish that we ate during the winter months when plastic freezer boxes were removed and emptied to reach the table when ice crystals were still clinging.

In our 1981 garden, **Mariner** will be replaced by two of the pickling varieties: **Pioneer** (51 days), and an All American Winner, **Saladin** (65 days) — both from Stokes. **Saladin** will not need the male pollinators that will be included with the **Pioneer** seeds. As was **Mariner,** these are resistant or tolerant to the ills of cucumbers. They, too, should go well with baking and freezing. Baked cucumbers are great favorites with us and our guests.

Two of the oriental "snake-like" cucumbers, **China** (75 days) and **Japanese Long Pickling** (60 days), both from Stokes, will produce thin cucumbers up to 18 inches in length. They are good in bread-and-butter pickles or raw in salads, and easily turned into strips for baking. They are tolerant to mosaic.

Seeds of the cucumber **Lemon** (65 days) are from Harris. The Lemon cucumbers are yellow and roundish with greenish flesh. They are sweetest of all — good for slicing, pickling and baking and at their best when just turning yellow.

If you plant only regular pickling cucumbers, long and slender oriental cucumbers and small "named" or real gherkins, you'll avoid the problems posed by the slicing cucumber — no getting them mixed in the picking pails or in the refrigerator, and no mixing of pollen either.

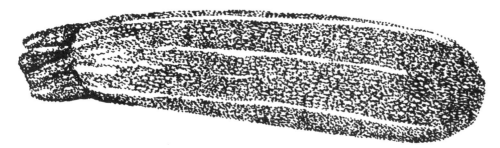

Squash and zucchini

No garden is complete without summer and winter squashes.

Only a few squashes are the bush variety. Others spread and spread. So, if space is important, read seed labels with care.

If the word "bush" is not used, the squash is a spreader. Good catalogs from good seed houses tell you plainly that **Table King** is a bush acorn squash and that **Table Queen** is a spreader acorn squash.

To us, the real great winter squashes are varieties of acorn, butternut and buttercup. We look for bush ones or those with short vines.

We like Table King (80 days), a real bush squash of the acorn type and All-American winner **Golden Nugget** (95 days), a butternut squash. To us, the flesh of a third variety is even more superior than its name, **Sweet Mama** (85 days), a buttercup type that has long vines but tolerates a "vine cut" when vines are four feet long. Seeds of these three are easy to find. See the catalogs of Burpee, Stokes, Park and Jung or the Northrup King and Burpee racks in garden centers.

A cousin, once editor of the Progressive Farmer magazine and now a tinkerer of plants and a doer of good deeds, gave me a Butternut type of huge winter squash that turned out to be our best — but for that year only because such types take up too much room.

For summer squash we have yellow crookneck and one or more of the green zucchinis. We are careful not to plant them close together. One year they were not separated and we picked green ones with yellow spots and yellow ones with green spots. They tasted good, but were hard to explain. Guests had difficulty in accepting the truth; one still insists that some oriental magic was used just to confuse.

These summer ones, from Jung, are three zucchini-like squash: **Aristocrat,** a dark green and high-yielding squash that was a 1973 "All American Winner;" **Black Magic,** not a true bush variety but a "compact" with small seed cavity and a glossy dark green peel; and **Hybrid Squash Gold Bar,** a fine yellow squash on very bushy plants.

Winter squash keeps well into any new year. Summer squash doesn't keep at all. Both can be frozen, but in entirely different ways.

Winter squash must be cooked and reduced to a pulp, which may be packed and then go directly to the freezer. But if it is to be canned, it must be packed in chunks in mason jars and canned at 10 pounds for 35 minutes if in pints, and 45 minutes if in quarts. In either case, it can be used for many tasty casserole dishes — even pies for dessert.

Summer squash may be sliced or diced and frozen for sauteing, baking and mixing with other things. It may be shredded and frozen, and, with shredded carrots, it provides a pleasing "bed" for fish and meats and other vegetables.

Zucchini has become one of our most versatile vegetables, and we plant lots of it. We eat it fresh from the garden, cooked or raw, when it's not more than six or eight inches long. We use it in soups, in breads, in desserts and in pickles, even dills.

Both summer and winter squash should be planted only after all danger of frost has passed. Plants must be covered when autumn frosts threaten. Even a touch of frost will cause leaves to wilt and plants to die. Fortunately, between frosts there are ample days for harvest.

7/They come up every year

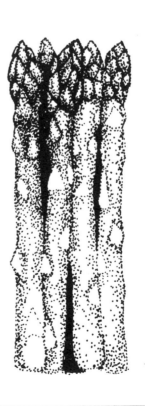

Rhubarb

We start rhubarb with root pieces from plants we like and not from seeds, which may not run true. We plant a hunk of root (the bigger the better) with one or two eyes just beginning to appear, perhaps to see the last scattered bits of snow that remain in the garden, perhaps to be the first to welcome spring.

To get these hunks, we dig, slice, pull and twist, as carefully as we can, the root-part that we want to remove from an older plant. We leave the rest of the root-eyes to become stalks that will find their way to the kitchen during the next few months.

That hunk of root we pulled loose may be planted in a new garden bed or row. In two years it will be firmly established, and then we can remove the stalks we want for the kitchen or freezer by twisting and tugging, never cutting, thus leaving a clean and harmless scar.

As years pass, even with yearly doses of fertilizer, rhubarb stalks get thinner and the leaves smaller — but the plant goes on. At some time we remove the old and start the new, but in a fresh bed or row. The old soil is exhausted for rhubarb, but not for other fruits or vegetables.

Briefly each spring, most nursery and garden centers and a few seed catalogs offer rhubarb roots for sale. Their stalks will be red, from roots to leaves — skinny, but red. The roots come in carefully wrapped packages, probably labeled **Chipman's Canada Red, Valentine** or **Honeyred.** They are the current favorites; they are the all-red ones.

The roots we dig from old beds grow stalks with red bottom halves and green upper halves. They are old varieties with lost names, cultivated for thousands of years. But the stalks from young plants will be like the baseball bats we call fungoes, and leaves will be like ears of an African elephant.

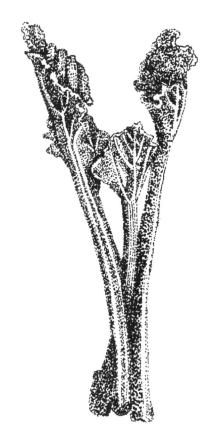

For red rhubarb sauce or pies, cut the stalks where the green joins the red, take the red parts to the kitchen and throw the green stalks and leaves in the compost heap.

However, if you're making rhubarb wine, use the entire stalk. They make the best wine, plain or spiced, especially when pulled in late autumn when they are weatherbeaten and tough with a strong flavor.

It's important that all leaves — even those of all-red varieties — go to the compost heap. They contain oxalic acid, which is poisonous and fatal in large doses. The big seed stalks (flower stems) that will sap the strength of the plants should be removed at ground level as they appear, and these, too, should go into the compost heap — but not too quickly. Before they open and become large and ungainly, treat and use them as cut flowers in tall vases. They make welcome gifts to friends.

One spring I dug complete roots from my 30-year-old bed, divided them and started a new bed — a double row of plants, 2½ feet apart, along the north edge of the 100-foot garden. First I dug bushel-basket-size holes, filled each with compost, chicken manure, commercial fertilizer and a scattering of trace minerals. This was mixed and sloped from the center to the edges.

Then with my hands I made a narrow hole in the center and filled it with ordinary garden soil. The rhubarb root should touch only the soil so it isn't shocked by immediate contact with

Summer was one of Uncle Jerry's favorite seasons because Grandma often made his favorite pie for him — pie-plant pie. Pieplant grows in our gardens and is on your menus today, too, but we know it by the name rhubarb.

strange chemicals.

I removed no stalks from the new plants that year or the next. After a second birthday, stalks could be pulled as needed — outer ones first. And these plants were gorgeous, huge beyond belief, making the old bed look even more dilapidated. Invitations went out for friends and strangers to start beds from the old clumps.

I have learned to make new beds after each decade of growth. And I'll stick with the old red and green plants that first entered recorded history in 2700 B.C. From the northern part of China, they have spread everywhere.

Rhubarb is still the springtime tonic of plain people worldwide. It has been used by witch doctors, traveling medicine men and now by scientists in pharmaceutical houses. Prospectors for Klondike gold used it to ward off scurvy.

Rhubarb is best in the spring. That's also the time to can, freeze or dry it for pies, sauces, jams and jellies for year-round use.

I prefer frozen rhubarb that is not blanched or sugared. Cut stalks into thin strips lengthwise. Slice them in small pieces, spread them on trays and quick-freeze them. Then you can package, label and store the rhubarb.

Lightly cooked, this rhubarb may be eaten cold or hot just as it is or with a trace of honey, sugar or saccharin. It will not be mushy.

My method is not for long-time storage, the experts say, but how long? I don't know, but the rhubarb in my freezer from last year's garden should last until packages of this year's take their place. That's long enough.

Commercial rhubarb in the market is apt to be "forced" by methods best left to the large growers. Still, the home gardener can force his plants by placing a bottomless pail or box around each. Thus protected, plants will reach for the sun and be ready to eat earlier.

Gardeners who can afford to destroy or injure a plant may dig it up in the autumn, put it in a hot or cold frame and enjoy still earlier rhubarb pies. Most home gardeners are content to wait.

Asparagus

What is asparagus, where did it come from and how do you grow it?

When my mother entertained her literary club, the platters she served were certain to contain her special chicken salad with a trace of black walnuts, two or three small, hot-buttered biscuits and several stalks of cold asparagus covered with a sauce that only she and Aunt Ann could make.

The asparagus was a lovely white. It came in cans, cooked. It was costly, served only to special guests. At our home now, we eat asparagus from our 20-year-old bed once a week or so, all year.

Our asparagus is green, not white. The difference between my mother's and mine is not just in color or even in taste. The difference is in knowledge.

Perhaps while at home from college I told her what I had learned from a lecture by a visiting Johns Hopkins professor of distinction. During his talk, I had written the word "vitamins" for the first time in my notebook marked "Botany." All who heard that lecture were stirred by a future seen dimly through a partially opened door.

What my mother and her guests didn't know was that the blanched pure white asparagus tips they enjoyed so much had about as much food value as a dish of newsprint.

But now we know that the vitamins in asparagus are A, B1 and C (especially rich in C) and that these vitamins are absent when the stalks are blanched by hilling, preventing light from turning them green. Almost all asparagus in our country is green — we want the vitamins, now that we know about them.

In Europe, a real white asparagus is grown, as is a purple, but not here.

Asparagus was first grown 2,000 or more years ago from the Eurasian steppes to the Mediterranean Sea. Some animal herds and some people ate wild asparagus.

Greeks, Romans and Persians grew it in their gardens — and wrote about it. Some authorities think the word asparagus is from Persian, others from Greek. No matter; all seem to agree on the methods of planting and harvesting. Cato, the Roman, wrote directions that can just about be followed today.

Not Cato's, but my directions:

Grandma would never let Uncle Jerry in her garden when he was smoking a cigar. She claimed the tobacco on his hands killed many of her plants. She was right as usual, and many years ahead of her time. It has since been proved that tobacco smoke, under some conditions, carries a blight that can infect growing vegetation.

You can begin with seeds; but only a few gardeners do. They don't mind the painstaking transplanting and cultivating and the three-year waiting period before harvesting.

Most gardeners will start with one-, two- or three-year plants. The older ones cost more and are likely to be more chancy, so most gardeners begin with the biggest one-year plants they can find. Seeds and plants may be found in some seed catalogs and in almost all seed and garden centers.

Mary Washington is the oldest and most-planted asparagus, but **Viking,** sometimes called **Mary Washington Improved,** is better, especially for the Midwest. Both are disease-resistant. Both can be had as seeds or as plants.

Asparagus roots are planted in a trench. It is easier if a rototiller is used to loosen the soil, which is then placed alongside, but not so close that it may be blown or washed back in.

The trench should be 18 or more inches wide — about the width of the tines of the tiller — and 12 inches deep. When digging is finished, two or three inches of compost, manure, 5-10-5 fertilizer and a scattering of trace minerals in varying amounts should in the bottom. Then, with the rototiller, this can be thoroughly mixed to a depth of six inches, then packed by walking on it.

Plants should have time to adjust slowly to new situations, especially when fresh roots first meet chemicals. So I next spread an inch or two of fresh soil loosely on the firmed mixture in the trench. Then, with both hands, a cap or cone of this soil can be made every 18 inches.

The roots are seated on the apex of the cone, spread carefully in all directions and covered and firmed with two or three inches of soil from the pile.

As sprouts appear, turn green and grow, rake the soil, a little at a time, from the pile into the trench and firm it around each plant. Before frost arrives, the trench should be filled and the ground made level. Harvest may start after two seasons have passed.

If additional trenches are needed, they should be five or six feet apart, because the root structure of asparagus may become a closely bound mesh reaching six feet from the row and six feet deep. Asparagus needs room to grow. A mulch of loose straw or leaves will prevent weeds from stealing food from plants.

Asparagus also needs food to nourish roots that send forth the tips that we eat and that, after harvest time, become tall, thick, willowy, beautiful plants.

Harvest should begin as the plants reach eight or 10 inches. Each stalk should be gathered; to do otherwise would lessen the number that the roots will send forth. It is not a good idea to cut the stalks below the surface where one can't see where the knife goes. Instead,

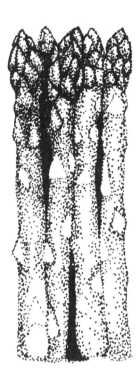

bend each stalk and let it break where it will.

Harvest should end the first of July. This will give the plants time to recover and reach full growth long before the first frost. After harvest each year, spread manure, compost or fertilizer over the bed and work it in.

If asparagus beetles arrive, you can't use a chemical spray on tips that are going each day to the kitchen. I stop cutting tips from one or two plants at each end of the row and let the beetles go there; they prefer the full plant to those that are being cut.

It may be possible, of course, if the wind is right, to spray only the plants on which the beetles live.

If you have no beetles, the dry plants each autumn may be cut to become part of the mulch. But if beetles have been present, put all stalks into the compost heap or far away from the garden, since beetles winter over in them.

The tender top of the stalk is the part that reaches the table. The tough bottom part goes to the compost heap; the middle may go into the blender and become asparagus soup.

Raw foods are growing in popularity. Food expert James Beard finds raw asparagus a tasteful addition to a tossed salad, and most gardeners will also.

Good cooks know that the tender top of a fresh asparagus spear needs less cooking than does the bottom. They stand the stalks in a coffee pot with boiling water covering only the lower part. That boiling water and its steam produce the asparagus we like to eat — no part is overcooked.

Try fresh asparagus that has been cooked this way for only a few minutes — say 10. Next time try eight minutes, then six, and adopt the cooking time that suits your taste.

Asparagus that is to be frozen must be blanched. The stalks are usually cut in inch-long bites. At our home the coffee pot is not used to cook frozen asparagus, which is always steamed.

8/Don't forget these

Peppers

What a change during the lifetime of this gardener!

Once he helped his father select and mark the most robust of the seed-producing plants — corn, tomatoes, beans, peppers. These were not to be used for food, but to produce the seeds for next year's garden.

Such seeds were dried in the sun and stored in bags of tightly woven cotton cloth with slivers of chewing tobacco strong enough to cause insects to go somewhere else. These bags were hung away from walls and rafters so as to frustrate even the smartest rats and mice.

In those days, neighbors swapped seeds. Still earlier, secretaries of garden groups arranged to exchange seeds with other groups. Such exchanges brought to northern gardens (with short growing seasons) seeds of plants that grew in regions where biennial plants could produce seeds in their second year.

Thus newfangled vegetables such as carrots could be planted in Minnesota — and in the Sandhills of Nebraska, as Mari Sandoz tells so beautifully in the book about her father, "Old Jules".

As a boy, I knew that the peppers in my father's garden were either sweet or hot, that the long yellow ones originally came from Mrs. Grogan's garden, and not much more.

Now this boy is a near-octagenarian, and his food garden will have only a few plants that remain complete and total strangers.

Good seed catalogs are good teachers of plant history. One "catalog company" (Stokes) lists and describes, with a line or two, sometimes more, each of 42 varieties of peppers it offers for sale. A bonus of value from this seed catalog: Something about the history and use and spread of peppers from the days of the Aztecs who first had peppers in their irrigated and well-planned gardens in old Mexico.

My garden always has hot and sweet peppers. Seeds of each variety will go into Jiffy 7 peat pellets (two seeds per pellet) that will stay under grow-lights until placed in a hardening-off box outdoors for a few days until acclimated and ready for a garden bed. By then, the weaker plant in each pellet will have been removed.

The small hot, hot, hot Jalapeno peppers (70 days from transplanting), actually perennials in hot climates but annuals in ours, are picked when mature but still green. They are canned in pint jars for frequent home use and much appreciated gifts.

I searched a long time to find a recipe for canning, but the Hennepin County Extension Service found one for me. To it, I added olive oil, as does a Texas cannery that specializes in Mexican foods Minnesotans seem to like.

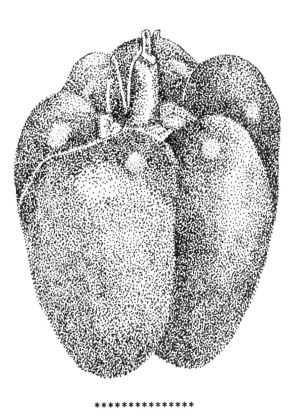

****

HOW TO CAN JALAPENO PEPPERS

First:

1. Wash 4 quarts of peppers, any size, green or red or mixed. Do not remove stems but use any without stems. Wear rubber gloves.

2. Make two small slits in each pepper.

3. Dissolve 1½ cups of canning salt in 4 quarts of cold water. Soak peppers in this solution for 12-18 hours.

Next:

1. In a cooking pot, enamel or stainless steel if possible, mix 10 cups of vinegar (the cheaper white is preferred); 2 cups of water; ¼ cup of sugar or Sugar Twin (which I use); 2 or 3 cloves of garlic (crushed or with slits).

2. Boil for 15 minutes.

Next:

1. Drain and rinse and rinse and rinse the peppers.

2. Pack in canning jars, pints preferred. Do these carefully for there is beauty as well as order in the result. You'll have an eye-catching display if you put a single red pepper in each jar, or, if many reds, space each with precision.

Next:

1. Cover all pods with the boiling solution.

2. Seal each jar and place in a boiling water bath for 10 minutes of boiling time.

Last:

1. Remove jars. Cover with a loose towel away from drafts and let them cool.

2. Next day, check seals, wash and dry jars. Label with name and date.

3. Stack in cool, dry, dark place.

(Exceptional jars make good Christmas gifts. But if you plan to use many as gifts, the garlic used should be whole and not crushed. Crushed garlic makes the jars cloudy if shaken but the great garlic taste will be stronger.)

****

The large hot peppers in our garden are the **Large Red Cayenne** (75 days from transplanting). At the end of the growing season, always before frost, when they are long and green or red, they are harvested.

Immediately, with thin needle and strong thread, we'll string most of them in four-foot lengths, taking care that the needle goes into the stem and not into the flesh of the pepper. These strings make ideal Christmas decorations; almost all of the green ones will turn red for the holidays.

When they are dried and red, the peppers have their stems removed and the pods are ground to a near-powder, bottled in airtight containers and protected from light, which will fade the pepper from fiery red to pale pink.

Those pepper pods not hung to dry are packed in glass jars of vinegar to make pepper sauce. The jars will look prettier if some green ones are included in each. Pepper sauce is on all condiment shelves in Southern kitchens and dining rooms.

When you handle any hot pepper — green, yellow or red — use rubber gloves because hands that have touched hot peppers will hurt eyes and skin scratches.

Our food processor, with its knife blade, is much better than our blender for the grinding because it reduces all the skin and most, but not quite all, of the seeds to pepper dust or powder.

But what does one do with hot pepper powder? Sausage makers and others use it to add flavor to mild food. At my house, breakfast includes eggs. For 40 years, my family has watched as I dipped a knife edge into the pepper jar and then tapped it to spread the pepper powder over the egg on my plate — whether that egg is poached, scrambled, steamed, boiled, fried, made into an omelet or, on rare occasions, eggs Benedict. I regret that no other family member has joined me — more than once.

This powder will clear sinuses better than snuff, but is not apt to be prescribed by doctors, I'm sure. In olden times hot-lipped belles used it to redden lips and cheeks to please their swain. This helped my mother's mother when she opted for and won her wounded Confederate soldier. Could it work even today?

A dozen **Large Red Cayenne** pepper plants should produce peppers to fill two or three small airtight and light-tight plastic containers when reduced to powder.

So gardeners, for whatever motive — food or clogged sinuses or winter decorations or rosy complexions — should gear the number of seeds they plant to the number of pints they expect to use.

But there should be neither inhibitions nor thrift in numbers or use when it comes to sweet peppers. One never has enough. We pass up all early reds, all yellows, all pimientos, all ornamentals, and all miniatures and will plant only **Yolo Wonder** (80 days) and **Keystone Resistant Giants** (80 days) because only big and blocky and thick-sided fruits meet our requirements.

Requirements? Of course, as with any garden plant. There are many more than just size. First, Yolo Wonders and Keystone Resistant Giants are tolerant to the virus disease called mosaic, which gardeners have learned to avoid. Seeds are listed in most catalogs and found on many seed racks.

Plants of these varieties will be leafy to protect the fruit from sun scald, important because peppers are tender and frost-shy plants. Pellets of pepper seedlings don't go into the garden until after Memorial Day.

Since most all plants in my garden are planted close together with only essential thinning, these seedlings in peat pellets are planted 12 to 15 inches apart within their beds. However, the plants on the edges of the beds will have an advantage because beds are three feet apart.

Plants of both hot and sweet peppers should be surrounded with a heavy mulch of leaves for weed control. Roots will be near rotted compost. A scattering of fertilizer and a smidgen of trace minerals, if available, will go into the soil when transplanting is done.

How strong should the fertilizer be? We've discussed soil testing in Part One of this book and a test is the only sure way to find out what fertilizer your soil needs.

Almost ghost-like in the early dawn, Grandma would "steal gardens," but it is not as bad as it sounds. On vacant lots in the village square, in front of the courthouse and library and entrance to the two cemeteries, she would plant seeds, divisions from her perennial flowers and spring seedlings from her garden.

Some years ago I visited these spots and there were flowers growing there. I hope they were descendants from her plantings.

Since tobacco is a frequent host to a virus mosaic disease often called tobacco virus, and since neither the manufacturing process nor the heat from smoking have an effect on it, one plant disease book suggests that no smoking be done in the garden, especially near tomatoes, eggplants and pepper plants.

Moreover, it adds that smokers should wash their hands between smoking and gardening!

About 80 days after transplanting, the Yolo Wonders and Keystone Resistant Giants will be ready to harvest at the same time — a great advantage for our purposes. Cut them from the stalks with scissors or knife.

The final harvest at our house of all sweet peppers starts when a few of them begin to turn red, or partly red. Some with red color are cleaned of seeds and cut into narrow strips and frozen (without blanching) for decorative use in salads and casseroles and on baked potatoes or whatever.

The rest of the just-turning ones end up as chopped peppers to be frozen in ice-cube trays, wrapped in foil, and stored in the freezer for use as flavoring, contrasting color or both. Try them with yellow corn, for example. The rest — by far the most — are used as stuffing peppers.

These are washed and sliced lengthwise to make two vessels of each. When cleaned of their seeds, each half is stuffed and frozen and then wrapped in foil for storage.

Blanched pepper halves are used by most gardener/cooks, but for the last two years we have used them raw and thus ours are firmer and, we think, tastier.

For the stuffing we rely on mixtures of raw chopped Egyptian onions with their green tops and cooked rice with ground beef, ground venison, flaked tuna fish or chopped cheese spread. If canned tomatoes are used, dried basil is added.

Note 1: Early on, pepper blossoms and fruit may suddenly fall to the ground and scare owners. If you leave the plants alone, other blossoms will appear when humidity increases. (And in Minnesota that will be day after tomorrow — any tomorrow!)

Note 2: The hot and sweet peppers in our gardens are in no way related to the pepper berries that grow on tropical shrubs. They are never in our gardens but always in our kitchens. The berries are ground to make fine or coarse black pepper and are also used whole. When the outer skins are removed, white pepper can be made. Black coarse pepper joins the red pepper powder on my breakfast egg, and probably goes on yours, too.

Cole plants

More gardeners ought to use the word *cole*. My dictionary says the word is rare, which is not encouraging. It also says cole plants are those of the genus *Brassica*, a word botanists rattle off easily, but practical gardeners may find as difficult as I do.

Brassica or cole plants include cabbages, Brussels sprouts, broccoli, Chinese cabbages, bok choy, kohlrabi, kale, cauliflower, collards, mustard, turnips, rutabagas and about 40 other plants rare in home food gardens.

Most home gardeners can point to corners or sides of their gardens and say, "My cole plants are there."

But why should home gardeners plant all but one of their cole varieties in one big area? (The exception is the rutabaga, which ought to be planted in soil never before cultivated — perhaps along a fence row.) One answer is that most pests and fungi that like one cole plant like all cole plants. So, if all plants to be sprayed or dusted are close together, a difficult job becomes easy.

There is a second good reason, maybe even better, for this togetherness. Gardeners who rotate cole crops will find it easier if all are in one area. No cole plant ought to be planted where any other cole plant has grown in the last three years. Most gardens have four corners; there is no better way to keep plants out of a given area for three years than by moving them around those four corners.

Broccoli, cauliflower, Chinese and savoy cabbage, bok choy, and Brussels sprouts and the ones called "greens" can be frozen, but if freezer space is limited, care should be taken to mix early, mid-season and late varieties, especially cabbage and cauliflower, in your garden and enjoy a longer eating period. Brussels sprouts, collards and broccoli are ready to be picked over a long time and after frost has appeared.

Knowing in advance just how any vegetable is going to be used can answer many of the gardener's questions. If the gardener and the cook are not one and the same, repeated conferences between the two are desirable.

The cook knows that red cabbage may be made into "red cabbage and apples," as in Germany, and that Savoy and green cabbage can be mixed with celery and carrots and peppers and made into coleslaw. Knowing that both these dishes may be frozen, the gardener-cook plants more seeds and seedlings.

The freshman gardener should know that, starting from the ground up, leaves of the Brussels sprouts should be removed from the stalks just as soon as the tiny sprouts reach match-head size. The gardener should know, too, that the cauliflower that reaches our tables is white only because its leaves are gathered at the top of the plants and tied to protect the heads from the sun.

Broccoli, Brussels sprouts, cauliflower, kohlrabi, leeks and celery, eggplant, okra, celeriac, salsify

Broccoli

There are two types of broccoli: A heading variety with a single large central head, with no side sprouts, or just a few (called "shoots"). Even if these liked our summers with their few hot and dry days, I would pass them up and plant only the second kind with a smaller central head and many more smaller sprouts.

It is these smaller sprouts that fill our larder. The variety in our garden is **Cleopatra** (75 days). This hybrid variety was a garden great for three recent years. Only one year did we think it a near-failure. But then the two other varieties did worse.

Our Cleopatra seeds are from Stokes.

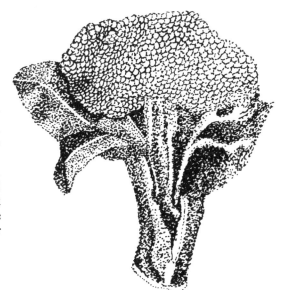

Brussels sprouts

Brussels sprouts first grew in Brussels, Belgium, where they have been for centuries. Perhaps the reason they have not spread everywhere is that they do poorly in a climate with lots of hot or muggy days and little or no frost.

But this means Brussels sprouts planted in Minnesota may think they are in their native country. They should grow in all our gardens for eating fresh or for freezing.

The single variety in our garden:

Jade Cross E (92 days). Not to be confused with the older Jade Cross. The *E* identifies the plants as of exceptional vigor, less subject to foot rot in rainy weather, and of a European style. (Harris, Stokes or other catalogs, or Northrup King seeds at your garden center.)

Bottom leaves should be removed from stalks as soon as the "little cabbages" on stalks just above the leaves are the size of the head of a kitchen match. These little heads won't grow much until cold weather arrives and will taste better if touched by frost.

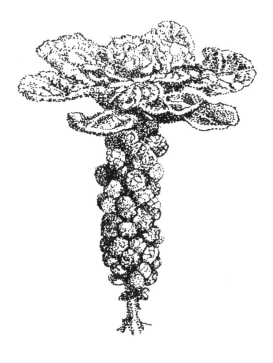

Cauliflower

There are two principal kinds of cauliflower: white and purple. The former is in great demand but difficult to grow. The latter is even better, though relatively unknown. But it is easy to grow and needs no blanching.

The big problem with the white ones: Bottom leaves must be tied to cover the heads, even when only the size of a silver dollar, to provide an umbrella to shade the heads and keep them white while keeping shoots from growing from the centers.

Now this can be done by the home gardener and, if results are good, he or she can strut with pride. But it is a chore. Cauliflower in our garden will be:

Snow Crown (50 days). A quick-growing hybrid, this plant produces wide and compact heads and large bottom leaves. When pulled together and tied, these bottom leaves make sunbonnets that protect and blanch the stem flowers. (Harris Seeds)

Royal Purple (95 days). The purple cauliflower is easier to grow because it needs no bonnet to bleach its purple crown, which turns green when cooked. There should be no confusion: Purple-headed cauliflower is an actual cauliflower, but with a different color. Don't be misled by those who insist it's some sort of heading broccoli. It freezes well. (Harris Seeds).

Kohlrabi

For many years just two kinds of kohlrabi, **Early Purple Vienna** (55 days) and **Early White Vienna** (50 days), went into American gardens. Odd-looking, they produce edible knobs that are actually swollen stems.

Inedible roots and near-inedible leaves that sprout directly on top of the knobs (like hair on a head) make up the rest of the plant.

Now there is a third variety, a hybrid called **Grand Duke** (45 days) that has larger knobs that taste milder. The plants are tolerant to black rot. Other varieties are not. Grand Duke was an All-American Silver Medal winner. Seeds are available from Joseph Harris, Burpee Seeds or Farmer Seeds.

Raw kohlrabi slices and sticks, with salt or a dip, or oil and vinegar, should be high on appetizer lists.

Kohlrabi freezes well and is good when cooked alone or mixed with other vegetables. Even the leaves of Grand Duke, I'm told, can be cooked either with the knobs or separately. This can't be said, at least with enthusiasm, of the leaves of the other kohlrabis.

Leeks and celery

Leeks and celery are grown in our northern garden from seedlings, not from seeds. Each is exciting and offers separate challenges to the experimenter who adapts what he learns from the seed catalogs.

As with cauliflower, blanched leeks and blanched celery are white because of actions the grower takes. In this case, the grower pushes soil against the stems as they grow.

To grow a few seedlings for the garden, fill a flowerpot with potting soil, scatter the seeds, cover them lightly, water them and keep them in a warm place.

When seedlings first appear, place the pot in a window with maximum sunshine or under grow-lights. When the seedlings have two leaves, each should be carefully lifted, by one leaf and never by the stem, and replanted in a peat pot or in a tray of the same potting soil.

The pots or trays should be kept moist and in as much window light as possible. A week before the seedlings are transferred to the garden,

they should be exposed to the outdoors for an increasing time each day to harden them.

When the garden soil has been made ready and is fairly warm, the seedlings may be planted, pots and all. Leeks go in a trench about a foot deep, to be filled slowly as they grow.

At our house we like celery leaves better than celery stalks. A variety with bushy leaves is **Tendercrisp** (105 days) from Stokes Seeds. Leaves are hand-rubbed when dry and packed in sealed, darkened jars. Stalks are sliced and canned; petioles are cooked to become soft and are then blenderized to make a puree which is frozen.

We have canned and frozen leeks — great for a thick leek and mashed potato soup. We generally plant **Electra** (100 days) from Harris, but any variety will provide the admirable taste.

Eggplant

Eggplants, fresh or frozen, bring something of the Near East to our house.

The one most used in our garden is **Black Beauty** (80 days from transplanting); it's quite large and round. Seeds from one of the newer eggplants from Japan will produce sweeter and more elongated fruit. Either does well in Minnesota gardens but must be started indoors.

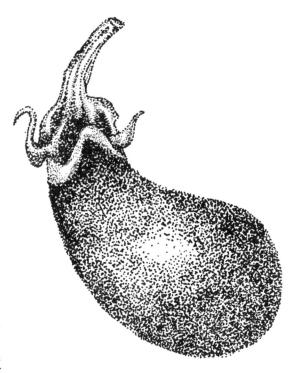

Most eggplants are peeled, sliced, dipped in egg, rolled in meal or flour and sauteed. They are delicious.

For a couple of hours before these slices were to be used, Grandmother used to pile slices on top of each other, put a plate over the pile, and then place a heavy iron on the plate. All of this was to remove the "poison" that she was sure was present. The juice that was squeezed from the slices was not even added to the slop that went to the pigs.

Grandmother was wonderful, as was her food. But what she did was simply remove excess water in the eggplant. We can do the same by soaking the slices in salted ice water for half an hour. But if we don't want to take that extra step, we can forget about the "excess juice" that in no way is poisonous.

We are not limited to fried eggplant. When sliced, mashed, baked whole or combined with other vegetables in casserole dishes, eggplant is a superior vegetable. And it can be frozen in any way you select and used when needed.

One of the best ways to use and preserve eggplant is to make large amounts of ratatouille from any recipe in any good cookbook.

For this dish, eggplant sticks, with those of summer squash, green peppers, and bunching onions, can be half-cooked, cooled and packed in boiling bags and frozen to be cooked again months later.

But first, just as my Grandmother did, surplus water from the eggplant sticks must be removed. We dip 2-inch sticks in a small amount of cold water heavy with canning salt and a little vinegar, handful by handful. Each handful is lightly shaken and placed in a large plastic container. When the water that will be removed almost covers the sticks, they can be drained and rinsed several times. Now the ratatouille that's made will be firm and not mushy with the extra water of the eggplant.

Okra

In northern gardens some plants are bewildered by cool weather and soil.

Their ancestors in the south did well for centuries and still do, in places warmed by the hot sun and moist winds. Here in cold country, neither such plants nor their owners are sure that they can make it before autumn frosts arrive. They need every extra day we can give them.

Okra is a plant that needs those extra days or some substitute for them.

So after soaking them in warm water for 24 hours, we plant the seeds of **Emerald** (60 days in the South but more will be needed here), which has pods that are green, round and spineless. Seeds come from the Geo. W. Park Seed Co.

By the side of the always-good-tasting green okra, plant some not-so-good-tasting red okra; how much depends on what you are going to do with it. Just a few stalks of the red will provide good garden conversation.

If pods of either are not picked for food before they reach three inches in length, just let them remain to dry. Arranged in a high vase, they will make an interesting winter decoration. If the red ones must be cooked, you should know that the boiling water turns the pods green.

Rather than in the soup, the red ones please us more in the eight-inch brass shell casings we use for flower vases. Seeds for red pods are more expensive. So far as I know, red okra has no varieties, it is merely "red okra." It isn't easy to find, unless you have the Park Seed Co. catalog.

Green okra pods can be canned whole with tops on, or cut into bite-sized pieces. Or they can be frozen in the same forms. Our pods are canned, used in soups, dipped in meal or flour and stir-fried, and also steamed or boiled, but only for Jo Nunn and me. The other members of the family are only surrogate southerners.

Only twice in a dozen years have my okra plants grown from seed in the garden failed to produce pods before the first full autumn frost.

Okra is good fried, steamed or boiled. No mixed vegetable soup is really good without it. It has a second name, gumbo, which tells of its thickening quality. Use the pods only while they are immature. They are easy to can or to freeze.

Celeriac

Celeriac is another seldom-used garden vegetable that shouldn't be ignored.

Sometimes it is called knob celery because only the large knobs at the tops of roots are eaten after they are two or more inches wide.

The knobs have a nutlike celery flavor. When cubed and boiled or braised, they usually appear in a cream or a cream-mustard sauce. The cubes also are used in soups and stews. Few guests have eaten this dish, but those who do pronounce it good. A packet of the variety called **Marble Ball** (110 days) is available from Harris.

Celeriac knobs are better if used when about 2 inches wide. And better, too, if not peeled until cooked.

Salsify

A native of Europe, salsify grows wild in much of our north country, and its purple blooms are found in many gardens of wild flowers. Roots are used for food. They can be peeled, chopped and cooked in a small amount of salted water until tender. Peelings, which give much flavor, can be added and then removed before serving.

To make a great dish, add chopped onions that have been sauteed in generous portions of butter or margarine, salt, black pepper, smidgens of garlic and red-pepper powders and finally milk and cream. Stir it together and heat, but do not boil, and serve in bowls with soda crackers and you have "oyster" stew. Salsify is known as the oyster plant. It's easy to grow.

The only variety I have ever used is **Mammoth Sandwich Island** (115 days) from Harris. I preserve the roots by loosely packing them in canning jars, each filled with boiling water and a tablespoon of flour. These jars go in the pressure canner for 20 minutes at 10 pounds.

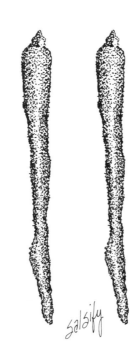

salsify

Peanuts

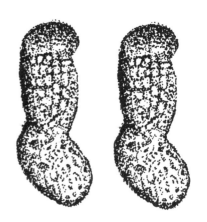

Peanuts are wrongly thought to be only for the Deep South.

They will grow in northern gardens. But they need many growing days and northern gardeners must plant them with misgivings

There are two kinds: One is the Spanish red type with fewer, but larger and longer shells and bigger kernels used chiefly for oil. These are also roasted and sold and served unshelled.

The second kind is the Mexican brown type with many smaller shells and kernels best known as the small, salted nuts found on bar counters and bridge tables and in baskets of vendors at stadiums and fairs when shells are not wanted.

In Georgia, peanuts may be planted four inches deep, but in Minnesota only 1-1½ inches deep. Plant four kernels, with skins, in hills 18 inches apart. When they are six inches tall, cultivation may start. When they're 12 inches tall, soil should be "hilled" high around each plant. Soon, lower flower-leaves will fall and slender peduncles appear. These will burrow back into the hills and each will produce a single peanut at its very tip.

Space between hills should be heavily mulched up to eight inches. Only after heavy autumn frosts have killed the tops should the plants be pulled from the ground, hung up and dried for about eight weeks. During this time, the kernels become the peanuts we eat. This drying should not take place in basements or open garages — try an unused bedroom.

Food gardeners with limited space may decide that a raid on the flower yard, or even on the rock garden, may be defended. The peanut plant is actually an herb and a very attractive one, so it could add interest to flower plantings.

It will add value to the food we eat, especially if eaten raw, for the number of units of vitamins in raw peanuts is truly awesome. In a single cup there are 50 units of vitamin A, 438 of B1, 240 of C, and 200 of G.

The modern world should thank the late Dr. George Washington Carver, of the Tuskegee Institute in Alabama, for much of what is known about or done with peanuts — and perhaps the Incas of ancient Peru who first grew them in their irrigated fields.

Peanut hulls shouldn't go out in the trash, but into the compost heap, for they are high in nitrogen.

From Park Seed Co. come either the smaller Mexican-type peanut or the larger Spanish type. Curiously, the name of the Mexican type from Park is **Spanish** (110 days); the name of the Spanish variety is **Valencia Tennessee Red** (120 days). Park also has a variety called **"Peanut Park's Whopper,"** the biggest of them all.

9/Herbs add spice to life

Among the loveliest of all gardens — some centuries old and some sparkling new — are those growing only herbs.

Plants are grouped in beds of circles, squares and triangles. There are areas of open sunshine and shade from vines and trees. We see walkways of stone and gravel and wood. Some walkways are snow white and others black-black and still others are of various reds and yellows and grays.

There are stone and iron benches for those who want to sit and silently admire the contrasting and complementary arrangements based on the shades of green and other colors and on the size of plants. All are the work of artists without pens, brushes or chisels.

Herbs add flavor, color and beauty to foods we grow. Because gardeners enjoy eating and serving the vegetables and fruits they raise, they ought not to stop with the more common herbs: dill, mint, sage, basil and chives. There are two good reasons to plant more.

The first is that all over the world thousands of plants are being harvested to give beauty and taste to the meals people prepare in their kitchens. Much of the "foreign" food Americans eat and enjoy is foreign only because of the herbs used — herbs that can be bought, and many that can be raised in Minnesota family gardens.

The second is that herbs can help restore the art of conversation and rekindle the togetherness of families. We need something to talk about, something of common interest and mutual aid.

Herbs are worth more attention. Let's start our discussion with the herbs almost everyone knows something about.

The basic herbs

Mint

Mint is a good one to start with.

It's the green liquid in the small bottle on a kitchen shelf, poured over ice cream and added to this and that; it's the last five half-pints of jelly marked "mint" that we serve with lamb or venison; it's the crushed, dried leaves firmly packed in plastic or glass containers, used whenever its flavor and color are needed; it's outside in the garden in the warm months and inside in a flower pot in the cold ones.

Most frequently it floats, slightly crushed in tall glasses of iced tea, of juleps of bourbon whisky or Virgin Islands rum, of slings of white or sloe gin or vodka.

Mint is a breath sweetener of good taste — found in chewing gum, candy mints, toothpaste, shaving lotions, scented soaps and in some of the medicines we take. We use a lot of mint. And it's easy to grow.

Most of the mint grown in our country is peppermint. It's generally not for home gardeners, but for commercial growers who get an average of about 50 pounds of peppermint oil from each acre planted. It's planted from roots and cuttings, not from seeds. Let's leave it where it is.

Also not for home gardeners are apple mint, which looks best of all mints when in a flower pot but has hairy leaves; orange mint, a funny mixture of green, purple and red that tastes like oranges; pennyroyal, which is bitter as well as minty; pineapple mint, which has striped leaves that no one will recognize as mint — and a lot of others.

Spearmint? Ah! That's the one for the home gardener; it's the mint that everyone loves.

Plant spearmint seeds and run, for mint demands the entire garden, quickly. Fortunately its roots are just below the surface and can be contained if metal strips enclose the growing areas. Mint likes sunny areas but will do pretty well in shade.

Mint leaves and sprigs may be picked whenever they are wanted. For drying, cut the foliage just as flowers appear — only from the upper half of the plant or a bit more.

Hang mint to dry in a ventilated but dark room. Rub the dry leaves between palms of hands and store in a plastic or glass jar, wrapped to exclude light.

If you want a pot or two inside for use in winter, switch plants from garden to pot in midsummer. Our grandmothers included mint leaves in the sachets of dried flowers and herbs they made each year to add fragrance to their bureau drawers.

Dill

Most gardeners know dill only as seeds purchased in small cans and used for making pickles or when a sauerkraut dish needs to be dressed up for company.

Dill is the easiest of all folk wines to make; it begins with dill seeds soaked overnight in unflavored brandy and ends with the compliments of friends.

Dill is an annual that scatters its seeds, even in a light autumn wind, all over the garden. Two points:

• The seeds we plant need light for germination and shouldn't be covered when planted. Just press the seeds in the bottom of the furrow to keep them from blowing away.

• Dill doesn't like to be transplanted, so don't try. Once planted, it continues to grow in the same area, year after year, just as if it were a perennial. Those dropping seeds make it do so.

Green sprigs and leaves may be harvested at any time; they're good in soups and salads and for garnishes.

When ripening, seed clusters may be cut with scissors and loosely stuffed in paper sacks to dry. The seeds, when sifted out, go into glass or plastic containers that are wrapped to keep out light.

We like to fill divided freezer trays with chopped parsley, basil or leaves of other herbs — even too-soft mashed bananas. These are frozen, wrapped in foil, and stored in the freezer for future use. Tender dill foliage does well if stored this way.

The adage "Seeds are where the flavor is," means only that foliage will lose flavor quicker than will seeds. Even so, we think that the best dill pickles, made with cucumbers or cauliflower sections or snap beans, have both dill seeds and dill foliage in their jars. And we add cloves of garlic, too.

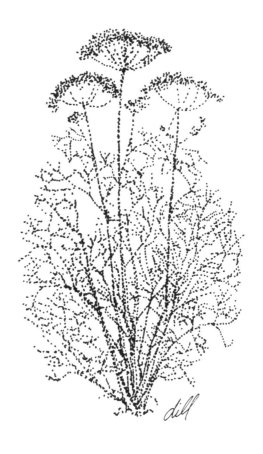

dill

Grandma used thin shavings of gum camphor -- still obtainable in drug stores -- on and under branches of evergreen trees that dogs were troubling. Also on places in the garden which were attractive to cats. Moth balls or naphthalene flakes will often repel these animals, and sometimes squirrels.

Chives

Chives are about the least troublesome plants in the garden.

Most gardeners plant the smaller chive with thin, tubular leaves and small purple flowers. A clump of these can be lifted into a flower pot and brought inside for fresh use during the winter. What's left will quickly restore itself if replanted in the garden in the spring.

Clumps divided and replanted every few years produce fatter leaves; otherwise the leaves get smaller as the plant gets older. These leaves may be cut and chopped and used any time.

They can be frozen — no blanching is needed — for winter use. Sprinkled on a baked potato, the frozen chives are just about as good as fresh ones.

In recent years many chives lovers have discovered and planted the Chinese chive. It has a much longer leaf, flat and gently curving, with a mild garlic flavor. Now that Park Seed Co. has included this in its list of herbs, its use will probably spread.

In my garden, between the old-fashioned and the Chinese chives, I have yet another flat-leafed chive that is much bigger, taller and fatter than the Chinese. This one's taste is purely onion and not garlic. The lady who sold a single pot of this plant to me a good many years ago said she thought it was an "arctic chive," and that the seeds were from Finland.

I ask every gardener/scientist who visits my garden to help me find a better name. All compare the leaves of this chive with those of the Chinese and say it is a different variety. Most have promised to "read some more" but I still have no name other than the two suggested by other gardeners: "Giant Chive" and "Great

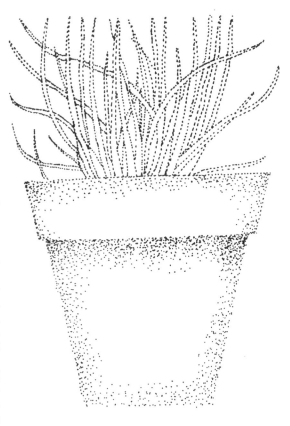

Chive."

Each year I give seeds or potted plants to visitors who, I suspect, give seeds to friends. If this continues, perhaps we should call it the "Minnesota Chive."

Either the "Minnesota" or the Chinese chives may be used just like the smaller chives. But these, even when chopped, won't get lost in stews or soups or salads; they are just too big.

Sage

There are so many kinds of sage that we ought to refer to the one we plant as "garden sage."

It may be started under grow-lights in early spring and transplanted to the garden when the soil has become warm. Sage seedlings can be bought in early spring at most garden centers.

Food gardeners should take care not to buy pineapple sage which is fragrant and lovely to look at but lacks taste. Leave this one to the flower growers.

Garden sage and pineapple sage are perennials and should be covered in the winter. Woody stalks should be removed each spring when winter covering is swapped for garden mulch. Leaves of garden sage should be harvested in quantity only from plants in their second year of growth.

If we remember to manage those woody stalks, sage does well in Minnesota weather —

better, I think, than in Minnesota kitchens or meat markets. In the latter, rolls of sausage are apt to be marked "hot" or "mild," which is a red-hot-pepper and not a sage matter.

Sausage is a finely chopped and seasoned meat, mainly pork. Its proper seasoning is sage, enough of which will turn ground pork, hot or not, into sausage.

If a sausage roll is found to be insipid, slices may be sprinkled and pressed with dried sage that the home gardener can make by rubbing leaves between palms or in a blender that will reduce the leaves to powder. The sage will make it better but hardly good.

Sage is also for dressing or stuffing for all meats, especially poultry. As stuffing, it has competition from soft bread and cream and chopped oysters, ham, apples, nuts and dozens of other strange items including the hard-to-get-rid-of gizzards, livers and hearts.

Odd dressings are better for conversation than for eating. But once while in Japan, I included in my stuffing fresh tangerines from the trees in my yard and sliced eels from the Inland Sea, which was the view from three sides of my house and its gardens. I thought this wonderful — my very own creation!

Years later my conversion was the work of Prof. W. A. Billings of the St. Paul campus of the University of Minnesota. He edited the much-fought-for "Turkey Letter" and was just about the most respected poultry specialist in the country. He preached his ideas about dressing to radio and auditorium audiences and to readers of food and garden columns over the whole land.

Nowadays the "soggy" supporters are coming back, but for me there has been no backsliding. I still do as Billings taught, though I use a bit more onion and an extra dose of sage.

His recipe: Two or even three completely dried-out loaves of bread, outer crusts removed and discarded, the rest reduced to hard chunks and then crumbled by a coarse grater (today's food processor does as well as the professor's grater) — all to fill a large pan. A dried onion chopped as fine as can be. Just enough salt to barely taste. Then powdered sage. In his own words, *"PULEEEEZE do not use too much sage — just enough to taste tangy, but not to gag you."*

Pour a pound of melted butter over the crumbs, stirring all the time. Then pour the dressing into the cavity of the bird. Don't press even lightly, not even with a weak spoon.

If there is any stuffing left, bake it in a separate pan. On top, place the neck, heart, gizzard and liver, whole. Billings always concluded with: "Sew up the incision."

Ah! When the bird is removed from the oven you have the best dressing that can be made — then and now! Sage makes it so.

Sage, fresh or dried, can make a wonderful sauce for pork, lamb or wild game. Cook it with gravy or with water or tomato juice to which onion or garlic powder or both are added, and maybe a bit of vinegar, too. Folk wine, and both morning and evening tea, can be made from fresh leaves.

And this is my best tip: Fill a blender almost full of burgundy or claret wine. Add a cup of fresh sage leaves and liquefy for a minute or two, then return it to the jug and mix. Indescribable pleasure.

The future of sage is for cooks and not for gardeners. Cooks must experiment, try new ways of using, mixing, serving — a mission that never ends.

Gardeners should know only that the new plants won't reach full maturity until their second year; that if you fertilize with fresh manure you will not like the taste of the sage, and that new plants are needed every three or four years.

Thyme

First, "thyme" ought to be spelled "time," for that's the way its name is pronounced.

Next, gardeners should not start with seeds because they take three or four weeks to germinate, and only after two years will plants reach usable size. Good gardeners are patient, but not that patient — especially since there are ways to speed things up.

Best way: In early spring every large garden center offers potted thyme. Frugal gardeners with patience buy a single pot and add to the thyme row with cuttings rooted in water. Affluent ones buy lots of plants to fill a bed or row.

When thyme is first planted, and every spring afterward, a small dose of bone or seed meal should be mixed with the soil around each plant. More fertilizer will bring winter-kill, even when extra mulch is used.

Plants should be divided every three or four years or they will become overgrown with tight stems and smaller leaves. You can harvest any time for today's use, but for drying and storage take only the upper half of the current year's growth just before flowers open.

Thyme, unlike sage, is not a kitchen problem.

It goes well with every meat and every vegetable and every salad, which probably accounts for the number of gardeners who try to raise it.

But thyme is not only for people. Since the days of old Greece, observations have been written about the allure the little blue-red flowers have for bees. For many years, I knew no better place than my thyme patch to observe bees, both my neighbor's Italian and my own Caucasian (which are black, you may like to know, and originated in the Europe-Asia area of the Caucasus mountains) which came to smother my few plants.

Plant thyme and grow better vegetables — for those same bees may return when other plants are rich in pollen and nectar and make biological pollination and fertilization more complete.

Celery leaves

Some gardeners in north Georgia raise celery. That is, they do if the path of the sun and the slopes of the mountains and the yards of cheesecloth and an adequate number of irrigation sprinklers will produce the climate that we in Minnesota can have just by stepping outside.

There are two kinds of celery — green and yellow. Each has many varieties. All are grown for their stalks, and judgments are not usually made of their leaves. But to me the stalks are by-products — delicious by-products — that are sliced slantwise as the Chinese do, packed in quart jars and canned in the pressure cooker. Wonderful for winter use — but still by-products.

It's the leaves of celery that I crave.

These leaves are picked, washed, then dried in the food dryer, rubbed between palms and packed in glass or plastic jars wrapped to exclude light. They are opened only when an herb of special merit is needed — in well-buttered,

salted and peppered mashed potatoes, or in a clear soup.

The celery I plant is **Tendercrisp** (105 days) from Stokes. This variety is bushy — topped with large leaves and long petioles from leaf to stem. Seeds are sown indoors and the seedlings transplanted into the garden the first week in May.

No other plant under grow-lights in my basement, with the possible exception of leeks and onions, does as well while the outside world is still white and cold.

In the garden, they are planted close together, not to have the plants blanch each other but to cause them to reach up for light and become bushy.

Most bunches will be undisturbed until early September when all will be dug, washed well and processed in one of the ways I have described.

Basil

When we talk of basil, we usually mean the common variety that is green while growing. It may be dried and crushed and stored in plastic or glass jars; packed in olive oil to be retrieved, leaf by leaf, as needed, or standing in big jars of white vinegar to make an herbal vinegar for salads.

When dried and crushed, basil may be poured, not just sprinkled, onto an empty plate and mixed with black pepper, powdered onion and garlic and a little salt. Then a thawed cut of the cheapest chuck or an unmarinated square of venison, patted dry but still damp, is rolled over and over on the plate to pick up the mixture.

Next drain the liquid from a quart of canned tomatoes, preferably Romas, for they have little juice. Then dump the pulp in a crock pot and add the meat. Make a tossed salad and — behold! — the perfect dinner for the hardworking husband/wife team. Basil makes it so.

What green basil can do, the other basil, **Dark Opal,** can do as well or better. Dark Opal is less frequently grown. That's a pity, for its

taste is richer. This one is native, as is its unidentical twin, to the South Pacific.

Its home now is surely Storrs, Conn. It was there, at the University of Connecticut's College of Agriculture, that long-time and intensive breeding changed a waif into an All-American medal winner.

There is no trick to basil growing — green or purple. Sprinkle seeds lightly along a row, cover with one-quarter inch of soil and firm the surface. Leave the plants alone and see that weeds do the same. Harvest by thinning or by cutting the upper two-thirds just before blossoms appear.

Harvest the entire plant before frost, for basil is an annual. Hang bunches on a string in a dry, darkish, ventilated room. Pack leaves, rubbed by hands from stalks and stems, in a light-tight, airtight container.

You learn that tomatoes and basil go together — good even when both are raw. But try basil in anything you fancy. However, don't mix a lot of herbs in a harum-scarum fashion for the flavor of all but the strongest ones will be lost.

Tarragon

One of the tarragons is called Russian, sometimes Siberian. It may be grown from seeds and it's a hardy, vigorous plant with a flavor considered by some to be rough and raw.

Another tarragon is called French. It may be grown only from cuttings from living plants. Its flavor is considered delicate and refined.

Russian is my favorite. Of all herbs in my garden, this one obviously likes both the garden and the gardener — the word lush is meant for Russian tarragon. Year after year, it's there, waving to attract attention, begging to be used.

At our house, it has just one use — herb vinegar. To make it, fill large glass jars with white vinegar from the grocery. Then insert with care sprigs of Russian tarragon the length of the jar. I increase its beauty by adding two or three flat and wavering leaves of one of the wide-leafed chives.

Herb vinegar from these big jars is not just for "oil and vinegar" dressing on tossed salads, It is a substitute for any vinegar.

I've planted seeds of Russian tarragon but, to persuade you to buy potted plants next spring, you need to know that my seeds were in the freezer for a week before they were planted — they are really Russian.

With care these went into flats, planted one-quarter inch deep, with the potting soil made firm. The flats were put in the sun each day and in a cool place in a shed each night. They were tested each day of 20 days to be sure that the soil was moist.

Herbs for tea

Many herbs are used for choice tea; let's consider just two that are easy to grow. Each is of special interest.

First catnip, which is really catmint. This native of Europe now grows wild everywhere. One reason: For years before real tea could be had, afternoon tea in English homes was made with this herb. And English homes were wherever English folk lived. Now anyone can grow it, or find it wild, for tea and for other purposes.

Seeds of two varieties of catnip are offered by Geo. W. Park Seed Co., each identified only by botanical names, *Nepeta Massinii* and *Nepeta Cataria*. The latter is the one that cats like, fresh or dried, leaves or blossoms. Leaves of both catmints are used for tea. If flower buds are removed each time they appear, more leaves will form — for a total of three pickings.

The plants will live in shade. Their leaves are easily preserved by drying and packing in airtight jars wrapped to keep light away.

But catmint tea has strong competitors. It's a matter of opinion, but most herb tea drinkers will agree that a better cup can be made from either one of the chamomiles (sometimes written camomiles).

Either one? Let's enter a fascinating jungle of confusion made worse by using the same name, spelled the same way, for two different unrelated and very uncommon aromatic plants, each of which makes a wonderful tea with an apple-like flavor.

One chamomile, **Nobilis,** frequently called Roman chamomile especially in England and parts of America, is a perennial that creeps to make a fine ground cover. If not mowed it may reach about six inches high.

Its flowers — a scant inch wide — are white or yellow. Flower heads are picked, dried and

chamomiles

used to make a fine herbal tea. When dry, they are about the size of the head of a kitchen match.

In the Sturgeon Lake area and other northern parts of Minnesota, where my plants first grew, these are now wild plants that can be had for the digging.

Why wild in Minnesota's Arrowhead? Let me guess. Once the woods were alive with lumberjacks whose faces and hands invited hungry insects — unless bathed in chamomile tea. The loggers left behind the plants that furnished their insect repellent and it's the descendants of these plants that now grow in my garden.

In England the "German" chamomile, **Ma-**

tricaria, is considered a weed. But in Germany the matricaria is the plant for tea, and Nobilis is the weed. Incidentally, the matricaria chamomile in my garden was marked "Hungarian chamomile" when I bought it.

By whatever name, matricaria is an annual that grows 2 to 2½ feet high and has daisy-like flowers with hollow disks, yellow centers and white petals.

Seeds of either chamomile, when planted, should not be covered but just pressed onto the soil. If covered, they won't sprout.

Is chamomile tea only for drinking? No, its other uses are as curious as the use of its name. It's a bug repellent, as we've seen. It's a good rinse for blonde hair. Spray it on other plants and prevent damping off. And on and on.

Seeds of Germanic or matricaria chamomile are offered by Geo. W. Park Seed Co. and by Burpee Seeds. Garden centers can supply potted plants of either chamomile, especially in the spring.

Nancy Moe, a member of the Hastings Garden Club, once reminded us that it was the comforting chamomile tea that Mother Rabbit gave Peter after his scary foray into Mr. McGregor's garden. (Flopsy, Mopsy and Cottontail had bread and milk and blackberries for supper.)

I suspect that Roman chamomile made Peter Rabbit's tea because the author, Beatrix Potter, was English.

Where do we go for seeds and plants of herbs? To me, the least confusing source of seeds is Park. This company offers far more herb seeds than any other garden seed company but not more than some of the great and famous merchant-herbalists like the Indiana Botanic Gardens in Hammond (zip code 46325) or the National Cathedral in Washington, D.C.

And in the spring, garden centers everywhere have potted seedlings of herbs for sale.

10/The gardener's tools

Hands are the gardener's principal tools. The sticks, stones and shells used by primitive man, and by some present-day primates, were projections of hands. So are the hoes, trowels, rakes and shovels that hang on the Japanese torii at the side of my vegetable garden.

For centuries, gardens were made ready for the seeds with a spade or a plow. And today's gardener is apt to use a spade if the area isn't large. A tractor does the job if the garden is large — an acre or more.

But the rototiller is the tool usually used. And there is one for sale or rent to fit the needs and the size of any garden.

Just after World War II, we began to hear about this European invention: a gasoline engine revolved tines that tore up the ground and moved the contraption forward. The user walked behind, guiding the machine by gripping plow-like handlebars.

On a summer midday, the University of Minnesota's Joseph Leverone and Jerome Tauer invited me to see a newfangled machine that the university had imported from England. They thought it might be useful in maintenance of the university grounds, Leverone's job.

The machine was called Gem, and its tines were in the rear. It was made for big, strong men. Even big, strong Jerry Tauer, who used it, thought so. None of us guessed that within 25 years it would become one of the principal implements of the garden worldwide.

I advise a gardener who plans to buy a rototiller to try them all. There are dozens of makes in the market: Those with front tines, those with rear tines, those that permit the users to walk by the side of the machine and not on the soft earth behind it, those with much horsepower and those with little horsepower, those driven by chains and those driven by belts.

Those with rear tines are preferred: Weeds and grasses — even cornstalks — won't clog their tines and demand constant removal. Bet-

ter yet, the user may keep out of the tilled soil and steer easily. Also, there are no rear wheels to disturb the freshly tilled soil. But these machines are costly.

Most gardeners get along with less-expensive machines with front tines, as I do. If weeds and grasses are too high and tough for front tines to manage, a rotary lawnmower used a day or two before will solve the problem of clogging.

Another drawback to these front-end tillers is that the rear wheels and the gardener's feet pack the freshy turned soil. Vibrations from the whirling tines shake the user, as the advertisements of competing machines with rear tines stress.

Honda introduced a quite different front-end rototiller. It had front tines, but with swivel handlebars that permitted the operator to stay outside the freshly turned soil. The rear wheels on this machine could be raised and locked so they left no deep marks to interfere with planting or the looseness of the soil. They were less exhausting to operate than others with similarly placed tines.

Every year more changes appear in the increasingly popular rototillers. Recent ones include rear tines in many models that previously had them in the front. Swinging handles are now more common. Hand controls are better placed.

As this book went to press, a new tiller with counter-rotating tines arrived in the market. In one sweep, it makes a seed bed that is almost perfect. Those counter-rotating tines (which have nothing to do with the movement of the machine) slam the soil upward against the covering lid — and when it falls the gardener has the tractable soil of his dreams.

Today's purchaser of a rototiller has more to read, see and try than ever. And the gardener must know about the companies that rent many tools, including rototillers, on an hourly or daily basis. The owner of the smaller garden may find it best to rent, rather than buy.

Many gardeners — perhaps most gardeners who own rototillers — use them not only to prepare the soil for seeds, but to cultivate during the growing season. This means, then, that every furrow is equally distant from every other furrow, and the width of the tines determines the distance.

For this reason, the two center tines should be as close together as possible and extenders should be provided for them when the machine is not to be used between the rows of plants.

Before the rototiller arrived, most gardeners who wanted surplus yields found the push plow, now generally called the garden cultivator, an indispensable implement. They are simple machines with handlebars reaching to the axle of a large wheel.

The plowshare, and other attachments as

Grandma always replaced her garden tools on or in their special hooks or bins in the toolhouse. Uncle Jerry was not so careful. Usually he would open the door and throw them in, much to Grandma's distress. One day he stepped on a prostrate rake and the handle flew up and hit him on the nose. The names he called that rake you won't find in the dictionary. Grandma ran into the house with her hands over her ears, but I think she was laughing.

needed, are mounted behind the wheel and near the feet of the one who pushes the cultivator along with slow thrusts.

Once the cultivators were heavy and awkward, but no more. Now they are made of lighter metals and plastics. They permit closer rows and for most garden work are considered superior to the hoe. Push plows and rototillers complement each other and both are apt to be found in the same tool shed.

The gardener needs other tools, too.

A cart can readily be found, but a satisfactory one will require more time and more dollars. One looks for large wheels, weather-treated wood for sides and bed, stout metal frames — all firmly put together in almost-non-removable fashion.

The front side and the bottom bed should fit at a right angle without slanting. Such a cart will permit the gardener to move almost anything without lifting. I've mentioned the Garden Way cart before but no discussion about garden tools is complete without a description of it.

The weight of the load can rest on the axle when the handles are raised. Thus human energy is used not to lift and carry objects by hand but to pull (not push) the cart. Anything that can be slid or rolled onto the front sideboard can be moved without ever being lifted.

A piece of plywood can convert such a cart into a table that can be moved about as needed. When not in use, the cart will stand erect on its front sideboard. In short, such a cart is a valuable garden tool.

After my hands, the cart is the tool I use most often in my garden. With it, vegetables can be moved to the house, even into the kitchen. Weeds and spent plants can be tossed into it and taken to the compost heap, fertilizer and compost can be moved to where they are to be scattered, stakes and a mallet to drive them can be moved to where tomatoes are to grow.

The gardener who misplaces small tools will be less frustrated if he wears a canvas apron with pockets.

Fancy aprons are available at fancy prices. They have a dozen or more pockets for tools the manufacturer thinks the gardener needs. These fancy aprons make interesting gifts for gardeners.

But a simple carpenter's apron with three large pockets is better. Inside one can carry a metal garden trowel, a pair of scissors (wonderful for gathering okra pods, peppers, cucumbers, dill heads and other herbs), a sweat towel, a pocket knife, canvas gloves, mosquito spray and, perhaps, paper, pencil and a small magnifying glass.

The experienced gardener long ago left behind any urge to be surrounded with seldom-used tools — cute as they may be. Only the manufacturer appreciates the multiple-use thing that is a hoe on one side and rake on the other, for example.

The gardener can get along well with only one hoe if it has a full-sized blade. For generations its edge has been the chief weapon in the war against weeds. The corner of the blade is excellent for making furrows for seeds. When turned over, it will smooth soil.

However, the affluent gardener may have three hoes: the one with the full blade, another with only a half blade for little weeds only half grown and a third with a triangular blade for furrows. Blades should be sharp.

Many gardeners have been stung in their eagerness to find new and better ways of doing things. Once my father sent a dollar in answer to a magazine advertisement that offered a sure way to get rid of the potato bug, then a greater threat than now. Tired of picking individual bugs and putting them in a jar of kerosene, we eagerly awaited the reply.

Back came two slivers of wood with instructions to place each bug between the slivers and press. My red haired, hot-tempered father, who taught a men's Sunday-school class all his adult life, roared as only he could do. New advertising policies were posted for the magazine.

If today's gardener is misled by anything he reads, he, too, should roar.

11/Garden care

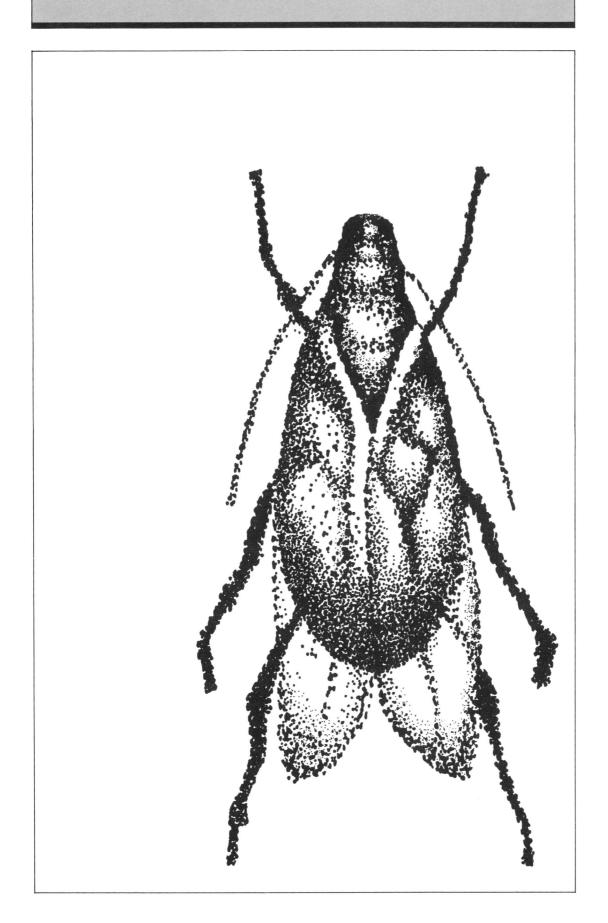

Chapter 1/Garden pests

The only job in my father's garden that I didn't like was killing potato bugs and destroying their eggs.

One by one, we picked off the bugs and dropped them into a can half full of kerosene — a tedious and tiring job, especially when the ground was wet. But worse, those yellow blobs of eggs we mashed on the undersides of leaves were messy — only a thumb and forefinger could do the job.

How pleased I was when the owner of the hardware store told my father about the Paris green that had just arrived at his store! In a few days we had no bugs on the potatoes. And if this green powder worked so well on potato bugs, it just might get rid of the green worms that ate the cabbages — and other pests, too.

It did. So we sprinkled Paris green on everything that grew — and resprinkled after each rain. But we always were careful to wash the lettuce leaves before they were brought to the dinner table; the powder didn't taste good.

My father's garden became a showplace for the finest vegetables around as people stopped to admire it. Soon we could boast that the Paris green had driven away the toads and that we

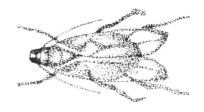

hadn't had to kill a copperhead for a long time. We no longer looked down each row before we picked pole beans; we were sure no snakes would be lying in their shade. And my Sunday school-teaching father became an apostle for Paris green.

There were no experts around to tell us that Paris green was arsenic with copper — two minerals that probably still permeate the Georgia soil my father once gardened.

Decades later, just after World War II, gardeners were presented with DDT, another insecticide they used just about the same way my father used Paris green. Or maybe it was worse, for Paris green was never used inside houses to kill insects and bugs that flew or crawled, as was DDT.

While we were enjoying the luxury of using this new chemical to kill pests, we used our hoes and plows less often to kill weeds, for we had chemicals called herbicides to spray on plants we didn't want. We had fungicides to spray or sprinkle about to confine plant diseases.

Our chemical world of gardening rested on insecticides, herbicides and fungicides. There were few, if any, rules or regulations; few, if any, inspections or directions; few, if any, laws or public agencies of concern; few, if any, gatekeepers to turn on red lights.

Never had production been so great or the future so bright. The word pollution was rarely heard, and then chiefly from those considered by many to be crackpots.

But now we know better. Now each box and bottle of pesticide must carry a registration number — meaning that the federal Environ-

Grandma had little trouble with rabbits on her farm. On bright, sunny days all during the winter she had Uncle Jerry do the necessary pruning of fruit and ornamental trees, berry bushes, and grape vines. The cuttings then were carried about a hundred feet away from the trees and placed in piles. There the rabbits found shelter. They ate the cuttings and did not harm the growing trees and shrubs. This plan just suited Uncle Jerry because he did not have to hurry. He was not permitted to shoot the rabbits because, as Grandma explained, "In a way they are our guests and they now trust us."

mental Protection Agency has approved its use, but only when label directions are followed and when the material is used only on the pests listed.

So one of today's issues is control of garden pests and plant diseases. A companion controversy revolves around enrichment of garden soil and the feeding of growing vegetable plants.

Two magazines are helpful. Organic Gardening, 33 E. Minor St., Emmaus, Pa. 18049, has become a guide to gardeners who use no chemicals at all. Seed catalogs are now offering untreated seeds and suggestions for their use. Their number is growing.

Another magazine, The Family Food Garden Magazine, (Webb Publishing Co., 1999 Shepard Rd., St. Paul, Minn. 55116), may become as widely known. It generally takes the position that only by careful use and control of chemicals can gardeners feed the world and not destroy it. Most gardeners agree.

By far the best single book about chemicals and insects that I've used is called "Pests and Diseases," by Richard H. Cravens. It is one of the books in the "Time-Life Encyclopedia of Gardening."

As it points out, there are natural means of controlling insects.

For example, gardeners need bird nests full of hungry babies fed continually by their parents with worms, caterpillars, grasshoppers, snails, bugs, grubs, beetles and their ilk — even by those parents who, themselves, eat more seeds than insects.

People go where invited; birds do, too. An invitation is the lid of a garbage can kept full of water just above things that grow and out of reach of cats. A bird feeder of any sort is another invitation, especially good if squirrels are barred.

I've lost count of the number of gallon and half-gallon milk cartons with round holes near their tops that are firmly attached to fence posts, trees and poles near my garden. About half of these are occupied each year and I'm sure the same wrens come to the same boxes year after year. Now they are almost tame.

Other invitations to birds include onion bags full of suet, boxes of thread, hair and twine and strips of cloth for nest-building.

If you want orioles enough to spend money to invite them, stick halves of oranges, cut sides up, on slender and flexible switches — not just once, but orange after orange, the whole summer long. The same pair of orioles so treated will surely be back next year. Their hanging nests are wonders of the world.

No invitation is needed for toads: just pick them up from anywhere (they won't cause warts) and put them in a holding pen of rabbit wire and hardware cloth anywhere in the garden with lots of shade and a little sun and a pan

kept filled with water. Turn them loose in a few days.

Toads need houses. I furnish mine with broken sewer pipes made of clay in various parts of the garden. The clay pipes are always cool inside. You can't have too many toads.

Field mice, which eat seeds and plants, and shrews, which eat insects, will be in your garden. You want the shrews but not the mice. This is unfortunate, for these two are "look-alikes." Only sharp eyes will see that the shrew has a long, pointed head, much of which is nose.

Both are easy to catch and examine. Snap traps baited with bread or wire-basket traps with meat or bread will do the job. So will butterfly nets.

Moles, too, are insect eaters. Some gardeners don't mind the tunnels they make. We do mind. We stick mothballs in mole tunnels and we attach hoses to exhaust pipes of cars or motorized garden tools and stick the hoses down the holes. But once declared, this is a war never won.

All turtles and spiders, and all snakes that have slender, pointed tails (the ones with blunt tails are poisonous) are welcome residents of the garden. They, too, are enemies of pests. Perhaps the best invitation is just to leave them alone.

If I were a garter snake that a child caught by the tail, I would not return to that place if I escaped. It may be my imagination, but I believe that the snakes in my garden no longer flee in panic if I happen to intrude. They seem to know that I will always say "hello," and wait for them to slowly get out of the way.

Do such garden residents really eat pests? Author Cravens reports that the shrew eats its weight three times each day; that one wren managed to gather 500 caterpillars and grubs in a single afternoon; and that one toad can eat 10,000 insects in a single garden season.

And in "Birds of Minnesota," by T. S. Rob-

Grandma had a method all her own for slugs. She placed a saucer half filled with stale beer in the garden with the saucer edge almost level with the soil. The following morning, the saucer would be almost full of dead slugs. We never knew whether they drowned or died of acute alcoholism. Grandma, an ardent prohibitionist, bought only a pint bottle of beer at a time and was careful to explain to the grocer how she was going to use it. She always showed the dead slugs to Uncle Jerry as a horrible example. He would sadly remark that the horrible part was such waste of a good beverage.

erts, we read of robins averaging an insect a minute, including one digging and eating 13 worms (six were cutworms) in 11 minutes and another six grubs in five minutes. Clearly these foragers are assistants to the gardener.

We accept Cravens's statement that North America has 86,000 species of insects and that 76,000 are harmless to man. From other sources and from experiences, we know that some of these harmless ones are actually helpful to the gardener — so helpful that they may be bought from seed catalogs and garden centers and turned loose where needed.

Ladybugs, lacewings, dragonflies, wasps and syrphid flies, which look like wasps or bees, and yellowjackets and praying mantises all get high marks. Some are predators that eat their enemies; others are parasites that lay eggs under or on the skins of their enemies for their larvae to feast on.

Ladybugs eat aphids and mealy bugs. Praying mantises will catch, kill and eat anything that gets in their way — including, unfortunately, any less-quick praying mantises. The larvae of lacewings are hairy yellow or gray worms that eat aphids and mealy bugs and scales.

Some wasps — and flies larger than the house variety — lay eggs on caterpillars; later their larvae dig inside and consume the host. Big dragonflies eat flying insects, from mosquitoes to horseflies.

Of special interest are advertisements in garden magazines and seed catalogs that offer for sale ladybugs and their larvae to combat bean thrips, chinch bugs, asparagus beetles and larvae, aphids, scale insects, the eggs of Colorado potato bugs; praying mantises to control caterpillars, tomato worms, mites, borers, maggots, flies, aphids and lice; the tricho parasites for cabbage worms, tomato hornworms, cabbage loopers, army worms, corn earworms, cutworms, gypsy moths; and milky spore bacteria for the Japanese beetle. And there are others.

Sources include: for ladybugs, King's, Box 640F, Limerick, Pa. 19468; for eggs of the praying mantis, Gurney's Seeds; for eggs of the tricho parasite, Millinger's, 23768 Range Rd., North Lima, Ohio 44452.

Those who buy these might consider a can of "Bug Bait," which, when spread about the garden, will (the ads say) keep the ones that are released and even attract others already in the area, from Stokes Seeds.

While most gardeners are now sensitive to the environmental impact of chemicals, and use them carefully, they do have a place.

Cans and bottles and boxes of legal insecticides, fungicides and herbicides are side by side with sprayers and dusters on the shelves of most gardeners. These containers and tools are isolated, and each is marked with a stripe of red paint. Also marked and isolated are cans and paddles and spoons used for mixing and applying. If an unmarked item once used for such a chemical is later used for simple watering, plants may die. Even a slight breeze will carry such sprays where they will do harm.

With care, believers in organic gardening and near-believers can have gardens reasonably clean of insects and worms. Such gardeners remove stalks and spent plants to the compost heap instead of leaving them in the garden as winter homes and food for borers, suckers, stingers and clingers. They remove a diseased plant, burn it or bury it elsewhere than in the compost heap.

Cutworms may be restrained either by poisoned bait or by paper collars, and the organic gardener chooses the collar. Wood ashes don't go out with the trash but are sifted and dusted over cabbages when the cabbage butterfly first appears. The ashes are a good source of potash. Dusts, if used at all, are those made from plants. Pyrethrum, rotenone, nicotine and malathion are examples.

Some plants don't seem to be bothered much by pests, perhaps because of their texture, odor, color or taste. Examples are marigolds from the flower garden, onions, celery, leeks, okra, eggplant, garlic, sage and other herbs, edible chrysanthemums, salsify and kohlrabi.

The gardener who doesn't like poisonous sprays may scatter-plant these among the vegetables that suffer heavy damage, such as cabbages, cauliflower, Brussels sprouts and broccoli.

Onions, hot peppers, garlic and sage may be liquefied with water in a blender; the liquid should be sprayed or poured on plants in trouble.

Two ounces of soapy water (from soap, not a detergent) in three gallons of water or a solu-

Grandma would never allow garter snakes in her garden to be molested. She knew that they ate vast quantities of slugs and other pests and were harmless. She was not fond of them, however, because they did startle her so frequently. They were not afraid of her. In fact, they were almost friendly. Uncle Jerry, the tease, would look dolefully at her and remind her that a snake and a woman were the original cause of evil. Grandma would become greatly exasperated with him.

tion made from oil spray bought from a garden store or a bordeaux solution from the same place are harmful to pests and fungi, especially those that don't fight back.

As a last unhappy resort, read the directions on bottles and cans of several of the all-purpose or specialized chemicals that crowd the shelves of seed stores. Select one that applies only to the plants that need help, and use it only on those plants. Take care not to eat what has been sprayed or dusted until well after the date recommended on the label.

Chapter 2/The compost heap

Many good gardeners for many good reasons pass up the many ways of preserving garden products for future use.

What does such a gardener do with his or her surplus? One choice would be to give it to neighbors who have no vegetable gardens.

But if such gifts have no appeal, the gardener may start a compost heap for such unwanted produce. And the compost heap will welcome all the weeds that you must pull.

The decision to have a compost heap promotes the gardener into a higher grade. It tells us that another gardener has learned that fresh, green, but unwanted plants are important — very important — garden products.

Into the compost heap goes everything that will rot — all garbage except glass or metal, rhubarb tops, bean and pea pods and shells, outer leaves of lettuce and cabbage, corncobs and stalks and shucks, children's hair cuttings, autumn leaves, twigs, sawdust, teabags and what have you. They join the weeds, the unused vegetables and the lawn grass clippings.

To make compost, everything in the heap must rot. There must be no odor, no unsightly objects, no haven for rodents or flies or maggots. Even if close by, neighbors should find nothing to complain about.

What's in the heap must end up as garden compost. It is a priceless addition to the soil; it makes things grow.

There are two methods for making it.

The older one goes back to work done in India by Sir Albert Howard, an English agricultural scientist, more than half a century ago. This is the aerobic method because it depends on microorganisms that live on air to rot what we put in the heap.

Most gardeners who make compost today use this method. Their heaps are in cylinders or rectangles of woven wire or wooden slats that admit air. To expose the contents to more air, the heap is frequently turned, generally by emptying one container and filling another. Care is taken to shift material that was on the inside to the outside in the new container. The more turning, the better the compost.

The top of the heap must be shaped basinlike, with higher sides than center, to catch and hold water. Water is essential to the rotting process and must be added from a hydrant if rain is inadequate.

The other method of making compost is the anaerobic (airless) method that depends on microorganisms that live only without air. These, too, will rot whatever is put in the heap. My own containers are made with sheets of metal clasped together at each end to make a round container and covered tightly with a sheet of clear plastic (clear only because it lets me see what's going on inside).

Air enters only when new matter or water is being added. These heaps rest on sheets of plywood that further insulate them from air.

One advantage of this method: It needs no turning. But remember, these heaps must never be inside because methane gas is created, which can be dangerous if released in a closed place.

Some notes:

I see no reason to add ashes, lime, commercial fertilizer or any of the "miracle" chemicals or biological aids to make compost better or faster or easier.

If you have chickens or other fowl or wild

Grandma had a lawnmower in later years, but there were no leaf-chopper attachments in those days. She had Uncle Jerry rake the tree leaves into long rows; then he would rush the mower through the rows repeatedly until the leaves were well chopped and reduced to about one twentieth of their original bulk, the better for compost or to be cultivated into the garden. Grandma knew well the fertilizing and soil-building value of leaves, even in those days.

animals about, add their manure to the heap and don't begrudge the food that made it possible.

A garden hose ending in a big plastic vessel (or a metal garbage can that does not leak) is valuable. Water stored there will be warmer, ready when needed and available for many purposes, not just to keep compost moist.

The inside temperature of a compost heap may move up to 140-160 degrees. It's this heat that kills weed seeds and accelerates the rotting. Fires have started in compost heaps so it's best to have them well away from buildings. When opening a heap after a winter, gardeners may find a core of ashes. Don't worry; the ashes are useful.

Heaps should be uncovered in early spring so that their contents will thaw faster. A pickaxe can break frozen heaps into pieces for quicker thawing and use. Or you can do as I do, let nature take its course and the slowly thawed compost can be used as a mulch after rows of plants are a few inches high.

Chicken feathers and offal, dead rats and such things can go into the heap but always should be buried inside.

Another reason for that clear plastic cover on the airless heap: Steam moves upward and condenses into drops on the plastic. These drop back into the heap. When the cover is removed for any purpose the dripping stops. Its start again will tell you that all is well inside.

Should compost be added in layers as some suggest? The scientist says "yes." The gardener says "nuts." Pea vines, cornstalks, green rhubarb stalks and flower stems, beet peelings after wine is made, hair after Junior's hair is cut, the mouse after it's caught — these and other composted things don't get ready in any orderly fashion. They are ready when they are ready and should be added without delay. The more moist they are, the better compost they will be.

Chapter 3/A new solution for weed problems

Roundup is a non-selective herbicide that is different. Sprayed on leaves of certain weeds, this chemical is carried to the very tips of the roots and the entire plant dies. Roundup has no residual soil activity that can affect next year's plants.

A few days after use on existing plants, new seeds or sets or seedlings may be planted if tillage is not needed. For tillage by rototiller, spade, plow or hoe, better wait two or three weeks until the sprayed plants turn deep yellow or brown, a sure sign that the chemical has reached those root ends.

Roundup is expensive; a gallon costs more than $80. It requires a glass or plastic sprayer because metal ones may explode. A plastic sprayer with a gallon capacity costs more than $20.

But if you use Roundup you won't have quack in Minnesota or Bermuda in Georgia, principal scourges to gardeners in those states.

Monsanto Chemical Company makes Roundup; H.D. Hudson Company makes a plastic sprayer. Both may be bought from seed exchanges, garden centers and nurseries.

Booklets of instructions come with each. These say that the sprayer will produce a mist easily carried by wind where it isn't wanted if a shield of plywood or cardboard isn't used — and such shields are chancy.

They also say that a turn of the nozzle tip will produce a coarse stream. If you are careful you can make the coarse stream reach a bad weed growing only an inch or two from a good plant, even with no shield. Use the coarse stream for quack anywhere near the garden, just enough to cover with no drips, or runoffs or mists.

Experts at the St. Paul campus of the University of Minnesota tell us that plants and roots killed by Roundup may be safely added to compost heaps.

Every gardener knows about quack and the need to get rid of it. Two pages of a special booklet with good copy and color pictures are devoted to quack. For a free copy write to Monsanto Agricultural Products Co., St. Louis, Mo., 63166. It will help in the decision-making.

Minnesota gardeners are more fortunate than those in Georgia because quack produces few (and weak) seeds and spreads principally as its underground rhizome system becomes thick and jungle-like. Bermuda has many (and strong) seeds and the same root system. Roundup has no effect on any seeds after they have left plants and lie on the ground.

If a weed is growing in the loose and friable soil of a permanent bed packed only by raindrops, it's not difficult to reach and remove every particle of each plant.

It's almost impossible if the weeds get started in the cement-like soil of a path and it's especially difficult if the walks are covered with wood chips. To remove these weeds, you'll need a mattock and a shovel. The hole will be deep, and the perspiration great.

But there were even better reasons for my use of Roundup. Years ago when the garden was laid out in part of a pasture, much of the pasture was left between the garden and the burr oak trees growing along the creek on the garden's north side. Space south of the garden was left for strawberries, raspberries, grapes, plums, apples and asparagus.

Later came our electric pump with rods of aluminum piping and overhead sprayers to provide water for thirsty plants and to save them from freezing in the late fall. But pipes had to cross the empty place north of the garden, then cross over the garden to reach the berries. To water the entire garden, pipes had to be moved three times.

But suppose those perennials south of the garden were moved to fill a part of the place between the garden and the burr oak trees? What a saving! Wonderful, except for the quack.

I remembered the hours with tractor and rototiller necessary to rid the area of the quack that made the pasture a pasture. Earlier, cows, horses, donkeys, sheep and goats had waxed fat and sleek there and had won prizes at county and state fairs during the years our four children were growing up.

I couldn't face the tractor/rototiller chore again. We turned toward Roundup. With timidity first and then with cautious confidence, we started spraying.

Results were startling. The quack died. Length of a plant's roots determines the time it takes Roundup to work — it may take days or weeks.

But Roundup does not control all the weeds in American gardens. It does control quackgrass and 36 other weeds, but does not control dandelions and countless others. Monsanto's list is specific — even down to the exact amount of liquid and water required for each kind of weed.

Chapter 4/Fertilizers: Two views

When gardeners get together they talk about their biggest and best — and how their nicest produce got that way. In other words, what part do fertilizers play? Our best advice is to learn about your soil, study the various fertilizers and what they do, and keep records from year to year. The subject is discussed here by both authors.

The soil must be replenished

By Leon C. Snyder

Growing plants on the same soil year after year robs the soil of fertility. This is particularly true where edible produce is removed from the vegetable garden and the fruit plantings.

Even in the flower border we cut flowers to enjoy indoors, and, in the fall, we remove the plants' remains. When the leaves fall from trees we take them up and remove them from the lawn area. Even pruning removes essential plant elements from the garden.

Unless the elements that are thus removed are returned to the soil in some manner, the soil will gradually decline in its ability to produce healthy plants.

In addition to the loss of essential elements by plant removal, there is also a loss of organic matter in the soil. Organic matter oxidizes and gradually disappears. Carbon dioxide and water, the same raw materials used in photosynthesis, are the end products of this oxidation process.

Organic matter is very important in garden soils. Without it clay soils become hard and difficult to work. Water, instead of soaking in after a rain, runs off and takes topsoil with it. Sandy soils become very porous, and plant nutrients are readily leached out following rains. Organic matter can also provide some of the plant nutrients required by garden plants.

On the farm, organic matter can be added by applying well-rotted manure each spring. In the city, organic matter is more difficult to obtain. A compost pile helps, but unless you gather plant refuse from your neighbors it will not be enough to maintain a high level of organic matter in your soil.

Growing green manure crops such as rye in the fall after your vegetables are harvested will help, but this is sometimes difficult.

Other sources of organic matter are old sawdust piles, peat moss and dried manures. Sewage sludge and manure from the stockyards can be used where obtainable.

Organic matter may be applied in the fall or spring. A layer one to two inches thick should be thoroughly mixed into the soil by spading or by using a rototiller.

Do not work a clay soil when it is wet. If you do, you'll have hard clods that will be a problem all summer. To determine whether the soil is dry enough to work, pick up a handful and squeeze it. If it crumbles when the pressure is removed it is dry enough. If it remains in a tight ball it is too wet.

Although organic matter will supply some of the mineral requirements of your garden plants, it is best to also supply a chemical fertilizer when soil is prepared. I use a 10-10-10 fertilizer at the rate of 15 pounds for each 1,000 square feet of soil surface.

This supplies the nitrogen, phosphorus and potassium needed for healthy plant growth. The nitrogen is needed for the synthesis of chlorophyll and for vegetative growth. The phosphorus is an essential constituent of each living cell and is especially important for flowering and fruiting. The potassium is a catalyst that is essential for the translocation of carbohydrates and for other vital processes in the plant. Potassium is associated with a strong root system and good stem development.

There are a number of other elements essential to healthy plant growth. Iron is a catalyst in chlorophyll synthesis. Magnesium is a constituent of the chlorophyll molecule. Calcium is a cementing substance to hold plant cells together and helps to regulate soil ph. Sulphur is a constituent of certain proteins.

Roles of other essential elements such as boron, zinc, copper and molybdenum are not clearly understood. These minor elements are not required in large quantities and are seldom deficient.

Occasionally we must add iron to soils that are high in lime. Some plants are very sensitive to iron deficiencies and show a yellowing of foliage if available iron is not present. The addition of an iron chelate or ferrous sulphate will usually correct this.

The best way to think of your soil is to compare it with your checking account. You cannot continue to write checks unless you put money into your account from time to time. Likewise, you cannot continue to grow healthy plants unless you replenish the organic matter and essential plant nutrients.

The importance of organic materials

By William L. Nunn

For ages the Japanese have used night soil as a natural fertilizer, organic in nature, without chemicals, indispensable to the production of food — and not dangerous to use.

Foreigners may object to the odors of Japan's farm and garden lands, but the Japanese do not. It's not that they can't smell. They find our barnyard odors objectionable. And the smell of cheese, even mild cheddar, will leave many pale and some ill.

It's important to remember that the Japanese did not pass through a pastoral economy of domestic animals with their milk and manure. We did. Our differences are in a state of mind resting on what we are accustomed to.

What the Japanese use so successfully, we Americans dump irresponsibly. We refine the refuse with costly chemicals and treatments and dump it into rivers from which we draw the water we drink.

Some dry fertilizer is now being made from sewage in a few cities. Milwaukee is out in front. Its Milorganite, made by the city itself, is widely used by gardeners in our area. It's a good fertilizer with no harmful chemicals.

We are experimenting with sludge on farm lands to learn how to treat it for use — how much to use and at what depth.

Such technical questions may be easier to solve than those resting on human fears, prejudices and ignorance. Even so, a new day may be ahead: first, clean rivers and lakes; next, less chemical (inorganic) fertilizer to produce the foods we eat.

Once our fathers and their fathers used organic fertilizers from their own pig pens, cattle yards, horse stalls and chicken roosts, but not from their own privies.

Some planted fields of rye that, when mature but still green, was plowed into the soil — green fertilizer, it was called. Those who did not do that just wore out their farms and moved elsewhere.

More than a century ago, discoveries in South America and on Pacific islands brought us a new fertilizer. For thousands of centuries the droppings of birds and debris under their roosts created mountains of organic fertilizer called guano. An organic fertilizer shipped to every American hamlet — and elsewhere in the world — in large and tough paper or jute bags, it was the solution for gardeners and farmers

Often Grandma would come home filled with indignation and disgust. She would explode: "I have just seen Mrs. 'Somebody's' flower garden. She asked for advice, and I gave her a piece of my mind. Her flowers are just starving. How anybody with a huge pile of fertilizer behind the cow barn can let their flowers die of starvation beats me."

who had no manure factories walking about their yards.

A few years ago, while helping a son-in-law with his garden in Bemidji, Minn., I was startled to find — and I quickly bought — sacks of imported guano in a local store. It was not from birds, but the droppings of bats, the labels said. It was like meeting an old friend.

Slowly most of the world's guano was used up. But by then inorganic fertilizer from chemical plants had begun to arrive.

Today's mountains of fertilizers come in stout paper bags and steel drums with precise and measured percentages of nitogen, phosphorus and potassium, 10-20-20, 5-10-5, and so on.

12/Come harvest time

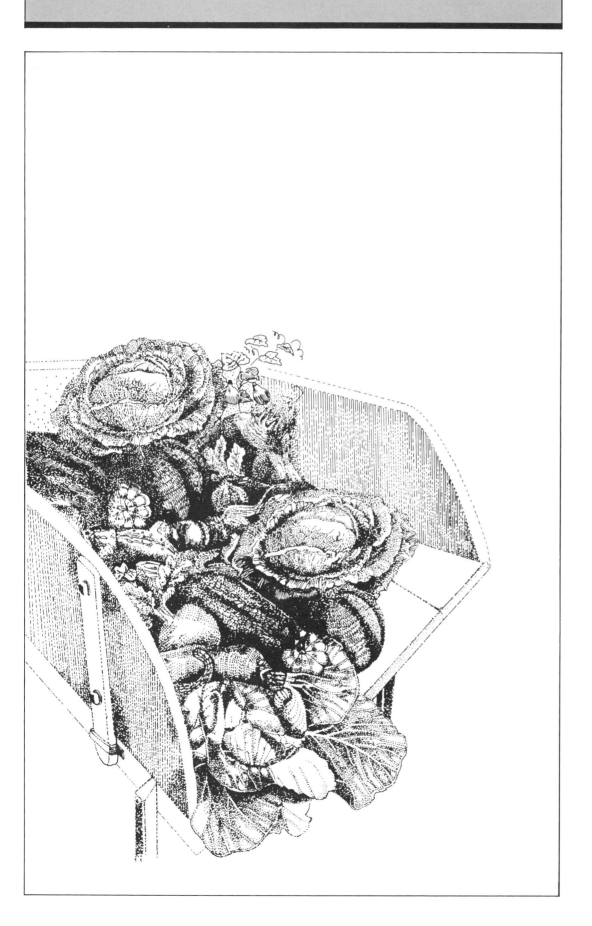

Chapter 1/An autumn scene

Days have grown shorter and turned chilly. The end of the garden harvest season is in sight. Now the best days are those that permit digging, storing, canning and freezing from dawn to bedtime. Home gardeners are grateful for Saturdays and Sundays.

Freezers are full and we have reserved drawers in the locker plant for more frozen food. Shelves are packed with canned food in mason jars, and dried foods are stored in jars emptied of store-bought food. Wine racks are sagging. Selections will be Christmas gifts to the Nunn children who live with their Trakehner horses in Wright County and those who live and work in the forests of Minnesota's wolf and bear country.

Nunn children in Florida, Texas and Hawaii are far away. But they, too, will share. They'll get jars of jelly and jam from wild and tame grapes and wild black cherries. There'll be folk wines for them too and dried chives and mint, sage, basil and tarragon. Such things can't be bought in stores.

The little yellow car is parked outside because the garage floor is covered with red and green and Savoy cabbages, acorn and butternut squashes, and Nantes carrots awaiting trips to the kitchen. No hurry about these; they will keep pretty well where they are.

Blue Lake pole beans, black-eyed peas and the pole Christmas and pole Lima beans were saved from the frosts by the water spray that whirled over the garden all night. Soon these will be picked.

Bush Lima beans, out of the range of the whirling water, were protected in a more conventional way — covered with strips of black plastic.

Some of the garden produce is under grow-lights in the basement. There the last of the near-green **Better Boy** and some of the Roma tomatoes are turning red. Most of the Romas are still in the garden awaiting their turn under the lights. They, too, were covered at night with black plastic when the weather bureau predicted frost in the air.

As autumn nears, the Roma's leaves have slowly disappeared, leaving stems and tomatoes piled on top of each other, jungle fashion. There the tomatoes grow, turning yellow and then red.

Potato tops, felled by the frost, tell us the tubers are waiting to be picked. Because potatoes grow in a mulch of leaves and not in garden soil there will be no digging — we'll just push the mulch about and lift the potatoes out.

Into the house go two baskets of bell peppers. We slice the smaller ones in the food processor and hold them in the refrigerator for ratatouille, a recipe for which appears in almost all cookbooks.

For this, we mix sliced green onions (actually green Egyptian ones with tops), sliced bell peppers, Roma tomatoes, curly-leafed parsley, sticks of eggplant and green and yellow zucchini (with water removed from eggplant and zucchini). We mix and then cook it all for about 25 minutes on top of the stove, then cool it, pack it in plastic boxes or boiling bags to be frozen for future use.

We fill the halves of the large bell peppers with either a mixture of rice, tomatoes, onions and ground beef or one with rice, chopped green onions, diced cheese and tuna fish. All go into the freezer. When frozen, each is wrapped and returned to the freezer for future cooking.

In October, when leaves were most colorful, Grandma would preserve them by pressing the not-too-dry ones with a warm iron. Sometimes she first would soak the whole leaf for two or three hours in a solution of one tablespoon of glycerine to nine tablespoons of rain or soft lake water. This would keep the leaf flexible.

Even a small branch of leaves could be treated by dipping in the solution several times, but not ironed. They would be beautiful for Thanksgiving decoration.

Another method she used was to place the stem of a branch in the solution for several days. The leaves would remain leathery and curled if they were not too ripe.

Chapter 2/Cleaning up the garden

September, October and November are the days when a gardener puts things away, cleans up and records it all.

When gardens are being prepared for winter, and final harvests are being completed, and seeds for spring are being planted, gardeners can't afford to sleep during the dwindling daylight hours. We listen to the newscasts and call the weather number to keep up to date on frost forecasts.

If frost is coming, gardeners enlist the family to cover plants with paper sacks, newsprint, boxes, jars, bed sheets, rolls of black plastic and anything else that can be borrowed. But, for a lot of reasons, everything in the garden can't be covered.

Some gardeners dig up vines and plants and hang them in garages, barns and empty bedrooms. There, with as much light as possible, green fruit will turn red and ripen. If plants are placed under grow-lights, the ripening will be startlingly rapid. And, curiously, tomatoes will ripen if wrapped in newspapers to exclude all light.

Frantic members of the garden family, in the face of frost, gather what can't be covered or removed to ripen elsewhere. Climbing cucumbers, cabbages, pole beans and peas, sunflowers, eggplants and squash from sprawling vines will be hurried to kitchen or garage.

But leave the collards, Brussels sprouts, broccoli and kale. They taste better if touched by frost. Harvest of beets, carrots and other root crops can be postponed because early frost will not damage what's underground.

Fortunate gardeners turn a switch on frosty nights and watch whirling wands of overhead irrigation systems scatter water on the plants that matter. The next morning these gardeners can invite neighbors for early coffee to enjoy and photograph a fairyland of glistening ice that covers everything from tomatoes to beet tops to the shovel that was carelessly left sticking in the ground. If the water runs until the ice has melted, no plant will be damaged.

When the neighbors go home and the ice has melted, the gardener can get on with ending a garden season and beginning another. So, too, can the gardener who, with the warmth of an early autumn sun, removes coverings from the plants saved from the frost.

The careful gardener will provide parsley, which is a biennial, and sage, thyme, winter savory, tarragon and strawberries, which are perennials, with covers of leaves or straw about a foot deep. If wind is a problem, the cover can be held down with a strip of wire fencing or similar material.

New Zealand spinach is a bed of thick and heavy growth that, if left alone, will provide a needed cover.

Other permanent guests in the garden are Egyptian onions, rhubarb, chives, horseradish, raspberries and asparagus. They do well if left alone. Carrots and parsnips may be left in the ground all winter if covered with bales of straw laid crossways over each row.

The gardener knows that some plants, like dill and edible chrysanthemums, will scatter seeds in the autumn that will sprout in early spring. Enough seeds will have dropped to produce next year's crops. Don't cover them; they need light to germinate. If dill seeds have not

Grandma would hustle out with Uncle Jerry when a killing frost threatened, and gather all the large tomatoes that were hanging on the vines. Each one would be wrapped carefully in a piece of newspaper and placed on a shelf in the cool cellar to ripen. Every week the tomatoes would be turned over. Almost all would ripen beautifully, and some years we would be eating fresh tomatoes in December. Grandma thought there was something in the printer's ink that prevented the fruit from decaying. Perhaps she was right; she usually was.

all been gathered, heads may be stuffed in paper sacks and seeds retrieved for use in soups, stews, wine and salads. Dill seeds are not just for pickles.

But most of the seeds that winter over in my garden were carefully planted in the last days of October or the first days of November.

Two beds, each 21 by 3½ feet, have been planted with **Cold-Resistant Savoy** spinach. Before this space is needed next spring, plants from these seeds will have been pulled, washed, blanched, packaged and frozen.

A third bed of Egyptian onions, planted in mid-August just after their bulbils were harvested, is now a thing of green beauty, for the tops are a few inches tall. Some seeds of spinach, green bunching onions, Japanese chrysanthemums (**Shungiku**), turnips, lettuce, collards, Chinese cabbage (if **Nagaoka**) and bok choy are others that can be planted in October to be harvested in early spring.

Remaining chores include the harvesting, shredding and freezing of Nagaoka cabbage leaves that were planted in early September, as were those of the spinach. Also on the agenda in late fall: harvesting, cooking and freezing the fully grown Egyptian onions.

On sunny, windless autumn days I sit outdoors on a milk box in front of a secure cedar block and chop up faded vines and stems with a hatchet. Five full compost heaps soon attest to the fact that most beds and trellised rows are clear of plants and roots. Such outdoor days and chores are princely gifts to me from the garden.

Stakes on which tomatoes grew must be pulled, cleaned and stored. Areas for rototilling have been covered with compost and turned into loose, black soil, ready for next year's seeds and plants. The end of the this year's garden is in sight.

But the gardening season does not really end until all produce under tarps in the garage has joined what's left from other years or until mason jars of **Concord** and **Beta** and wild grapes have been turned into jams and jellies.

Perhaps the end does come when the handles of garden trowels, hoes and rakes have been rubbed with linseed oil and their metal parts with engine oil; when the rototiller has been cleaned, drained and covered with a plastic sheet; when all the plastic collars that kept the cutworms away from the seedlings have been washed and counted; when all the nearby holes and runways and dens of gophers, field mice, moles, shrews and woodchucks have been found and rodent-bombed; when the pump is pulled from Elm Creek and the aluminum irrigation pipes removed to the racks alongside the hay barn.

Perhaps it all never ends, but just blends into next year's garden.

Grandma was ruthless when frost threatened. Everything in the house that could be used for cover went into the garden, even her prized Irish table linen that was used only on holidays and when the minister stayed for supper. Poor Grandpa grumbled bitterly when he had to sleep between scratchy blankets. Grandma had borrowed the sheets from his bed to protect the plants. Or, if frost threatened on an almost windless night, she would have several smudges of hay or straw covered with partly dried grass. The smudges were put in old metal washtubs covered with coarse wire netting to prevent sparks from flying. They often smoked all night, forming a protective canopy over the garden.

13/Food for the winter

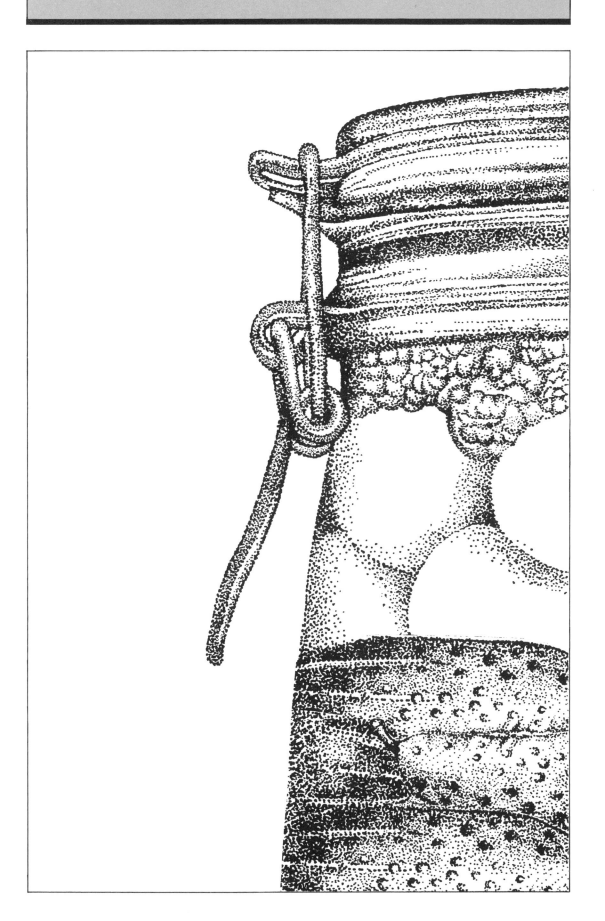

Chapter 1/Canning

The tin can and the glass jar are as basic to gardening as buttons and buttonholes when it comes to holding things together.

Canning provides far more security than does freezing. If jars are kept in a dry place, their lids will not rust and contents will not spoil. If they are stored in the dark, the color of what's inside will not fade. Once prepared, there is no cost.

With freezing, you can't be so sure. Freezer burn may limit the time frozen food may be stored and thus may send aged frozen food to the compost heap. Even after preparation, the cost of electricity continues.

A recent garden year at our house was a good one for beans. The score in terms of jars and packages of beans was higher than ever before. But ours were not just "beans."

Mason jars were marked purple beans (19 in number), wax beans (83), green bush beans (67), Italian beans (58) and Blue Lake pole green beans (95). Freezer packages were marked Blue Lake pole (95), Italian (4), and wax (26).

University of Minnesota Professor Harold Wilson asked, "How do you use all the food from your garden? You must have guests for dinner every night." No, just families of Nunn children living close by, he was told.

Still, 447 packages of string beans, besides Lima, Christmas and edible soybeans, does sound like a lot of beans.

How about cabbages?

Just about all the red and green cabbages in stores ship and keep well. Only a small percentage of green cabbage produced in America goes into sauerkraut, in contrast to central Europe where almost half is preserved this way and used in ways quite foreign to us.

For example, try sauerkraut cooked with wine and grapes or with pineapple chunks and juice. But you must know that every recipe over there begins with "Drain the sauerkraut, wash it thoroughly under cold running water, and then let it soak in a pot of water for 10 to 20 minutes, depending on its acidity. A handful at a time, squeeze the sauerkraut until it is completely dry."

Brining is a far cheaper — and easier — way to preserve cabbage than freezing or canning. Only in America do so many insist on eating the salt.

At our house we plant few green cabbages, more red cabbages and many Savoy cabbages. All our green cabbages go into sauerkraut, made in a big crock that left Red Wing, Minn., many years ago.

After it's shredded in the food processor, the green cabbage is turned over to Jo Nunn, who lightly salts every shred. (Three tablespoons of canning salt for each 5 pounds of cabbage) Packed in the crock, the cabbage is carefully covered with a moist cloth and a plastic plate on which rests a weight heavy enough to bring water to the surface.

Jo Nunn began a career in sauerkraut-making many years ago. In the early days, she kept records of everything she did and consulted books and articles.

Now she takes quick looks when refreshing the cover cloth each day and gets a whiff or two. There comes a day when she announces that the crock no longer holds cabbage, but sauerkraut. We hot pack it into mason jars and put them into boiling water baths for 15 minutes.

Gardeners curious about the history of what they harvest may be interested in knowing that what Jo did with our green cabbages was described by the early Romans, but widespread use of the cabbage is credited to Genghis Khan's Tatars from Asia who overran Middle Europe in the 13th century and left behind the method of making, and an appetite for, sauerkraut.

The history of canning should be of interest to most gardeners and cooks.

Back in 1809, Paris chef Nicolas Appert won 12,000 francs when he developed a crude form of canning by boiling foods in a corked bottle. The prize was offered by a government hard-pressed for new methods of feeding soldiers and sailors fighting in the Napoleonic wars.

Today Appert is known as the father of canning.

An American, Thomas Kensett, developed the tin can 14 years later. And in 1858 another American, John L. Mason, invented a glass jar that had a threaded opening on which a metal cap could be screwed tightly against a rubber ring.

But the heyday of canning was delayed until after the work of two professors — Harry L. Russell of the University of Wisconsin and S. C. Prescott from the Massachusetts Institute of Technology.

At the turn of the century they proved that exclusion of air was not the key to food preservation, as had been believed since the days of Appert, but "the (varying) death points of bacteria in all foods." Our job, then, was to discover these "death points."

Soon it became common knowledge that snap beans in quart mason jars had to be processed at 10 pounds of pressure for 25 minutes, while carrots required 30 minutes and corn needed 85. We learned, too, that only a boiling water bath was needed to can fruits and most tomatoes.

But first people had to convince themselves that canned food was safe to eat — especially someone else's canned food. Both government and the canning industry had to take action.

I suspect that today's buyers seldom pay much attention to the circular seal of approval and the stamped numbers on cans of store-bought meats. I wonder if most buyers know what they mean. The seals certify that inspectors of the United States Department of Agriculture are "on the floor" of the plant that produced the product, enforcing laws and orders that protect us.

Moreover, these seals and numbers identify the plant that supplied each can. Some duties relating to canned vegetables and fruits are assigned to another federal agency, the Food and Drug Administration.

The government's interest in the quality of canned vegetables and fruits did not end with establishment of regulations for commercial canners. Hundreds of booklets, brochures and fact-sheets of vital information are printed with tax dollars for nationwide distribution to gardeners. Most are free.

If a problem appears, the home gardener-canner should call the county office of the agricultural extension service and ask for information. A postal card to your congressman in Washington will bring you a list of all booklets about gardening available at the Government Printing Office. Review the list and order those you wish.

The home gardener-canner should have at hand the answers to common questions about canning. In my opinion the best source is the "Freezing and Canning Cookbook" edited by Nell B. Nichols (Doubleday). Nichols is the food editor of the Farm Journal. The book has a down-to-earth quality and tells exactly how to can or freeze each vegetable or fruit. Even more, it tells about many things that will appeal to those who like to give and serve out-of-the-ordinary dishes of home-grown food.

Many gardeners can far more of their produce than they freeze or dry. Small wonder: Fresh vegetables keep in prime condition only briefly after removal from the garden, and even more briefly after removal from the vegetable market.

Greens wilt, potatoes and onions sprout, asparagus shows bracts, carrots become limp, corn, peas and beans lose their sweetness — all in spite of water sprays, cubes of ice and plastic bags with holes.

Vegetables go into jars when they are at their very best. The entire family gets into the act. Vegetables are washed and cleaned. Blemishes are removed. Jars are made ready and packed.

Be sure to watch dials on the pressure cooker and hands on the clock and heed the timer's bell. Hot jars must be removed from the canner, placed on a board out of a draft and covered with a cloth. When the jars are cool, each lid should be tested, and bands (if used) removed for use on the next batch.

Jars with tops that pop up and down just don't seal. These lids should be discarded and the jar's rim inspected; if it's smooth, the jar and its contents may be canned again. At our house such jars are marked "F" and reach the table when only family members are present.

As canning goes on, full jars accumulate. Each is labeled, not with a sticker which can get lost, but with a heavy felt-tip marker and permanent ink. We write everything we know on the side of the glass, not on the lid. Soapy hot water and steel wool will remove the words easily. If you use nail polish remover, words will come off quicker and you can remove only the ones you want to. That's especially appropriate when jars become gifts.

What do we do with the leaves and stalks of much that we grow, or with the middle pieces of cut asparagus or with the hollow stems of spinach? Simple. We boil the best in the smallest amount of water possible and then liquefy them in the blender. Then we pour the liquid into plastic boxes or boiling bags for storage in the freezer.

No longer do we use mason jars to be canned 90 minutes at 10 pounds pressure as we and others did for many years. Reason for the change: fears that the heat from the canner would not always reach the center of the thick puree in each jar. Result: The finest and safest puree for soups.

What tools are needed for canning? The most

important one is an aluminum pressure-cooker-canner. It's best to choose the one that will hold seven quart jars or 20 pints. It's the largest and should last for years.

Along with this pressure-cooker, but for different purposes, some canners use a large, covered pan holding a rack in which quart jars may be placed, covered with two inches of water and boiled. This one should be an enamel pot, not aluminum, for it can be used to make folk wine, sauerkraut, or any kind of pickle. Fruits, tomatoes, and vegetables with added vinegar cabbage for sauerkraut, can be mixed in these enamel pots; if packed in mason jars, these can be canned in the same pot.

All others that contain acid can be canned in the pressure canner. This includes beets, cauliflower, beans, cabbage, zucchini and crookneck squash, onions, peas and end-of-the-garden odds and ends gathered in October and November.

Consider, too, the juice from tomatoes, especially the thick juice from the Roma-type, or the juice from apples, especially if made into "country cider" by only rough straining. Also, you might want to boil and can the juice of Concord, Beta or wild grapes, which is best canned to drink rather than turned into poor wine.

Chapter 2/Freezing

During World War II people were asking questions about a new way of preserving food by freezing: Have you ever eaten such food? Does it taste fresher than canned food? Do you think freezing food will catch on?

One young navy lieutenant who was a friend of mine spent his spare time dreaming and blueprinting a future business involving refrigerated trucks (he called them refrigerated stores) that would have regular routes on Chicago streets to permit housewives to enter and select frozen food for evening dinners.

He never expected any appreciable number of grocery stores to install refrigerated equipment to handle such food. The very thought was laughable.

Today's markets, of course, even those in the smallest places, are equipped to store and manage frozen food. Many families own freezers, have freezer space in their refrigerators or rent locker drawers.

Now, more than ever before, we eat a great variety of things at home, for we are no longer dependent on the seasons. The freezer makes it possible for us to eat strawberries in months that have the letter "R" in their names and oysters in the months that do not.

Probably the main reason for rapid growth in food-freezing is that we respond to reports from our taste buds. From them we know that most frozen foods are double first cousins to fresh foods.

With freezers we save money; leftovers may be frozen for later eating. Or we may cook food in quantity and freeze it. Instead of one casserole, we cook three or more at once. A big batch of a great Japanese dish, sukiyaki, or corned beef and cabbage, or Bill's thick soup may be made, packed into freezer boxes and stored for eating months ahead.

With a freezer, dinner for the unexpected guest is a joy. Before the martinis are finished, dinner can be served. Sukiyaki, frozen six months before — made from store-bought tofu (soybean paste) and vermicelli and shōyu sauce, and from our own strips of beef, green onions, bean sprouts, celery, spinach, Chinese cabbage and slices of mushrooms — may be taken from the freezer, heated and served on rice.

Before packages are put in storage, the food must be sharp-frozen at much lower temperatures. Some locker owners make a small additional charge for this, but others make no charge and may even move your food from the sharp-freezer unit into your own space.

Before renting locker space, look at several locker plants, ask questions and then decide. Compare the yearly rental with the payments you would make if you bought a freezer on installments. You may decide to do the latter.

Before selecting a freezer, look at those owned by your friends and listen to what they say. You will learn that "frost-free" means that more power and perhaps more maintenance must be paid for. An "upright" will use more power than a "chest." But it is far easier to keep track of things stacked in orderly rows on shelves than in a big box.

Chapter 3/Drying

Graduates of the Anoka Senior High School who were fossil hunters know a lot about dried foods — what foods to select, how to dry and store them, and how to prepare them.

As students, they went with Prof. Lyle Bradley and an ever-changing pair of "moms" to the fossil digs in North and South Dakota, Montana and Wyoming, with the blessings of the Smithsonian Institution. Under blazing summer suns they dug, found, cleaned and classified fossils, including dinosaur bones — and ate foods they had spent hours drying back in the classroom.

Why dried foods? Their fossil-digging spots were far from markets. Dried foods take little space. No ice is needed; only water for cooking and drinking need be carried. And dried foods taste good.

Backpackers, canoeists and mountain climbers have discovered the advantages of dried foods.

City dwellers who don't have room for hundreds of sealed mason jars and even more packages of freezer foods should know that eight to 12 pounds of fresh vegetables will weigh only a single pound dried. As much as eight pounds of fresh fruit will dry to just a pound.

Thousands of us who are neither digging fossils nor exploring a wilderness have joined the hordes of dryers. But people in every stage of civilization have dried foods. The sun and the wind provided the first methods of preservation. So what's new?

Almost everything is new. Our grandfathers put shelled beans, peas and corn — allowed to dry on the vine — in small cotton bags with dark slabs cut from plugs of chewing tobacco to discourage weevils. We can do better. We can pasteurize our field-dried vegetables in a preheated oven (175 degrees F.) for 15 minutes and we won't have the problem of keeping the chewing tobacco fresh for another year.

Our grandmothers threaded yards of fresh purple and yellow and green string beans and hung up the strings. The beans, thus strung up, were called "leather britches." And that leather consistency has relegated most of the leather britches we made three summers ago to their glass containers. They are pretty and visitors find them interesting.

We can do better with our beans. We can freeze, can or dry them, but we won't improve on some of the things our ancestors did. We, too, may string red hot peppers on lines and wait for them to dry completely before packing them into jars, to be kept in a dark place until needed.

Just as our forefathers did, we pack peppers in jars of vinegar for pepper sauce.

But even with crushed dried pepper and with pepper sauce, we will plant much less than our grandfathers did, for they used lots of red pepper in the preservation of meats.

Like our grandmothers, we cut our basil, chives, marjoram, sage, savory, mint and parsley just before flowers appear, being very careful that our scissors leave enough of the bottom of each plant to grow for further cuttings.

These herbs should be cleaned of sand, bunched and tied by rubber bands or string and hung on a line in a well-ventilated room without direct sunlight. When completely dry, the leaves will go through the blender — very slowly and very briefly if a powder is not desired — or will be rubbed between our palms.

Dill is different. The strength of dill is chiefly in the seed clusters at the top of each stem. These may be clipped just before they shatter and placed in large paper bags. When very dry the seeds may easily be shaken loose. They are used in pickles of many kinds, in some sauerkrauts and in crockpots of meats.

The young plants make interesting additions to salads and are frequently stuffed along with seeds into mason jars when cucumbers, beans or strips of zucchini squash are being made into pickles.

Jars of dried foods should be stored in the dark. The sun's rays fade the colors of dried herbs.

Unlike the many demands of canning and freezing, the drying of vegetables and most fruits need not assault the pocketbook. We can start with a blender (really a perforated double boiler) sold everywhere, a cutting board and sharp knives, frames on which to spread the cut fruits and vegetables, an assortment of jars of any size or shape — but always with tight-fitting lids — and a source of heat.

The heat may come from the bottom, never the top, burner in a kitchen oven, from hot plates or electric light bulbs in a dryer.

You can start with the kitchen stove to get the feel of it, but soon you will want to make your dryer or buy a factory-made one. The cost of either will be a fraction of the cost of a freezer.

How do we proceed? What's first? Simple. We spend $2.95 for a 125-page paperback book called "How to Dry Fruits and Vegetables at Home." It was written by the food editors of the Farm Journal. Your bookstore can get you a copy from Doubleday, or from the Farm Journal.

The authors will tell you quite candidly that drying is not the best way — from the yardstick of taste — to preserve vegetables that are to find their way to the dinner table. (Corn may be an exception. Many of us find kernels of dried corn when cooked with strips of green and sweet red peppers to be equal to the fresh corn we have long enjoyed.)

But, with cogency, the authors will praise the use of dried foods in stews, casseroles, soups and mixed salads. Perhaps you may already know about this from using dried lentils, peas and beans from the grocery store. But we may add green beans, cabbage, potatoes, okra, corn, eggplant, beets, broccoli, carrots, cauliflower, tomatoes and still others to the list of the vegetables we may dry.

The book on drying will tell you how long to blanch each vegetable and fruit (if you are to blanch it at all), how long you dry it and into what sizes it should be cut. Blanching not only sets the color but stops action of enzymes that will ripen vegetables (and eventually cause them to spoil if that action is not stopped). This, of course, is the very heart of all food preservation — the stopping of enzyme action.

If you dry your vegetables in the kitchen stove, keep the oven door partly open for the entire drying time. Put a thermometer on the bottom tray, far in the back. Try to maintain an inside temperature of 160 degrees, using only the bottom burner. If you have an electric oven, start with the door only an inch open and if you have a gas oven you will start with the door open four to eight inches. Open or shut the door to maintain this 160-degree temperature.

Perhaps the best pages in the book are those that provide exact drawings and dimensions of a natural draft dehydrator and a more elaborate and more costly electric food dehydrator that uses both a fan and a battery of 75-watt bulbs. The electric dryer with a thermostat will, of course, maintain that 160-degree temperature.

With a dryer you will be on your way.

Chapter 4/Irradiation

Home gardeners struggling with pressure canners, dryers and freezers may wonder if there is a better way to preserve vegetables and fruits.

Remember that for a long time we were skeptical of the tin can. Later we were skeptical of aluminum pots and pans. And it took us a very long time to learn that the tomato is not poisonous.

History has shown us that little understood and somewhat feared processes have come to be used successfully to preserve food.

So what's next? It could be the preservation of foods by irradiation. Let's see about this one first, even if it's a long way off.

Unfortunately, what most of us know about irradiation of foods reaches us only in occasional short news items or in sensationalized feature articles. As this is written in 1981, research is at a standstill in the United States.

So we can be grateful for the scholarly article by Willard Libby, former atomic energy commissioner and 1960 Nobel laureate, and retired Brig. Gen. Edwin F. Black published in the Bulletin of the Atomic Scientists, February 1978. The authors tell us a lot.

In the United States, the Interdepartmental Committee on Radiation Preservation of Food has existed since 1956. Represented are ERDA (Energy Research and Development Agency, which succeeded the Atomic Energy Commission); the Departments of State, Agriculture, Commerce and Health and Human Services; the army; the Food and Drug Administration (FDA); the National Aeronautics and Space Administration; the Bureau of Standards, and other agencies.

Most American research on preservation of food by irradiation has been done by or for the army at its Natick, Mass., research center.

This research has dealt principally with meats. The Department of Commerce and ERDA are investigating the use of radiation to delay or stop the sprouting of stored vegetables, to disinfect grains and to prolong the edibility of vegetables, fruits, flour and ocean fish.

Fifty-five governments are doing this type of research, and 27 pilot plants were operating in 1970 — all begun since World War II. The U.S. Atomic Energy Commission in 1970 believed that the use of radiation in the preservation of food "has been more thoroughly tested than any other method . . . . "

We have learned much:

Radiation can delay spoilage of all fruits and vegetables for varying periods. Certain irradiated meats, poultry and marine products can be kept for as long as 16 months without refrigeration. Potatoes and onions can be stored in cool, dry places and kept from one crop season to another. Radiation can destroy all insects, insect eggs and fungi in grains.

Patients with reduced or with no natural resistance to germs — those badly burned, for example — can be fed irradiated foods without danger from infectious microorganisms.

Astronauts traveling to the moon in 1972 enjoyed irradiated ham-and-cheese-on-rye sandwiches. Russian and American spacemen on the Apollo-Soyuz hookup ate irradiated broiled beef and ham steaks, smoked turkey, corn bread and breakfast rolls.

But Americans who don't fly to the moon will not enjoy irradiated foods — at least for a while. The reasons lie in two forces, each formidable.

One is our fear of anything that relates to atomic energy, as, of course, irradiation does. The second is closely associated with the first.

U.S. laws and regulations have decreed that irradiation is not a physical process like heating or freezing or drying, but is an additive, although no one can identify what is added. All this is best expressed in the 1958 food-additive amendment to the Federal Food, Drug and Cosmetic Act.

This act requires lengthly tests before irradiated food can be sold. For a single prescribed test, Libby and Black believe that quarter of a million dollars and from three to five generations of experimental animals would be involved. The test would require that 30 to 50 percent of these daily diet be composed of the foods under test, which is a sure way to cause death or illness to the animals and cause them not to produce the offspring demanded by the law. So the technology may be developed elsewhere.

In 1973 the Japanese began a potato irradiation center with a capacity of 10,000 tons a month. Thailand, Turkey, Iran, Singapore — all countries that have experienced the horrors and problems of food shortages — are close behind.

At this point, those who hope irradiation will not be excluded as a food preserver can make two points: (1) Irradiation is not an additive, and nothing is added to food by irradiating it, and (2) all tests thus far of irradiated foods have found them to be safe for human consumption.

But there is always something new — sometimes here before it is seen or tested. And any "something new" is apt to be based on much of the "something old." Getting rid of the causes of spoilage is the aim of irradiation: heat and packaging were heavily involved. Now a "something new" is about to shout: "Look at me." Let's see about this new "something new" that is exciting so many people in the world. Let's start with milk.

The milk of my youth was evaporated — Pet was the brand we liked. Only ice boxes could keep milk cool; home refrigerators had not arrived. Little fresh milk could be bought in the small towns of America, unless a farm family could spare a gallon.

In my Japanese days, the milk I used was powdered whole milk from vacuum packed cans — packaged in America and very expensive. There was nothing else.

Still later, much later: within a few days after my boss, Harry Hopkins, tossed me into the troubled Federal Surplus Relief Corporation (FSRC) I knew about dried skim milk that under regulations could only be packed in the same vacuum packed cans I used in Japan. Too expensive, even in America. On the FSRC staff was a "borrowed" scientist, dedicated to problems of spoilage, who had bags of dried skim milk stored in odd places from one end of our building to another — in conditions of heat, steam, cold, wind, dripping water, dust and dirt. Bemis and Betner, makers of bags and boxes, had "something new." We liked what we saw and heard.

In those New Deal days, some regulations, hoary with age, were too antiquated to be mended. So they were broken; there was no time to do otherwise. So millions of bags of dried skim milk went on their way to people who needed milk. Sacks? Of paper? No, indeed. This milk was in laminated bags — made of thin layers compressed into sheets impervious to outside factors of any kind. "Something new" had been added to the ordinary paper sack. It's still here, widely used.

And now? You and I may soon buy milk that never saw ice or a cold spot. And sliced raw fruits packed months earlier that are served for lunch, made cold only if guests like them that way. And meats and vegetables in packages not made just to keep items from falling out, but to keep air and microorganisms from getting in and contents from spoiling for long lengths of time. Some of these, after being packaged, will have been heated to sterilizing levels, and the new packaging will keep them that way.

With all of these, we must learn a new language that the Japanese, some Europeans and some Canadians already know. Here are some of the new words: retort pouches, sterile aseptically packaged (we will know it as sap), ultra-heat-processing, shrink wrap, modified atmosphere packages — and others too. And some packages of liquids will always be full until the last drop is used, for the package will shrink as contents are removed!

Who's doing all of this? In America, the giants in the food preservation industry: Kraft, Reynolds, American Can, Ludlow Packaging and others — and with the approval of the U.S. Department of Agriculture and the Food and Drug Administration.

And even now Atlantans and Columbusites and residents of a few other test areas are trying them out. They may soon be in supermarkets down the street.

There is always something new.

14/A loaf of bread, a jug of wine...

Chapter 1/Wines from the garden, not the vineyard

Some garden plants may be made into excellent wine. There are three good reasons to do so.

First, wine making is an excellent way to use food that otherwise might be thrown in the compost heap or left to wilt and die with the arrival of winter.

By these I mean: Those big red beets that are just too tough for the table, even as pickles; that spinach in the bed where every seed germinated to provide an unexpectedly bountiful harvest — with a freezer already holding a year's supply; those rhubarb stalks that don't make it into pies or breakfast fruit and stand around all summer begging to be used.

Next, making wine is fun. Every member of the family can help — from the first washing of plants to the labeling of the bottles that should lie on their sides, shaded from fierce light, for at least a year. Wine needs time to ripen and mellow.

But let the bottles lie where they can be seen, for wine makers never tire of admiring their handiwork. The pride they have in their wine runs deep — much deeper than with their canned beans.

When wine is given as Christmas presents, "thank you" notes are prompt. Friendships are cemented with wine; acquaintanceships are turned into companionships.

Finally, serving homemade wine is a good way to greet guests. Those who just pop in can be given a glass filled from a bottle already opened; those invited can have a glass of sherry-like rhubarb wine before dinner, and a glass of port-like beetroot wine afterward — poured from fresh bottles.

When you are alone with a good book by a wood fire, a glass of wine can end another good day.

All over the world gardeners make wine from growing things: Wine from rice, wine from yucca, wine from potatoes, wine from grapes, wine from beet and carrot roots, wine from spinach and parsley leaves, wine even from onions and oak leaves. It was so in colonial days in North America.

The recipes of North American colonists not only make fascinating reading, but tell us about their kitchen gardens.

In Time-Life's "Foods of the World" Mrs. William Penn tells how she "lett . . . her . . . gousberys . . . boyle . . . in a furnis . . . and . . . Run through a gelly bagg to be ready to drinke in three weeks." First her gooseberries had been steeped in water and sugar in amounts equal to that of the berries themselves. Today her wine might win a blue ribbon at a county fair.

European settlers in North America brought apple trees and seeds with them. Left to itself, sweet cider would become hard cider, which could be improved if left out in freezing weather. That way the water it contained would freeze and could be removed.

In any form, cider brought warmth and good feeling wherever people gathered. It was a widely used promoter of fellowship and a protection from chills and fever. President John Adams began each day with a tankard.

We, too, wanted to make wine. So we bought fermenting vats, measuring sticks, stirring paddles, presses, crushers, casks, carboys, spigots, pressing and straining bags, water seals, a corking machine, a saccharimeter and a hydrometer jar.

Our vocabulary increased to include fining, racking, must, acetic bacteria, Campden tablets, sulphiting, maturing and fermenting.

We read books like "The Art of Making Wine" by Canadians S.F. Anderson and Raymond Hull, published by Longman's of Canada; "Successful Wine Making at Home" by Britisher H.E. Bravery, published in New York by ARC Books (Bravery's liquid measurements are British, not American), and "Winemaking at Home" by Homer Hardwick, published by Funk and Wagnalls.

We read "The Amateur Wine Maker," a monthly magazine from England, or bought copies from its American agent, our own Semplex of U.S.A., 4805 Lyndale Av. N., Minneapolis.

Prohibition taught us much. Then wine (other than sacramental) could not be sold or shipped. But prepared concentrates and extracts, long made for the food industry, with sugar and preservatives removed, could be offered with instructions to the home wine maker.

The repeal of Prohibition did not end the use of these preparations for homemade wine. We had found the taste good, the cost lower, the method easier and quicker, the pride of accomplishment exhilarating.

From Spain, California and Cyprus, concentrates, mostly wine grape, are now offered in wine specialty shops that can be found in the yellow pages of telephone books.

A recent publication is a great teacher. The book, "Folk Wines, Cordials and Brandies — Ways to Make Them, Together with Some Lore, Reminiscences and Advice for Enjoying Them," by Dr. Moritz A. Jagendorf, published by Vanguard Press, Inc., New York, lives up to its full name.

Born in Austria, Jagendorf came to the United States when he was 13. He became a New York City dentist and lived on a nearby farm for 30 years. There he and his wife, a former dancer, became gardeners and wine makers. At one time his racks held 32 kinds of wine.

Jagendorf, who died in early 1981, traveled over much of the world — always searching for foods and wines and tales of common folk. He was an active participant in food societies of note, both here and abroad. He always wore a boutonniere. To him, sleep was a waste of time; it interfered with his work.

His book is beautifully written and easily understood. Its recipes, models of simplicity and clarity, are interlaced with folklore. Amateur wine makers, as well as lovers of good books, will enjoy it.

Until a few years ago, all wine makers needed a license from the federal government to make even one bottle of wine. With the license, one could make up to 200 gallons, tax free. But the last request for renewal of my license was returned with the notation that licenses were no longer required. Wonderful!

Chapter 2/How to make vegetable wines

Just how is wine made?

Let's start by recalling how we made carrot wine late one October, with the thought that it might be served to guests in two years. This is the process:

Twenty pounds of carrots are scrubbed (but not peeled) and cooked until soft in 4½ gallons of water. In the water 14 pounds of sugar had been dissolved and on it during cooking floats an ounce of ginger root.

The carrots themselves end up in the compost heap; they are not palatable — tough skins and too sweet.

The boiling-hot strained carrot water and the piece of ginger root go into a vat (actually a plastic wastebasket) that contains eight sliced unpeeled oranges, four peeled and squeezed lemons and their thinly pared rind, juice and seeds, and 1½ pounds of raisins chopped in the food processor.

Carrying on, let the contents of the vat cool. While waiting, dissolve four quarter-ounce packages of dry yeast in a half cup of lukewarm water. When finger testing tells you the liquid in the vat has become lukewarm, pour in the dissolved yeast and stir slowly and briefly.

"Must" is the winemakers' name for what's in the vat. The vat is covered with a muslin cloth (an enamel pot cover holding it in place) and put in a warm, non-drafty spot among plants in the bay window. Bubbles starting to rise a few hours later are evidence that the must is fermenting, that wine is being made.

Twenty days later, the bubbling stops. Now strain the contents of the vat through a muslin cloth. Rinds and seeds go to the compost heap.

Pour the cloudy liquid that is left through a plastic funnel into a five-gallon carboy, which is a big glass bottle. If the bottle isn't quite full, a cup of commercial white dry wine may be added to leave only an inch of space in the neck of the bottle.

At our house the carboy stands on a bench passed by anyone who leaves the house by the back door. A quick check ensures that liquid is always in the air lock.

Carboys — and bottles of any size — must be corked in a special way to prevent outside air from entering and to let inside gas escape. Stoppers to do this are sold under various names: Fermentation locks, air locks or water seals.

Now the sediment, called "lees" by winemakers, sinks slowly to the bottom of the carboy. When the light of a match held on one side of the carboy can be easily seen from the other side, the clear (the winemaker says "fine") liquid is siphoned off, leaving the lees. This probably will not happen until springtime.

While waiting, reread other pages of Jagendorf's book and select the other folks wines you would like to try. Our own favorites are the wine from beet roots, parsley leaves, rhubarb stalks and dill seeds. But note: Each has its own recipe and winemaking procedure.

Now how do you fill the bottles?

I own a siphon with plastic tube and bulb, but rarely use it because there is a far cheaper and, I think, a better way of making one. To do this I use a thin wooden dowel stick, two rubber bands and about three feet of plastic tubing. The tubing is banded to the stick in such a way that its end is held down close to the lees about an inch off the bottom of the carboy and does not wiggle about.

With the carboy on a table, I sit on the floor with bottles ready. With a little dexterity and a quick thumb-index finger operation I siphon the lees and fill the bottles — with only one initial suck on the tube.

Corks are soaked in hot water and, with the indispensable help of a hand corking tool, bottles are corked and the necks dipped in hot red wax. Bottles are then labeled and stored in racks on their sides. The wax ensures the seal and adds to the beauty of the bottles when opened a year from the storage date.

Let's see about some other wines.

The celery-leaf Italian parsley plants that first saw grow-light in my basement did remarkably well in the garden. Exactly six pounds of leaves and stems went into wine.

Here is what Jagendorf says about parsley wine: "Let me introduce you to a wine with a rare, fantastic taste that becomes more pleasurable the more you drink. Not only is it rare, excellent and stimulating, but it is famous through herbal medicine as a specific against arthritic pains — which seem to afflict every other person I know. But it is the flavor and the bouquet of this wine that fascinate me. It was completely new, delicate, haunting, provocative, and when prepared with other herbs . . . became a creation of truly Oriental wizardry with a bouquet and taste out of a poet's imagination. One might call it a mysterious iridescence of flavor and taste . . . . Parsley was an important plant to the Greeks and the Romans. Garlands of parsley were the prizes often awarded by the Greeks to those who won athletic contests. . . ."

Jagendorf's recipe for a batch of parsley wine: You need: 2 lbs. parsley (2 glass quarts filled, but not pressed down), 2 gals. water, 2 lemons, 2 oranges, 4 lbs. sugar, 1 slice toast, ½ oz. yeast (2 packages). 1. Put fresh parsley leaves into the water in an enamel pot. 2. Pare thinly the rinds of the lemons and the oranges and put them in. If oranges are out of season, you can double the number of lemons. 3. Bring the liquid slowly to a boil and let it simmer for a full 30 minutes. 4. Strain into a crock, squeezing the parsley through a cloth. 5. Add the juice of the lemons and oranges and the sugar. Dissolve the sugar well. 6. Prepare a slice of toast. Cover with the yeast, dissolved in ½ cup warm water, and add both to the crock. Cover; set the crock in a warm place (65-70 degrees) to ferment. 7. When the fermentation has ceased, strain the wine into glass jars and let stand to clear. If it does not clear, fine with eggshells of isinglass, siphon off and bottle.

Home gardeners will find great delight and challenge in Jagendorf's recipes for wine from potatoes, tomatoes, parsnips, celery, beets, carrots, spinach, dill, parsley, mint, sage, strawberries, rhubarb, plums, apples and pears.

They may be surprised to discover recipes for wine made from pesky dandelions, clover, goldenrod, oak leaves, beet tops and roses.

So leave the apparatus of earlier winemaking where it is or sell it. Gather a few — a very few — everyday tools, make a few more, buy still fewer and become one of Jagendorf's students. Wine made at home from garden produce is a bargain — cheaper than wine made from concentrates and cheaper than gallon jugs from commercial wineries.

Chapter 3/The paraphernalia

Wine makers know wine is best if metal (other than stainless steel, which is expensive) is not used in its making. Pots should be enamel, spoons and paddles, wood.

You can avoid the agony of cleaning wooden kegs or barrels by using ordinary plastic trash cans for vats in which the wine ferments. Siphons and tubes should be rubber or plastic. Measuring cups should be glass or plastic.

All wine-making involves straining; some involves squeezing. There are metal strainers and like gadgets, but don't use them. Instead, use an old pillow case or a piece of a sheet, if it has no holes. These and hands are good for squeezing. There is no need to buy a wine press, though if a friend offers one as a gift, take it.

When you want color, as with beet wine, cut finer, boil the vegetable longer and the liquid will get redder, the beets whiter. No squeezing is needed. (Hands used for squeezing without rubber gloves will be stained and require lemon juice or bleach to come clean.)

Wine-in-the-making in a plastic vat should be removed as soon as the fermenting stops. After the straining, the liquid is poured into its carboy or gallon jug. This should be of untinted glass, for it must be easy to clean — and transparent to provide a clear view of what's happening inside.

It should have a mouth that can be plugged, but only with water seals. Whether big or little containers are used, they must be filled to an inch of their stoppers, for it's liquid and not air that ought to fill each jug. Air heads the list of wine's enemies.

Most wine makers clean and store the empty jugs of clear glass that bring gallons of cider, vinegar and cranberry juice and some store-bought wine into the house. A neighbor probably would save them for you, too.

Some wine makers may fancy the five-gallon carboys that hold spring water. They are easier to handle. Yellow pages list their sellers under "Bottles" and "Wine Makers' Equipment." Most wine makers won't bother with these; they cost too much.

Don't use regular corks, even if new, in gallon jugs or the carboys. They either will be blown out or the glass containers will shatter. The war between the yeast and the sugar produces both alcohol and gas. The gas must escape. So be sure to use fermentation locks or water seals.

The store-bought water seals that I use are made of clear plastic and have a bottom tube that fits tightly into a rubber stopper which in turn fits tightly into the mouth and neck of the container. This and everything else needed were bought from Minneapolis' nationally known Semplex of USA.

Once the jug has been closed by the water seal, it should be put in a warm area (65-70 degrees) where it should remain untouched for the months needed for the dregs to settle. This process can be hastened if eggshells or a small amount of isinglass are crushed and floated on top to slowly sink to the bottom carrying dregs with each bit.

I don't do this, though. To me, making good wine is a slow process; I want no part of it to be hurried.

With help or not, the sediment finally will settle on the bottom in a fairly tight and smooth mass. The clear liquid above can now be called wine. It is raw and needs to age a year or more in air-tight bottles. Pouring it into bottles will just stir up the lees.

There is only one other way — siphoning out what's clear and leaving what's cloudy. The winemaker calls this racking. Some makers will rack their wine more than once to be certain that it is fine (clear) and will remain so.

New bottles may be used, but so can any others that can be closed with a wine cork. The bottles may be filled as soon as the liquid is clear and no gas bubbles can be seen. They should be stoppered as soon as they are filled.

Once I used the cheaper plastic stoppers but became tired of leaks and drippings that had to be wiped up when bottles were on their sides. Each leak meant that air was entering and the wine inside was deteriorating. So I turned to corks — new wine corks from Spain and Portugal.

I know of no way to cork a wine bottle without the proper tool, since the corks are larger than the mouth of the bottle. Each cork is taken from hot water and inserted in the corking tool — a hard squeeze of the hand and a push and the cork is in the bottle.

Where do you get bottles? You can buy them or you can forage for them. Once I used non-returnable pop bottles, which are the curse of the countryside. Nowadays friends put their wine bottles aside for me to use. Strangers who bid high and get bottles of my wine at silent auctions for good purposes join those who provide bottles. It's a high order of foraging.

I have described myself as a "born-again" wine maker who works with simple things and leaves the measuring of sugar and alcoholic content to others. The only tests I have are taste and appearance. But I confess that I am a back-sliding maker of wine. At least Jagendorf would have thought so.

Years ago, those who wrote about winemaking taught me to dissolve sodium metabisulfite powder or Campden tablets in water and rinse every pot, bottle, paddle, cork, fermentation lock, spoon and anything else that touched the wine I made. One crushed tablet in one gallon of water does no harm to cultured yeasts but is an effective sterilizing agent that will control the wild yeasts and spoilage organisms that are just about everywhere.

I still do this. Maybe I would have no spoilage if I didn't, but with the Campden tablets I don't worry about it.

What plants, shrubs and trees may be used by home gardener-cooks to make wine in their own kitchens? A partial list:

From the home garden: carrots, beets (roots and leaves), parsnips, turnips, tomatoes, celery, rhubarb stalks (not leaves), ordinary chives and those with wide flat leaves, onions and Egyptian onions, mint, dill, parsley, edible crysanthe-mums, all garden-grown berries and cante-loupes and like melons.

From the flower beds, lawns and fence rows: dandelions, geraniums, marigolds, cowslips, roses, chickweed, woodruff, lamb's quarters, clover, daisies, apples and all other edible fruit from trees and shrubs.

Fruit you can grow in Minnesota

Leon C. Snyder

1/They grow on trees

Chapter 1/Some things to think about

Before planting tree fruits you should consider the advantages and disadvantages. Let's take a look at a few general aspects of growing fruit trees before we get specific about the different fruits.

Most tree fruits, especially apples, require a very thorough spray program to control insects and diseases. This can be quite expensive and it requires weekly attention. If you miss one spray or use the wrong material you can end up with wormy fruit.

On the other hand, if you are successful in controlling insects and diseases, you can enjoy high-quality tree-ripened fruits to eat fresh, to process or to store.

You need a large enough space for planting. Tree fruits require considerable space and should be planted where they will receive full sunlight. Dwarf fruit trees help to solve the space problem and should be planted whenever possible. Not only do they save space but they are easier to spray and harvest.

The dwarfing is brought about by the kind of rootstock used. Dwarfing rootstocks are mostly from the Malling Experiment Station in England, so they are not fully hardy and a winter mulch of hay or straw around the bases of the trees is a good idea.

Only the size of the tree is affected by the rootstock. Fruits are normal in size and quality.

The only tree fruits hardy in the Upper Midwest climate are apples, pears, plums, cherries and apricots. Not all varieties of these tree fruits are hardy. Your Agricultural Extension Service office will have a list of recommended varieties to plant.

If you use dwarf fruit trees, space them about 10 to 20 feet apart. With standard apple trees you will need 30 feet between trees. Apples do best in well-drained clay loam soil. Avoid low areas where frost settles. A slope is fine for most tree fruits.

Apples are best grown in sod. With dwarf trees it is advisable to mulch around them to protect roots from extreme cold. Mice can be a problem with all fruit trees, so protect the trunks with a mouse guard. We have found that cylinders of quarter-inch hardware cloth make excellent mouse guards.

Pears aren't usually grown in our area. But **Parker, Patten** and **Luscious** are hardy varieties and, with care, you might succeed with one of them. Their culture is the same as for apples.

Plums, cherries and apricots have similar culture requirements. But remember, plums differ in pollination requirements. **Mount Royal** and **Dietz** are self-fruitful; you can get fruits even if you have just one tree. **Superior, Red Glow** and other varieties of hybrid plums are self-sterile and require a special pollinizer variety such as **South Dakota** or **Toka** to set fruits.

The sour or pie cherries are the only ones hardy in our climate. **North Star** and **Meteor** are good varieties to plant. North Star is a natural dwarf and is best if space is limited.

Commercial varieties of apricots aren't hardy, but several varieties of Manchurian apricots have been developed and can withstand Minnesota winters. **Sungold, Moongold** and **Scout** are the best ones. Because of their very early bloom and the resulting danger of frost and lack of pollinating insects, a full crop of fruits does not occur every year.

Peaches are sometimes planted in our area but seldom reach a fruiting age. The flower buds of peaches normally are killed at about 15 degrees below zero F. If we do have a mild winter and peach trees do set fruits, the trees often are winter-killed the following winter. Some varieties are reported to be very hardy, but we have not found any to be reliably hardy in trials at the University of Minnesota Horticultural Research Center.

All of the above stone fruits do best in soil that is cultivated to control weeds. If they are grown in sod, a mulch should be used under the trees and a nitrogen fertilizer should be used to compensate for competition from the grasses.

All tree fruits require a spray program. You will need a good sprayer, one that will cover the entire tree with a fine mist. The chemicals to use and the timing are very important. The Agricultural Extension Service has a home fruit spray guide that is revised each year. You should get one.

Pruning of fruit trees is very important. This usually is done in late winter. There are no fast rules for pruning. It is done on young trees mainly to space the branches.

The house that Grandfather brought his bride to was of the large, solid brick type, similar to most of the farm houses in lower Ontario at that time. They were practical, but not beautiful.

However, in a very few years, Grandma transformed it into a bower of loveliness with vines, blossoming climbers, shrubbery, with a background of evergreen trees.

Greeting you at the front door were Jacqmani, clematis and climbing roses. Over the back entrance was an arbor covered with honeysuckle, where Grandma peeled potatoes and the bees were always busy. The side door had wisteria and bittersweet. Over the cool summer house were grapevines that bore large bunches of large, blue, sweet grapes, and the hen house was cool with a mass of scarlet runners, wild hops and wild cucumber vines.

Grandfather and Uncle Jerry always kept the vines so neat and well-trimmed that the hen house was never damp or stuffy.

Even in winter the house was most attractive, especially after a snowfall when, from a distance, it appeared like a toy house enclosed in a basketweave of dormant vines nestling against a background of evergreen trees.

Chapter 2/Apples and pears

The planting of apples and pears should not be attempted unless one has adequate room to grow them and is willing to give them adequate protection against insects and diseases.

The site selected for growing apples and pears should be in full sun, and the soil should be a moisture-retentive clay loam. Apples and pears do poorly in sandy soils, especially in northern parts of our area. An east or north-facing slope is ideal, but not essential.

Dormant, bare-root plants are most economical to plant. Planting should be done as early in the spring as possible. Balled and burlapped or container-grown trees may be planted later in the spring, but they are more expensive.

Make the planting hole large enough to accommodate the tree's root system without crowding. After unpacking the dormant tree, plunge the roots into water for a few hours before planting. Prune back any broken roots. Place the tree in the planting hole with roots spread out and enlarge the hole if necessary to avoid crowding the roots.

The tree should be planted at the same depth as it was growing in the nursery. This depth can be determined by laying a board over the hole next to the trunk of the tree. It may be necessary to adjust the depth by digging the hole deeper or by filling in with soil.

With the tree held in place, fill in with good topsoil and firm the soil around the roots to eliminate air pockets. Leave a shallow depression around the base of the tree for watering. Add a bucket of water if the soil is at all dry and water the tree during dry periods for the first year.

Spacing of apple and pear trees is important and will depend on whether you are growing dwarf or standard trees. Standard trees are grafted on seedling roots and need at least 30 feet between trees. Dwarf trees are grafted on dwarfing rootstocks and vary in size depending on the rootstock used.

Trees grafted on East Malling IX rootstocks are only about seven feet tall and eight feet wide. These trees could be spaced about 10 feet apart. Trees grafted on semidwarfs grow to a height and width of about 15 feet. Such trees should be spaced about 20 feet apart.

If you do plant dwarf trees, be prepared to mulch the trees with hay or straw in late fall, because the root systems are not as hardy as the seedling roots of standard trees.

Pears are planted the same way apples are. Most pears for this area will be grafted on seedling roots. The trees are more upright than apples, and a spacing of 20 feet should be adequate.

Pruning at planting time is important to balance the top with the reduced root system. Remove all lower branches to a height of two feet. Thin out the branches so they are spaced about six inches apart.

Select wide-angled branches to make the framework for the tree. Branches that are left should be pruned back to an outward-facing bud. Follow-up pruning should be done each spring before growth starts. A little pruning each year is better than too much pruning at any one time.

The varieties of apples and pears to choose will depend on personal preferences. Only varieties adapted to this area should be planted. For early apples plant **Oriole, State Fair** or **Beacon.** For midseason plant **Red Baron, Sweet Sixteen** or **Redwell.** For winter use plant **Honeygold, Haralson** or **Fireside.**

In 1979 the University of Minnesota's experiment station and Department of Horticultural Science and Landscape Architecture introduced a new hardy apple that can be planted in some areas of the Upper Midwest.

The variety was **Keepsake,** a late-maturing variety that keeps until spring. The trees are very hardy, but the fruits mature late in the season, making the variety unsuitable for the far north. It does well, however, in southern Minnesota. The apples are medium-sized, irregular in shape, and with nearly flat sides. The skin is red with scattered white dots.

At harvest time the fruits are hard and the flavor is tart. The quality improves strikingly in storage, and by late winter it is one of the finest of eating apples, crisp and juicy with a sprightly flavor. It is also excellent for pies and sauce.

Few pear varieties are hardy enough for our area. **Parker** and **Patten** are dependable. **Luscious** is a new variety from South Dakota that has excellent quality. There was some winter injury on this variety in the severe winter of 1978-79 but none observed since then.

Pest control is the No. 1 problem in growing apples and pears. Apple scab and cedar-apple rust may be controlled by including ferbam or zineb in the first and second cover sprays.

Fire blight is very difficult to control. It is a bacterial disease, quite common each year on mountain ash and other susceptible plants as well as on apples and pears.

The tips of the branches are affected and the leaves look as if they had been scorched by fire. Unfortunately, there are no very good controls for fire blight. Overly vegetative trees are most susceptible so go easy on the nitrogen, which favors succulent growth susceptible to blight.

Insect pests of apples and pears include aphids, curculios, codling moths and apple maggots. Red spiders can also be a problem.

The adult of the apple maggot or railroad worm is a fly. Early in July, and continuing through the summer, this fly emerges from the soil after pupating as a larvae. The flies feed for a while and then lay their eggs just under the skin of developing apple fruits. To ensure maggot-free apples spray weekly until harvest time.

Control of insect and disease problems requires a regular spray program. The fruits must be covered with a general-purpose protective spray at all times. Get a copy of the Home Fruit Spray Guide from your county Agriculture Extension Office and follow recommendations.

Rabbits and field mice can be problems, especially in the winter. A cylinder of quarter-inch hardware cloth will protect the trunk from mouse injury. A chicken-wire barrier will protect against rabbit injury.

A word about grafting

Fruit-growing is always challenging and rewarding. It can be creative, as well. The ancient art of tree-grafting is responsible for many of the improved varieties we now grow and enjoy. Try it; it's not just for the professional horticulturist.

Suppose you have an apple tree grown from seed. The fruits are worthless. Must you replace the tree? If it's a healthy specimen, maybe it's time to try grafting.

That's how you force desirable cuttings from a tree with good fruit to grow on small lateral branches of your seedling tree.

The cuttings are called scions. They should be cut from vigorous new wood that grew last year. These scions must be taken while they are dormant and stored in a cool, moist place until the buds on your seedling tree start to swell in spring.

The storage temperature for your scions should be just above freezing and below 40 degrees F. Unless you have a cool place with the desired temperature, it is best to wrap the scions in aluminum foil and store them in a refrigerator near the freezing element. The scions must not dry out.

In late April the grafting is done. There are several types of grafts that can be made but the cleft-graft is the easiest. Take a side branch that is about an inch or less in diameter. Saw it off about a foot from the trunk. With a sharp knife split the branch at the tip. Use a screwdriver to hold the split open.

Take a portion of the scion variety about four inches long, make slanted cuts at the base with a sharp knife to form a wedge that can be inserted in the split stock of the seedling tree. The cambium (growth layer) of both stock and scion must be in contact. Two scions, one on each side of the cleft, can be inserted. Remove the

Grandma would be making "pomanders", or clove apples, every year about this time. She made them for her closest friends to place in their linen chests and clothes closets and also to hang on Christmas trees. This is her recipe: Press whole cloves into a medium-size, uncooked apple, continuing until the entire fruit is a mass of clove heads. Allow it to dry for a couple of weeks -- it won't spoil or decay -- then roll it in powdered cinnamon and, if you can get it, orris root. Tie a bow of ribbon to the stem or hang it by a double loop of ribbon or tinsel cord. These enchanting spicy balls will last for years. I have one that Grandma made over sixty years ago, and it is still delightfully fragrant.

screwdriver and the pressure will hold the scions in place.

The cut must next be sealed to prevent dessication. Grafting wax can be used or a rubberized electrician's tape can be wrapped around the stock and the basal part of the scions. It is important to use only dormant scions and to make a clean cut in contact between both stock and scion.

Some common questions about apple culture

Q. We have a tree in our yard that our neighbor calls the **Minnesota Delicious.** Last year it had a bad case of fire blight. We would like to plant another tree like it in case it dies. Our nursery does not know of a tree called Minnesota Delicious. Does this tree have another name?

A. The **Regent** is a variety of apple introduced by the University of Minnesota. It is a seedling of the Red Delicious and much hardier. This is probably the variety you have. It should be available from most nurseries.

Q. I am thinking of planting some apple trees this spring. I have a catalog that has varieties for zones 5 to 8. Would these be hardy in Minnesota?

A. Most of Minnesota is in zones 3 and 4. Varieties for zones 5 to 8 would probably lack hardiness. Get a list of fruit varieties recommended for Minnesota from your county Agricultural Extension office and buy your trees from a local nurseryman who sells trees grown in this area. Oriole, Beacon, Haralson, Fireside, and Regent are good varieties for southern Minnesota.

Q. We planted four apple trees five years ago. Two of these, both Haralsons, have been fruiting for several years. The Fireside and **Northwest Greening** have never flowered or fruited. This spring I read in a gardening book that if I hammered a branch no less than 1½ inches in diameter, gently breaking the bark, that blossoms would form. I did this on the Fireside and Northwest Greening. The Fireside bloomed but the Greening did not. What I would like to know is when do the flower buds form and did the treatment actually work?

A. Flower buds on apples are initiated in June for the next year's bloom. Your treatment in no way affected this year's bloom. Fireside and Northwest Greenings are not precocious bearers like the Haralson. It normally takes five or more years from planting to the first flowers and fruits. Your Fireside would have bloomed without the treatment. The treatment, however, could affect next year's bloom. The interruption in the flow of manufactured foods from the leaves to the roots will provide more sugars in the branch treated and this will favor blossom bud formation.

Q. I would like to plant a Fireside apple this spring. My dilemma is this. We have bought Fireside apples from several growers, and the quality seems to vary greatly. Some are delicious, and others are quite tasteless. Are there several kinds of Fireside apple? Will the apples from a dwarf tree be equal to those on a standard tree?

A. There is only one Fireside apple. The quality differs greatly depending on the soil and season. The fruits on dwarf trees are equal to those from standard trees. The **Connell Red** is probably a red sport of the Fireside. The quality of this variety can also vary.

Q. We have a Haralson apple tree that has produced a crop each of the last four years. Each year the fruits are filled with what has been called the railroad worm. The fruits are useless and we have thrown them out. What can we do to get rid of these worms?

A. The only answer to your problem is a complete and thorough spray program. The Agricultural Extension Service publishes a folder entitled "The Home Fruit Spray Guide," available from your County Extension Office or from the Bulletin Room on the St. Paul campus

---

Grandma had on her farm a cave in the side of a hill with a front wall of grass sod and a double wooden tar-papered door. It was called the root house, and potatoes, other vegetables, and barrels of winter apples were stored there. It was not heated, but nothing ever froze. And all winter long we had good fresh vegetables, while the apples seemed to taste better as winter wore on.

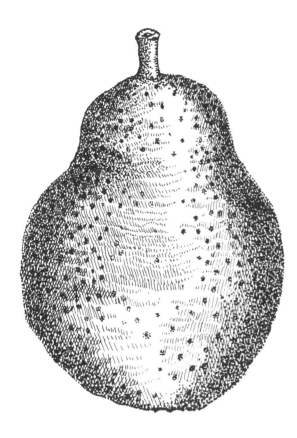

of the University of Minnesota. Get a copy and follow recommendations. Commercial apple growers spray their apples about 16 times during the season to get clean fruits.

Q. Will apple trees grown from seed bear fruits, and will the fruits be like the parent tree?

A. An apple tree grown from seed will bear fruits, but you may have to wait 10 years before you get any. Seedling apples are usually inferior and seldom resemble the parent tree. Chances of getting a worthwhile apple from seed are rather slim.

Q. Please tell me how I should plant an apple seed to get it to grow.

A. The problem is not how to get an apple seed to grow, but what the resulting tree and fruit will be like. The chance of a worthwhile apple is very slim. We grow thousands of seedlings at our University of Minnesota Horticultural Research Center for every variety worthy of introduction. Apple seeds should be extracted from the core of the apple. They should be stored over winter at temperatures between 32 and 40 degrees F. Placing the seeds in a plastic bag with a little moist sand and then placing the bag in a refrigerator is a good way to keep the seeds cool and moist over winter. The seeds can then be planted in the spring with a fair chance of germination.

Q. I have a **Wealthy** apple tree and this year the leaves are covered with orange spots that have fingerlike growths on the under surface. What causes this and how do I prevent it?

A. The Wealthy apple is susceptible to cedar-apple rust. The disease spreads from red cedar trees to the apple following rains in late May. Ferbam or zineb are good fungicides to control this disease. Spray about a week after petal fall and again a week later.

Q. Three years ago I planted three apple trees. Last spring the tops killed back. New sprouts are coming from the base. Could I train one of these sprouts into a new tree?

A. If the sprouts are coming from above the graft union, one of the sprouts could be selected and trained as a new tree. Cut the main stem above the sprout. If the sprouts are coming from below the graft union it would not be worthwhile to keep them. The graft union is usually at about the soil level.

Q. I have several dwarf apple trees in my yard and would like to keep them from getting too large. How much of the top can I remove and when is the best time to prune — fall or spring?

A. Dwarf apple trees can be pruned to control size if this is done in late winter or early spring before growth starts. The amount to cut back is a matter of judgment. A little pruning each year is better than pruning too much at one time. Make clean cuts and avoid leaving stubs.

Q. Last spring three of our eight-year-old dwarf apple trees died from some type of disease. The leaves wilted on one branch at a time

When the ground under Grandma's five apple trees was thoroughly frozen, she would cover it with a four-inch layer of sawdust, which the sawmill gave to her.

This mulch would hold back too-early blossoming in the event of a prematurely warm spring, often followed by a killing frost.

At first Grandfather laughed at Grandma and her notions, but he did likewise after he lost several apple crops in his big orchard.

until the entire tree died. What killed these trees?

A. It was probably winter injury. A sudden freeze early in the winter will often cause this. We can expect a winter about once every 20 years that will kill fruit trees. The Armistice Day storm in 1940 killed many fruit and ornamental trees.

Q. How does one distinguish between winter injury and fire blight on an apple tree?

A. In winter injury, the leaves may open in the spring and then suddenly wilt and die. The bark usually is dead and loose near the base of the trunk. When a branch is cut diagonally, the cambium and sapwood are dark colored. With fire blight, the disease shows up in late spring or in summer. The tips of the branches wilt suddenly and turn black. The disease progresses downward from the tips of the branches. The bark shrivels and becomes dry.

Q. I planted some apple trees about three years ago that have not produced fruits. I have been told by someone to mulch them with six to eight inches of straw out to the tips of the branches, keeping the mulch about a foot away from the trunk, and then put manure on top. Someone else has told us not to mulch, since this would stimulate vegetative growth and delay fruiting. Whom should I believe?

A. The use of a mulch will have little or no effect on flowering. Very few apple varieties start to bear until the trees are six to eight years old. Even on dwarf rootstocks you will get little or no fruit until the trees are four or five years old. The use of a straw mulch is advisable with dwarf trees to protect the roots from winter injury. I would go easy on the manure, since it encourages late growth in the fall, and this could result in winter injury.

I keep my dwarf trees mulched with straw and use a commercial fertilizer high in nitrogen about May 1, and I have good production.

Q. I would like to trim the suckers on my apple trees. I also have a problem with my apples. I get a large crop of apples, but the fruits are small. Can you tell me what is wrong? Would it help to prune the trees? Will I need to paint the cuts to prevent bleeding?

A. The size of the fruits is often influenced by the number of apples set. If there are too many apples, the amount of food manufactured by the leaves will not be sufficient to mature the fruits properly. The result is small and often poorly colored fruits.

Hand-thinning of fruits would help. Pruning would also reduce the numbers of fruit set and would favor new vegetative growth. The additional leaves would help develop the apples to a larger size. Late winter is the best time to prune.

Remove all suckers from the base of the tree and any water sprouts along the main branches. Prune one branch of any set that cross and rub each other. Thin out the branches in the top of the tree to let in light.

Bleeding is not a problem. Whether you paint the wounds is optional. Usually wounds under 2 inches across are not painted.

Q. Our pear tree is about 10 years old and produces a crop each year. The problem is that the fruits are covered with black blotches. What must we do to prevent these?

A. Pears are susceptible to about the same diseases as the apple. I suspect your problem is scab, a fungus disease. The only control is a regular spray program. You can get a spray guide from your agricultural extension office or from the Bulletin Room of the University of Minnesota.

Grandma had a tree in her orchard that bore freak apples. The upper half of the fruit was a bright yellow and tasted sweet, while the lower half was rosy red and tasted like a very tart crab apple. Today horticulturists call these apples chimeras. They result from the fruit's taking on characteristics of both stock and scion in grafting. They are not considered desirable. But this apple tree of Grandma's was quite a curiosity and folks came from miles around to see and taste the apples every autumn. Uncle Jerry always exhibited a plateful at the county fair, but never won a prize until he donated five dollars for first prize in a special class for the most curious exhibit of fruit. Then he won his own money for years. He sold cuttings from the tree for two dollars each.

Chapter 3/Stone fruits

Stone fruits are fleshy fruits with pits. A thin epidermis or skin surrounds the fruit. The pit is a hard endocarp that surrounds one or more seeds. Between the epidermis and the endocarp is the fleshy, edible portion of the fruit.

Plums, cherries, cherry-plums, apricots, peaches and nectarines are familiar examples.

Most stone fruits are borne on small- to medium-sized trees, best grown in a garden area where the soil can be kept cultivated. They do not compete well with grass or weeds. If they are grown as lawn specimens, a mulch should be used around them to smother grass-and-weed competition.

The mature size of the tree should be ascertained, and spacing between trees should be such that the trees can grow to maturity without crowding. For most varieties this means about 20 feet between trees.

Plums are grown for dessert, sauce and preserves. Two species, the **American** and the **Canadian,** are native. They produce tart fruits, excellent for preserves.

Hybrids between cultivated plums and the American are very hardy and are commonly planted. **Red Glow, Superior** and **Pipestone** are examples of these hybrid plums. Being hybrids, they are self-sterile and must have a pollinizer such as one of the wild plums or one of the cultivars such as **Toka** or **South Dakota.**

The Italian prune, a variety of European plum, is not hardy, but a few of the European-type plums can be grown at least in southern Minnesota. **Mount Royal** is a blue plum of excellent quality for eating fresh or for sauce or preserves. **Dietz** is a smaller plum that makes excellent sauce. The advantage of these European plums is that they do not require a special pollinizer.

Cherry production is limited to the sour or pie cherries and to the **Nanking** cherry. **North Star** and **Meteor** are two varieties introduced by the Horticultural Research Center of the University of Minnesota. North Star is a natural dwarf and should be planted where space is limited.

The Nanking is a bush cherry that produces clusters of small red cherries that are pleasant to eat and make a fine jelly.

Birds are especially fond of cherries, and some means of protecting the fruits must be used. A plastic bird netting draped over the tree is the best method.

Apricots are planted as much for their ornamental value in the landscape as for their edible fruits. The pink blossoms in early May are always welcome. Leaves turn golden yellow in the fall, adding to the beauty of fall colors.

Only the Manchurian apricot and some of its hybrids are hardy in our climate. The university has introduced two cultivars, **Moongold** and **Sungold. Mandan** and **Scout** are other cultivars that might be planted. It is necessary to plant

Grandma would not allow water to become stagnant anywhere around the farm, because she knew it encouraged mosquitoes. If it could not be drained, it was treated with kerosene. (Grandma called it coal oil.) Where she got the idea I don't know, but it was at least 50 years before this treatment was in general use.

two or more kinds to assure cross-pollination.

The size of the fruit crop is usually reduced by late-spring frosts or cold weather at blossom time that interferes with bee activity. The fruits, when they do develop, are smaller than commercial varieties and more tart. They make excellent preserves.

Another stone fruit, planted mostly in western parts of the state and in North Dakota and South Dakota, is the cherry plum. These fruits are hybrids between the native sandcherry and the plum. They are small bushy trees that seldom grow taller than about eight feet. The fruits are intermediate in size and prized for making jams and preserves.

Opata and **Sapalta** are the most common varieties. Being hybrids, these fruits are self-sterile, and the **Compass** cherry should be planted for a pollinator. Cherry plums are inclined to be short-lived.

Peaches are sometimes planted, but seldom prove successful. The flower buds are hardy to only about 15 degrees below zero F., and most winters it gets colder than that. Occasionally a tree will have a few fruits, but usually the tree winter-kills following such a crop.

For this reason we do not recommend that you plant peaches. Some of the dwarf types might be grown in tubs that could be moved into an unheated garage or other building during the winter.

All stone fruits are susceptible to certain insect and disease problems. Plum curculio and the plum gouger are the principal insect pests. Brown rot can affect the fruits in a wet year. For the control of these and the other pests, obtain a copy of the Home Fruit Spray Guide we've mentioned.

Some common questions about stone fruits

Q. I have a Pipestone plum five years old. It flowers every spring, but no fruits develop. What's my problem?

A. The Pipestone plum is self-sterile and requires a pollinizer. A wild plum will provide the necessary pollen, or you could plant either the variety Toka or South Dakota. Cutting flowering branches of the wild plum and putting them in a bucket of water near your flowering Pipestone might help until your Toka or South Dakota reaches a flowering age.

Q. I have **Superior, Waneta** and Pipestone plums. Could I use a Dietz for a pollinizer?

A. The Dietz is a good plum and needs no pollinizer. It would be best to plant a South Dakota or Toka to pollinize the hybrid plums that you have. A wild plum would also work.

Q. Last year I bought a peach tree that was supposed to be hardy in our area. It came through last winter and leafed out this spring and even bloomed. Shortly after it finished flowering, the leaves started to turn yellow, dried and dropped off. I believe that the tree must have been infected with fire blight. Will the tree leaf out again next spring, or should I remove it now?

A. I doubt that your peach tree had fire blight. Fireblight affects apples, pears, mountain ash and cotoneaster, but I have never seen it on peaches or plums. What probably caused the death of your peach tree was winter injury. If your soil was a heavy clay, the roots could have been killed by too much water in the soil.

Q. We have heard a lot about the Nanking cherry but I am not sure what kind of a cherry it is. Does it produce big cherries that are worth growing? Are the fruits sweet or sour? Are they hardy? If this is not a good cherry to plant, what would you advise?

A. The Nanking cherry is a bush cherry that will grow to a height of about eight feet. The fruits are small, about a quarter of an inch in diameter. They are sweet to the taste and make a nice fruit drink. They can also be used for jelly. The fruits are usually produced in abundance, but birds are also very fond of them. The fruits are rather small for making pies or sauce. The Nanking cherry is an attractive ornamental shrub with an added bonus of producing edible fruits. The plant is perfectly hardy. We cannot grow sweet cherries in Minnesota. Northstar and Meteor are pie cherries that can be grown. The fruits are tart but do make excellent pies.

2/Grapes: the climbing fruit

Grapes for home use can be grown in all parts of our area. Success depends on site selection.

Full sunlight and high temperatures are required to ripen grapes and to mature the wood of their vines before winter sets in. In the north, grapes should be planted on a south-facing slope or on the south side of a building.

The soil should be well-drained and preferably a sandy loam with high organic content.

Grapes grow best when cultivated to reduce competition from weeds. A fall cover crop of oats will help to mature the wood and thus reduce winter injury.

Grapes are vines and must be trained on some kind of support. Usually they are grown in rows with wooden or steel posts spaced at regular intervals. Two or three wires are stretched between the posts, with the first about 2½ feet above the soil. The vines are tied to these wires in the spring after pruning.

Grapes should be fertilized regularly. Well-rotted manure, applied in fall or early spring, helps maintain a proper level of organic matter in the soil. About May 1 use a complete fertilizer high in nitrogen at the rate of about a pound per 20 feet of row.

A proper choice of grape varieties for your area is essential. Some are hardy without winter protection, while others must be removed from the trellis and covered for winter.

Beta is one of our hardiest varieties and can be grown in most parts of our area without protection. **Concord, Fredonia, Van Buren** and **Worden** are blue grapes of American origin that require winter protection in all but the southern part of our area.

I grow the Worden without winter protection and usually have a good crop, although there is occasionally some winter injury. For me, Worden has been the most productive of the blue grapes.

Edelweiss and **Interlachen** are white and

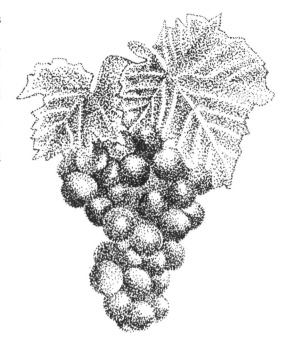

green grapes. Edelweiss is the hardier of these two. **Delaware** and **Swenson's Red** are red grapes. They require winter protection.

Edelweiss and Swenson's Red were introduced by University of Minnesota horticulturists in 1979.

Edelweiss is a sweet, high-sugar, white grape with good production. The grapes are of medium size and excellent for eating fresh or for wine-making. The fruits mature early, and the vines are vigorous and disease-resistant. Plants have survived without protection to 25 to 30 degrees below zero F. If it gets colder than that, winter protection is advised.

Swenson's Red is a high-quality red table grape with medium-large, firm-textured fruits. They mature in early September with high sugar content and a very fine flavor. The plants have about the same degree of hardiness as the Edelweiss. Swenson's Red makes a high-quality white wine.

Some growers plant European or French hybrid grapes such as **Foch, Seyval** and **De Chaunac.** These are all tender and must be given complete winter protection.

Tender varieties that require winter protection require special training. Select a strong cane and tie it to the lower wire. Lateral branches that develop from this cane should be tied to the upper wire or wires.

In the fall, after the leaves have been killed by frost and the wood has hardened, cut back these lateral branches to two or three buds and remove from the trellis. Cover the cane with soil, and when the ground freezes apply a mulch of clean straw or marsh hay.

Remove the mulch in early April, and, when the soil is dry, lift the cane and again tie it to

Grandma was making grape jelly one autumn and she told Uncle Jerry to throw out in the field, a long way from the house, a large pail of discarded grape skins and seeds. Uncle was "tired", so he put the pail behind the barn for later disposition, and then forgot it. The discarded fruit fermented, the geese and ducks ate it and became, well, just plain drunk. They hilariously hissed and quacked at each other, and then promptly went to sleep. Uncle thought it was a big joke. Grandma was indignant, and Granddad just smiled quietly — he always played safe.

the lower wire. After a few years another cane should be selected to replace the old one, since repeated pruning of the lateral branches will result in a cane that is difficult to cover. Allow this renewal cane to develop to fruiting size before removing the old cane.

With hardy grapes, training and pruning are different. Pruning is usually done in late winter while the plants are still dormant. Plants are trained with one upright stem from the base and lateral branches in opposite directions on each wire. The object is to leave about 40 buds per plant. Since fruiting occurs on one-year-old canes, pruning should retain a maximum of such growth.

After pruning, tie the canes to the wire, using binder twine or a similar material.

Bleeding may occur if pruning is done in late winter or early spring. There is no evidence that bleeding harms the plant.

Pruning should be done every year. Old neglected vines are difficult to prune, since there will be little new wood close to the main stem. To renovate such plants it may be necessary to sacrifice most of the crop for a year by pruning severely to force vigorous new growth close to the main stem.

Grapes have their share of insect and disease problems. Black rot and downy mildew are common diseases. Leafhoppers and grape phylloxera are common insect problems. Follow the recommended spray program for grapes given in the Home Fruit Spray Guide.

Grapes should be harvested as soon as they are fully ripe. Use a knife or pruning shears to cut the clusters from the vines.

Birds can be a problem for ripe fruits. A nylon bird netting is the best protection.

Some common questions about grapes

Q. We have a four-year-old grapevine. Last year and this year the vines were covered with flowers, but no fruits set. What's up?

A. Some wild grapes produce only male or female flowers and require a pollinizer. Most grape varieties produce perfect flowers and are self-fruitful. If you have a male plant, it will never produce fruits. If you have a female plant, you will need to plant another variety that has perfect flowers. The only time you can determine the sex is when the plant is in bloom.

Q. I planted 20 grape vines last spring that are doing well. Next spring I would like to put up a fence on which to train them. I have steel posts and some woven-wire fencing. Could I use this type of a fence?

A. I have seen grapes growing on a woven-wire fence, but it is difficult to prune them properly since the vines grow through the mesh fencing. A better type of a trellis is made by using two heavy wires stretched between posts. The lowest wire should be 2½ feet from the ground and the upper wire about 4 feet. Wood posts are best to use, but since you have the steel posts you could use them.

Q. I am planning to plant grapes next spring. I would like some white grapes for eating and some blue grapes for jellies and juice. How many plants will I need? Can several varieties be planted in the same row?

A. Edelweiss is a good white grape of good eating quality. I have had excellent results with Worden for a blue grape. Other blue grapes are Fredonia and Concord. If space is limited, I would suggest one plant of Edelweiss and possibly two plants of Worden or one of the other blue grapes. These can all be planted in the same row. Plants should be at least 10 feet apart.

Grandma's pride and joy was her grape arbor. She grew luscious bunches of red, white and blue grapes. We children thought this was most patriotic, and the arbor the most delightful place on the farm on hot days. It was always so cool and fragrant with bunches of ripening grapes hanging within our easy reach.

If we children could eat a grape without screwing up our faces, Grandma thought the grapes were safely sweet and ripe, and our capacity was our only limitation.

3/They're the berries

Chapter 1/Strawberries

Many home gardeners can find room for a few small fruits, even where space is too limited for tree fruits.

Ripe strawberries and raspberries picked from your own garden are a real treat. Blueberries, currants and gooseberries are other small fruits that you may wish to try. Let's learn about them, starting with strawberries.

June is the month for home-grown strawberries. No fruit is easier to grow or returns more for space used.

Strawberries are of two general types. The June-bearing varieties produce a single crop that matures in June and July depending on the variety and location. The everbearing varieties produce a fall crop as well as one in the spring.

There are two systems of culture: The matted row, which we recommend for June-bearing varieties, and the hill system, recommended for everbearing varieties.

In the matted-row system, young plants are planted as early in the spring as possible. Dormant plants are best. If you use freshly dug plants, plant immediately after digging.

Space the plants from 18 to 24 inches apart in rows that are five feet apart. Make a deep slit in the soil with a spade, insert the plant with the roots fanned out and the crown at soil level.

At this time of year, Grandma insisted that Uncle Jerry spend as much time weeding as he did fishing, and for peace's sake, Uncle agreed. Grandma used to say, "Weed and thou shalt reap," and Uncle would sadly retort as he thought of the good fishing time being wasted, "Weed and you will weep."

Remove the spade and firm the soil with your foot to elimimate air pockets.

If the soil is dry, water the plants, using about a cup of water per plant. Remove any flowers that develop, but allow runner plants to develop.

By the end of summer you should have a matted row. Do not let the row get more than about 18 inches wide. Limit the width of the row by cultivation, thus cutting off surplus runner plants.

You may need to fertilize the plants during the first growing season. A pound of a 10-10-10 fertilizer used as a side dressing after the plants are established should be sufficient to develop strong runner plants.

Keep the space between the rows cultivated and remove any weeds that develop in the row.

The hill system differs in a few details. Space plants a foot apart, remove the first blossoms and keep the runners cut off. If you need more than a single row, the rows can be a foot apart with a picking aisle between every third row. After July 1, allow blossoms to form for a fall crop.

Be careful not to allow the roots to become dry. If the soil is dry at planting time water the plants. A starter solution will help to reduce the shock of transplanting.

There are many strawberry varieties to choose from. Different varieties perform differently on different soil types so it is a good idea to try several to determine which ones are best for you.

Veestar, Cyclone, Redcoat, Sparkle, Trumpet-

er, **Toplight** and **Badgerbelle** are recommended June-bearing varieties. **Ogallala** is the best ever-bearing variety. It has given the best performance in my garden.

Many commercial growers dig their strawberry plants in the fall and store them over winter in a cool, moist storage room for spring planting. Such plants should be dormant when planted. If you move plants from your own plantings, do it early in the spring before growth starts and replant immediately.

The soil for strawberries should be high in organic matter and contain adequate plant nutrients to assure good growth. I use a 10-10-10 fertilizer at the rate of one pound for each 25 feet of row. I apply this at the time of planting and again after runners start to form.

Strawberries require winter protection. The flower buds are formed in the fall and these can be injured by temperatures lower than 20 degrees F. About Nov. 1 apply a straw or marsh-hay mulch over the rows to a depth of about 2 inches. This mulch is lifted from over the rows and placed in the picking aisles about April 20.

The straw between the rows helps to control weeds and enables you to harvest the berries during wet weather without getting muddy. With everbearing strawberries it is best to use a summer mulch to keep the fruits clean for the fall crop.

Strawberries can be renovated immediately after the harvest period. If your plants show any leaf-spot disease, go over your rows with a rotary lawn mower. Rake out the removed tops and old straw. This material should be added to your compost pile.

Next narrow your rows to about six inches wide. Use a power rotovator or a hoe or spade. The row that is left should be slightly to one side of the original row so all plants will be young runner plants.

Remove any weeds in the newly established row and thin the plants to a spacing of about a foot apart. Apply fertilizer at the same rate recommended for a new planting. A flower pot can be used for this job. Let the fertilizer run out through the hole in the bottom of the pot.

Keep the renovated planting cultivated and weed-free for the remainder of the season. By late fall new runner plants will have formed and the rows will be about 18 inches wide with plants that should produce an abundant crop next spring. With proper renovation each year a strawberry planting should last for three or four years.

With everbearing varieties it is best to start a new planting every spring but they can be renovated like the June-bearing varieties. Plants started in spring produce the best fall crop of everbearing strawberries.

Insects and disease can be a problem for strawberries. Watch carefully for insects and spray as necessary to control them. The strawberry weevil and the tarnished plant bug are the main insects but cyclamen mites can also be a problem.

Kelthane is a good control for mites; leaf diseases and fruit rots may require a protective spray with a good fungicide such as captan. If virus disease should appear, start over with virus-free plants. There are no practical controls for virus.

When Grandfather passed on, Grandma threw out all the cuspidors. She did not know that Uncle Jerry chewed tobacco — he never dared tell her — and she did not know why her big Boston ferns died. But Uncle Jerry knew why. About every month, all winter long, Uncle would buy her another fern to replace the last stricken one. Come spring, the fern would last until the next winter. Grandma was grateful to Uncle for the new ferns, but she would exclaim, "The gardeners are not growing hardy ferns like they used to, or there is something in the winter air of this old farmhouse that kills them." I wonder if Uncle Jerry, the rascal, had a guilty conscience.

Some common questions about strawberries

Q. We have a strawberry bed that did well last fall and fairly well this spring. The fall crop this year is not very good. Should I thin the plants and remove the runners?

A. I have always had best results by starting a new planting every spring. I leave just enough runners to have vigorous young plants to transplant in the spring. I leave the old plants for a spring crop the second year. If you do not plant a new planting each year, it would help to thin out the plants in your old planting. Plants should be no closer than eight to 10 inches apart.

Q. I have always read and believed that the flower buds in strawberries were formed in the fall. How do you explain the following experience? Last May, my husband was burning some leaves and the fire spread into our strawberries. The straw and the leaves of the strawberries burned to the ground. I was tempted to plow up the patch, but my husband suggested that we leave them and see if they might not recover for next year. Much to our surprise, the plants developed new leaves and in a few weeks the plants were white with flowers. We have never had such a good strawberry crop.

A. The flower buds are in the crown of the plant. The burning of the straw did not create a temperature high enough to kill the flower buds. The flowers and the fruits developed from the flower buds that were formed the previous fall.

Q. We spend our winters in Arizona but spend our summer at a lake home in Aitkin County, Minn. We would like to plant a strawberry barrel but are wondering how we would winter the plants.

A. The easiest way to grow strawberries is in ground beds, where the plants can be protected over winter with a straw mulch and normal snow cover. The flower buds that form in the fall of the year are killed at temperatures below 20 degrees. It would be difficult to protect the plants in a barrel unless the barrel could be moved into an unheated building in the fall. Even then you would need to cover the entire barrel with straw or some other insulating material. You could, of course, plant the barrel each spring using purchased plants of an everbearing variety. These would start fruiting in August.

Q. You recommended Ogallala as a good everbearing variety of strawberry. I have been told that a new variety called **Gem** is just as good and much hardier. Is this true?

A. The Gem is certainly not new. It was grown at least 50 years ago. It is quite hardy, but I would question whether it is hardier than the Ogallala. The Gem fruits are quite tart, but acceptable with cream and sugar. My preference would still be for the Ogallala.

Q. My strawberry planting is badly infested with a creeping clover plant. It is nearly impossible to remove the clover by mechanical means. Is there a spray that I could use to kill the clover that would not hurt the strawberries?

A. I am afraid you're out of luck. I do not know of a selective weed killer that would kill clover without injuring your strawberries. It would be best to start a new planting in soil that is free of clover.

Q. We have a large garden, and this year we planted some everbearing strawberries. Our soil is a sandy loam. We fertilize our vegetables with garden fertilizer, but we have been told that strawberries need other minerals than those contained in the garden fertilizer. Can you advise me on what to use on strawberries?

A. On a sandy loam soil it would help to incorporate well-rotted manure or compost into the soil before planting. This would improve the water-holding capacity of the soil. I would also till in a complete 10-10-10 fertilizer at the rate of one pound per 100 square feet of surface or at the rate of one pound for each 25 feet of row. I would also use the same application following renovation of the planting. I am not aware that strawberries have any special mineral requirements. I have grown excellent strawberries using these practices.

Chapter 2/Raspberries

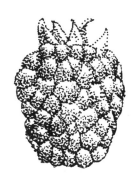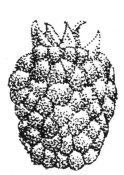

Raspberries are best grown in rows, but they can be planted in odd spaces. As with strawberries, there are two types; the summer-bearing and the fall-bearing.

Boyne is a good summer variety and **Fall Red** and **Heritage** are good fall varieties.

There are several systems of culture. I prefer the staked-hill system. Vigorous young plants that are virus-free should be planted.

Plant by making a slit in the soil with a spade. Insert the plant with roots spread. Remove the spade and firm the soil around the roots. The depth is not as critical as with strawberries, but try to plant them at about the same depth as they were growing.

Space the plants about 30 inches apart and space the rows eight feet apart.

Cut back the canes to about 18 inches. New plants will form from buds on the roots. In the summer-fruiting varieties, fruiting occurs only on second-year canes.

In the everbearing varieties, fruit occurs at the tips of first year canes in the fall and again the following summer on the same canes on lateral branches. Once the second year cane has fruited it gradually dies.

After removing the old canes, tie the new canes to stakes or wires so the berries will be held up off the ground. Failure to do this will result in dirty berries because the weight of the fruit will bend the canes over, splashing the berries with soil following a rain.

Birds may continue to share your fruit crop. The best defense is to use a bird netting to cover your fruit. This plastic netting is available from most garden centers.

With the cost of raspberries rising each year, more and more gardeners are growing their own.

The red-fruited raspberries are the most popular and the easiest to grow. The black raspberry is grown to a limited extent and requires different training methods.

Red raspberries send up sucker plants from the roots, and new plants may come up 10 feet or more from the original plants. The black raspberries reproduce mainly by tip layering. A long, arching stem bends over, and, where the tip of the cane touches the soil, roots form and a new plant is started.

It is the suckering habit of the red raspberries that causes most of the problems. If all of the sucker plants are allowed to grow, you will end up with a thicket. In a few years the berries will be of poor quality because of overcrowding.

The root system of the raspberry is perennial. It lives for years. The canes are biennial, living for two growing seasons. Canes of summer-fruiting varieties that have finished fruiting will die before winter and are of no further use to the plant. The sooner they are cut out the better. They should be removed with a raspberry hook or pruning shears. Cut them off at or near the soil line.

The new canes that came up last spring will fruit next year in those varieties that produce a single crop. In the everbearing varieties, such as Fall Red and Heritage, these new canes will produce a fall crop this year from flowers that form near the tips of the canes.

You probably will have too many of the new canes formed for optimum production. These canes should be thinned either in late summer or fall or early spring. The number of canes to leave will depend on the method of training.

If you grow your raspberries in a hedge row you should leave two to three strong canes per foot of row. If you grow them in hills and tie the canes to stakes, leave five to seven strong canes per hill.

The work of thinning the canes can be reduced by cultivating between the rows with a rotary tiller. The sucker plants are removed while still small. Do not let the row get wider than about 18 inches.

I space my rows about eight feet apart and tie my canes to stakes spaced 30 inches apart in the rows. Tamarack stakes are best. Redwood stakes are also durable.

If you use other types of wood, the portion underground should be treated with a wood preservative such as cuprinal. A seven-foot stake should be used for tying. Tie the canes tight so they cannot move.

In the case of everbearing varieties, new canes should be tied to their support immediately. Before tying, remove old canes and thin the new canes to five to seven per hill. After the last berries have been harvested, the tops of the canes should be cut off. This pruning may be delayed until spring.

A summer crop will be produced on lateral branches that will develop next spring. Some growers sacrifice the summer crop on everbearing raspberries by cutting all of the canes off in the spring.

With raspberries, you should pick the ripe berries every other day until the crop is harvested — early in August.

Winter protection may be required on some varieties. This protection is given by bending the canes over and holding them down with soil. Snow will usually cover the basal arched portion and provide adequate protection. I have had success with the Boyne, Heritage and Fall Red varieties without any winter protection. With the **Latham** variety, winter protection is usually beneficial. It is usually best to give winter protection to black raspberries.

Diseases can be a problem. Virus diseases such as mosaic are most destructive. The leaves are mottled, the berries are crumbly and plants usually lack vigor. There are no practical controls for the virus diseases. Affected plants should be destroyed.

Anthracnose and spur blight are fungus diseases that affect the canes and reduce production. Sanitation and proper pruning and cultivation are usually sufficient to control these fungus diseases.

Attention must also be paid to maintaining adequate soil fertility. A fall application of compost or well-rotted manure will help to maintain adequate organic matter in the soil. I also use a 10-10-10 fertilizer in the spring at the rate of one pound for each 25 feet of row.

When Uncle Jerry would come in just before supper on one of those hot, muggy days, stretch out on the couch and groan about how tired he was, Grandma would remark pointedly — but with a twinkle in her eyes — "Yes, Jerry has worked hard all day in the shade of one tree."

Apropos of nothing in particular: "An old gardener never dies, he just spades away."

Some common questions about raspberries

Q. Is it a good idea to prune raspberry canes in the spring? I've heard pros and cons. My canes have grown very tall to more than six feet.

A. The primary reason for pruning canes back in the spring is to provide proper support. The height is optional depending on the method of support. In a hedge row, four feet is the commonly recommended height. If you tie your canes to stakes the height will be determined by the height of the stake. Five feet is the usual height for staked plants. Pruning back the tips may also help to force lateral branching. Pruning and tying should be done in the spring before growth starts.

Q. I have an old patch of raspberries that doesn't produce much fruit and rabbits have chewed most canes down to the ground. Can I plant new plants on the same soil after it is plowed and the old canes removed?

A. It would be best to start a new planting in a new location. It is difficult to get all of the roots out, and these old roots will continue to send up suckers. There is also the danger of infecting your new planting with the virus disease called mosaic if your old planting was infected.

Q. I have a raspberry thicket. When would be the best time to prune out the surplus plants?

A. It would be best to wait until early spring. Cut out all old dead canes that fruited last July. Reestablish rows. Leave about three young canes per foot or row and space the rows eight feet apart. Remove all other canes.

Q. Last year I transplanted some raspberry plants in the fall and they all died. When is the best time to transplant raspberries?

A. We generally consider spring to be the best time to plant raspberries. Late April or early May should give good results. We have also transplanted them in late September with good results.

Q. We have some plants that produce black fruits. We are not sure whether they are blackberries or black raspberries. How can you distinquish between these fruits?

A. The difference is the shape and structure of the berries. Blackberries are elongated, while black raspberries are round. When you pick the black raspberry, a white, thimble-shaped structure remains on the plant, and the fruit has a hollow cavity at the stem end. In the blackberry this central core breaks off and is a part of the fruit that you eat. The canes of the blackberry are also much larger and usually more spiny.

Q. Last year I purchased plants of the Robertson black raspberry. This year the new canes are sprawling on the ground. If I tie these canes up to a stake will this affect their fruiting?

A. The canes of most black rasperries have a tendency to bend over and touch the ground. I recommend tying these canes to a support. It should not affect the fruiting. Fruits develop only on second-year canes.

Grandma always encircled her little vegetable garden with bright-colored annual flowers. She explained that she and the birds enjoyed the colors and, incidentally, the birds enjoyed the cutworms and other grubs. She never forgot to keep her birdbath filled. She knew that parent birds have not only their own thirst to satisfy, but also many little babies that are crying for water. The birds were so numerous that often the bath had to be refilled several times each day. Perhaps that was the secret of Grandma's pest-free garden.

Chapter 3/Blueberries

Growing blueberries has always been a challenge. Varieties currently available are not very hardy and winter injury can be a serious problem. If the plants are to be successful, they must grow in acid soil. All in all, there's a good deal of work involved.

Highbush blueberries are the only ones available from commercial sources. Numerous named varieties are on the market.

Rancocas, Weymouth and **Bluecrop** have performed well at the Horticultural Research Center near Excelsior, Minn. It is best to plant two or more cultivars for cross-pollination.

The highbush blueberry, *Vaccinium corymbosum,* is native from northern Michigan to Nova Scotia and south to Indiana and Pennsylvania. It is usually found growing on moist, acid soil with a high water table.

Select a site with moisture-retentive soil in full sunlight. Have your soil tested for acidity, which is measured in "pH," unless you already know what it is. If the pH is above 5.5 you will need to modify the soil to lower its pH value. This can be done by working liberal quantities of acid peat moss into it.

Chemicals are also used to lower the pH. Aluminum sulfate is effective, but continued use can result in an aluminum toxicity. I have found ferrous sulfate to be quite effective, too,

and safer to use. Agricultural sulfur is also used, but its reaction is slower. Fertilizer used on blueberries should react with the soil to make it more acid.

Blueberries should be planted early in the spring in soil that has been modified as we have described. Plant at the same depth that the plants were growing in the nursery. Avoid deep planting, because roots need oxygen as well as moisture.

Water the plants thoroughly at planting time and use a surface mulch such as weathered sawdust or compost. Blueberry roots are shallow, so it is best to control weeds by mulching rather than by cultivation and hand hoeing. Water during dry spells.

The flower buds on highbush blueberries are usually killed at temperatures under 15 degrees below zero F. This means that the flower buds will be killed most winters unless the plants are protected. Since it is impossible to depend on snow cover as a means of winter protection, some other method is a must in Minnesota.

A simple method is to erect a large cylinder of chicken wire about 3 feet in diameter around each plant. This cylinder should be filled with tree leaves, marsh hay or straw about Nov. 1.

In the autumn Grandma had Uncle Jerry barrow in several loads of good garden earth to bank her roses and shrubs before the freeze-up.

The first time, uncle thought the excavation would be a dandy hole in which to dump ashes and rubbish. But Grandma made him fill it with tree leaves, load after load, and then tramp them down.

So she always had a convenient source of loamy compost to draw from every summer.

The mulch material should cover the plant. Allow enough space for the mulch to settle. If the mulch settles to expose some of the flower buds, add more mulch. Remove the cylinders in spring and spread the mulch around the plants.

Each year remember to maintain the soil acidity and supply the nutrient needs of the plants. Organic matter used as a mulch uses nitrogen in its decomposition, so additional nitrogen will be needed to replace it. Ammonium sulfate is the best form of nitrogen to use. About two ounces per plant will be needed to break down the organic matter and supply nutrient needs of the plants. Any fertilizer recommended for evergreens or azaleas could also be used.

The color of the foliage and the new growth each year will tell you whether your plants are healthy. Yellowish foliage and short terminal growth indicate that the pH is too high. A dark green color and vigorous shoots indicate that everything is fine.

If you are successful in getting fruits to set, you will need to protect them from birds. A nylon bird netting draped over the plants and tied securely at the base is best.

If all this sounds like too much work, you may enjoy picking your own blueberries from wild stands of native plants. These are the lowbush blueberry, *Vaccinium angustifolium*. These plants depend on snow cover for winter protection. Late spring frost can also kill the blossoms on developing fruits.

Some years production is plentiful, while in others you may have to hunt for a suitable place to pick the fruits. There is nothing better than wild blueberries for pies or for an ice-cream topping.

Some common questions about blueberries

Q. In your Minneapolis Tribune column you mentioned that the highbush blueberry is not too hardy and that it requires an acid soil. I have the **Saskatoon** blueberry that thrives on neutral soil. The berries are fine for jellies and pies. Is this plant not the same as the highbush blueberry?

A. The Saskatoon is a juneberry belonging to the genus *Amelanchier* and the species *alnifolia*. It belongs to the rose family. The fruit is quite different from the true blueberries that belong to the genus *Vaccinium*. Where you cannot grow blueberries, the Saskatoon makes a fair substitute.

Q. I have large quantities of pine needles. Would these pine needles be a good source of fertilizer for my garden? I have been told pine needles will turn the soil sour. I have also been told that they make good fertilizer.

A. Decomposed pine needles make an excellent mulch for acid-loving plants such as blueberries. It is true that pine needles have an acid reaction in the soil when they decompose. A limited quantity could be safely used, but I would not apply more than about a bushel to 100 square feet of surface for most garden crops. As with most organic materials, the benefit comes from improving the soil structure rather than from the fertilizer value that the needles contain.

Grandma always stored in the cellar for use during the winter a tub of potting mixture consisting of good garden earth, sharp sand compost or loam and screened cow or sheep manure.

One autumn Uncle Jerry thought it would be a fine place to store earthworms for winter fishing, and he put a few worms in the tub.

The worms evidently found the cool cellar and rich earth very much to their liking. Nature had taken her course, and Grandma was horrified when she found she had almost more worms than earth. Uncle then had to find other housing for his worms.

Chapter 4/Currants and gooseberries

Currants and gooseberries are grown primarily in the home garden for home consumption. They may serve a dual role as ornaments if they are planted in a shrub border.

Neither berry is readily available on the fresh-fruit counters of supermarkets, but only a few plants are needed if you want a supply.

We have two plants each of the **Red Lake** currant and **Pixwell** gooseberry, and we produce more fruits than we can use.

Currants and gooseberries belong to the genus *Ribes*. There are several native species and several that have escaped cultivation. The distinction between currants and gooseberries is the manner in which flowers and fruits are produced.

Gooseberries produce fruits singly or in small clusters of two to four. Currants produce their flowers and fruits in drooping clusters that hang downward like clusters of grapes.

Another distinction is the presence or absence of spines on the stems. Gooseberries have spiny stems, while the stems of most currants are smooth.

The cultivated gooseberry is probably of hybrid origin. The English gooseberry, *Ribes uva-crispa,* is large-fruited, but is not reliably hardy

this far north. Varieties grown in this area have either been selected from our native *Ribes hirtellum* or are the result of hybridization between *Ribes hirtellum* and *Ribes uva-crispa*.

Many varieties of gooseberry have been tested and grown over the years, but only two are readily available from nurseries. These are Pixwell and **Welcome**.

Pixwell was introduced by North Dakota State University, and Welcome was introduced by Minnesota's Horticultural Research Center. Welcome has a larger fruit than Pixwell, but the foliage is more susceptible to the powdery mildew disease.

Most of our cultivated currants have been developed from *Ribes sativum*. The fruits are typically red, although white-fruited varieties are known. Like gooseberries, many varieties have been tested and grown. Today, we recommend only the **Cascade** and Red Lake. Both varieties were developed and introduced by the Horticultural Research Center.

Cascade has larger individual fruits, but Red Lake produces larger clusters. The black currants, *Ribes nigrum,* are popular in Europe,

Grandma's mosquito repellents — sixty years ago — were extracts of wintergreen and citronella. She smelled like a drug store — only nicer. Uncle Jerry's mosquito repellent was a powerful dark oily linament that was marked "good for man or beast". He smelled like a race horse with a strained tendon. No self-respecting mosquito would go near him, but neither would we.

but are seldom grown in this area. I grow my gooseberries in a cultivated row along one side of my vegetable garden with the plants about six feet apart.

They require little care except for weed control and pruning. The best fruits are produced on two- to four-year-old stems.

Pruning consists of the removal of the oldest stems at ground level in early spring before growth starts. This pruning will keep the shrubs young and fruitful many years.

Currants and gooseberries have few insect and disease problems. Powdery mildew can be a problem on susceptible varieties of gooseberry such as Welcome. Most currants and gooseberries are susceptible to white pine blister rust.

Rust spots develop on the undersurfaces of the leaves and hairlike projections hang downward from these spots. The disease does little injury to the currants and gooseberries but can prove fatal to the more valuable white pines.

The currant worm often feeds on the foliage and may defoliate the plant if not controlled. Sevin is a good insecticide to use. The currant aphid may cause a curling of the leaves, especially in early spring but a malathion spray when the leaves are about a half-inch long will control aphids.

A permit is needed to grow currants and gooseberries in certain northern Minnesota counties where white pine is an important tree crop. Check with your county agricultural extension office.

Red currants may be used fresh, as a sauce, and they make excellent jelly. We freeze the ripe fruits and use them in salads and desserts throughout the year.

Currants are ready to pick as soon as they are fully colored. The fruits will stay on the plants in good condition for several weeks after they are fully ripe.

Gooseberries are used for preserves and pies. Pick them just as they are starting to turn from green to yellow. When fully ripe, the fruits will have a reddish tinge. Fully ripe fruits become quite sweet and may be eaten fresh.

Grandma no more would think of killing a mole than she would a robin. She knew both were gardener's friends and consumed vast quantities of cutworms, grubs, beetles and other harmful insects. The mole does not eat roots or other vegetation. If they became too numerous, Grandma washed sand and ashes down their runways with a stream of water.

4/The wild fruits

Wild fruits are abundant in most parts of Minnesota and adjoining states. They grow on uncultivated land and are more abundant in the north, where less of the land is under cultivation.

Among them are wild strawberries, raspberries (black and red), blackberries, grapes, currants (black), gooseberries, blueberries, juneberries, highbush and lowbush cranberries, pincherries, chokecherries, black cherries, sand cherries, wild plums and roses.

Some of these wild fruits, such as strawberries, raspberries, blackberries, juneberries and blueberries, are eaten fresh or can be frozen or canned. Syrups are made from rose hips, blackberries, chokecherries, pincherries and blueberries.

If jellies interest you, look for rose hips, highbush cranberries, pincherries, gooseberries, sand cherries and chokecherries. I like jams from wild plums, gooseberries and blackberries, and wine can be made from most wild fruits.

The quantity of wild fruits differs greatly, depending on the season. Winter injury, late-spring frosts and summer drought may reduce the crop or eliminate it.

Information on the location of good blueberry patches is hard to get. Local residents are reluctant to share their blueberries with outsiders. Sometimes forest rangers can help you find them, for wild fruits may be picked on state-owned land. Often fruits may be picked along highway rights-of-way. On private lands you should get permission from the owner.

It takes longer to harvest wild fruits than tame ones. They are usually much smaller, and it takes time to find the plants. If you live in areas where fruits are plentiful, it will pay to harvest what you can use. If you have to drive long distances and spend time finding the fruits, you may want to compare costs of harvesting them with the cost of cultivated fruits.

But that may be a little too crass. Think of

wild plums

berry-picking as a recreational pursuit. It's rewarding to get into the wilds of northern Minnesota or Wisconsin and the berries are a fine bonus.

If you are new at picking wild fruits, you need to know when each fruit ripens and the type of area in which to look for it. The exact time varies with the season and the location.

Wild strawberries ripen in June. They grow best in open areas where the plants are exposed to the sun. They prefer an acid soil and can often be found along roadsides and in abandoned fields. They are especially abundant along the shores of Lake Superior.

Raspberries, red and black, ripen in July. Look for them in cut-over areas and on the edges of woods. They are most common in the southern part of the region. Red raspberries occur throughout the region, but are most abundant in the north. They can be found in abandoned fields and along old logging trails.

Blackberries ripen in August. Some years there is a bountiful crop, and in others they are hard to find. Blackberries flower and produce fruits on second-year canes. If there is deep snow, the canes are killed above the snow line.

Blueberries are the wild fruits that most folks look for. Fine fresh or frozen, they make excellent pies and are delicious served with cream and sugar. Fresh and frozen berries also may be used for blueberry muffins and blueberry hotcakes.

The berries grow only on acid soils in northern parts of the area and are usually abundant after land-clearing operations and forest fires. After a few years, though, shrubs and weeds grow up and subdue the blueberry plants. Clearings in jackpine forests are likely places. Blueberries also grow on rocky outcrops and

Grandma had three low, wide pots of parsley, mint, and chives growing all winter long in her window. These she lifted from her garden in November, cut off most of the top growth, and potted them in ordinary garden soil. They supplied her with fresh seasoning until spring.

sometimes in sphagnum bogs.

They ripen from early July through August depending on the season and the location. Bog blueberries usually ripen later than the upland berries.

Chokecherries grow in most of Minnesota but are most abundant in the north. Birds also like chokecherries and often eat the fruits before they are fully ripe. But up north there are more chokecherries than the birds can eat, so that is where you will find the best picking. Chokecherries are black when fully ripe.

There are several species of juneberry. All produce edible fruits. Locally they may be called Saskatoons, sarvisberries, serviceberries or shad-bush.

The Saskatoon *(Amelanchier alnifolia)* variety produces the best fruit. Abundant in northwestern Minnesota and in neighboring parts of North Dakota and Manitoba, the fruits resemble large blueberries and make excellent pies. Although these fruits are called juneberries, they seldom ripen before early July.

Birds are fond of the fruits and usually eat them before fully ripe, except in areas where the plants are abundant.

Grandma knew that the odor of cedar was distasteful to many insects. So from the sawmill she got a hundred wide red cedar shingles, thick as shakes. These she placed under her ripening watermelons, muskmelons, and citrons, and these fruits never were touched by slugs, worms, or decay. Grandma counted her shingles at the end of harvest, and woe to anybody who took even one. She would have much preferred the loss of a melon to the loss of a shingle. She was of Scotch descent.

5/Pruning

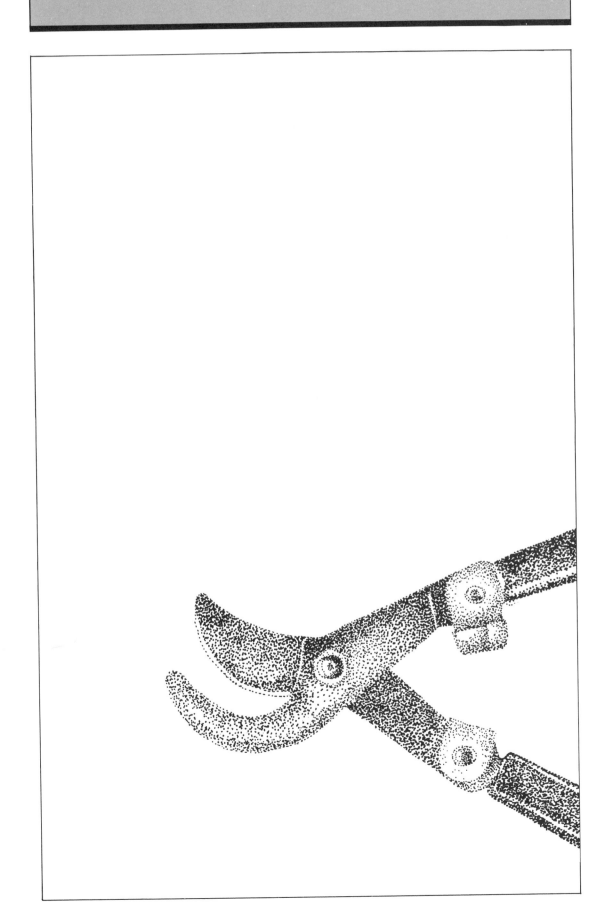

When snow disappears and the weather moderates, it is time to do some pruning. This annual chore is avoided by many gardeners not because of the work involved, but because they lack knowledge of how to do it.

Pruning is an art that few people really understand. First let's look at reasons for pruning and how a plant grows because that knowledge is the key to a proper job. Each plant is different, so a person can become an expert pruner only after years of experience and study.

The reasons for pruning are several. The most common are:

• To limit the size of the plant.

• To improve the size and quality of flowers and fruits.

• To improve the health and appearance of the plant.

Pruning to limit sizes is seldom necessary for fruit trees. If your tree has grown too tall, it can be lowered by cutting back some of the upper branches. This will make it easier to spray and it will be easier to harvest the fruit.

Pruning to improve size and quality of flowers and fruits makes more sense. The best flowers and the highest-quality fruits are produced on young, relatively vigorous wood, usually two to four years old. By cutting out the old wood and encouraging new growth, a plant can be kept young and fruitful for many years.

The third reason, to improve a plant's health and appearance, can be accomplished by removing dead or broken branches and by eliminating narrow crotches and branches that cross and rub each other.

There are other reasons for pruning: To remove lower branches of trees that interfere with the flow of traffic and to thin tops of trees to allow light to filter through to the fruits.

Pruning starts with the choice of tools. Buy top quality. Cheap pruning shears and saws are virtually useless. Pruning shears with plastic-covered handles are easier to use than all-metal

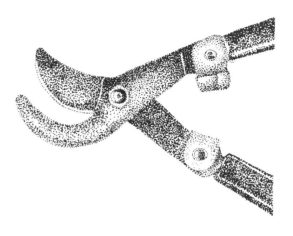

shears. Several excellent brands are on the market but try the shears before buying them. See how they feel in your hands.

For some pruning jobs, a pair of hand shears is all you will need. But a pruning saw is essential for removal of large branches and, for intermediate branches up to 1 1/2 inches in diameter, a long-handled pair of loppers is useful. For pruning hedges, you will need hedge shears, either hand or electric.

There are a few simple rules to follow in pruning, In removing a branch, make the cut close to the main stem. Never leave a stub. The wound heals quickly when the cut is close to the stem. When a stub is left, the cut surface fails to heal, and decay sets in. In cutting back a stem, make the cut just above a bud or lateral branch. Make the cut about one-fourth of an inch beyond the bud and at the same angle as the bud.

When there is a choice between removing a branch with a wide-angled or narrow crotch, always remove the branch with the narrow crotch. Wide-angled branches are stronger and less subject to storm damage.

Two general types of pruning are recognized, tip pruning and renewal pruning.

Tip pruning is accomplished by cutting back the ends of branches, stalks or vines. This causes lateral buds to develop that were inhibited by the terminal buds. A dense, bushy type of growth is produced that is quite unnatural for the plant. This type of pruning is used to restrict size and for formal hedges. It must be repeated every year and sometimes several times a year.

Renewal pruning is a more natural type. It improves flowering and fruiting. On fruiting plants, such as currants and gooseberries, pruning is accomplished by removing the oldest

Grandma would prune all her shrubs during the summer and Uncle Jerry would attend to the tree branches that had not leafed out. Grandma explained that dead wood absorbed some of the life-giving sap that should go to the living wood. As I remember, apparently dying trees and shrubs usually would make a vigorous comeback after this treatment.

stems at the surface of the ground. New stems grow to replace those removed. This results in a shrub of natural form that has a maximum of stems of optimum age to produce a good crop of fruits.

On fruit trees, renewal pruning is accomplished by removing some of the older branches that have become unfruitful and by removing narrow crotches and branches that cross and rub or grow toward the center of the tree.

In tip pruning, one should cut back either to a lateral bud or to a side branch. In renewal pruning, make clean cuts close to main stems or branches. Never leave stubs that will die and cause wood-rotting fungi to spread into the main stem.

The time to prune is important. Early spring is the time to prune most fruit trees.

The thinning of fruit branches results in renewed vegetative growth. This reduces the number of fruits set and provides the necessary leaves to provide a reserve of food for developing fruits. This results in larger fruits. Thinning out the top of the tree also results in better light conditions and permits a better job of spraying.

Grapes are pruned heavily to reduce the number of grape clusters and increase the size of those that form. Grapes fruit on year-old wood; 40 buds will produce an optimum crop of quality grapes. Since most grape vines will have up to 400 buds, it is necessary to remove about 90 percent of last year's grapes.

Don't worry if the cut stems bleed. This is bound to happen, but there will be little or no harm done.

Raspberries are pruned by removing all old, dead stems at the ground and by thinning out the young canes to about three per foot of row.

Grandma knew what to do to keep shrubbery, fruit trees, and evergreens from being crushed by heavy snow. She had Uncle Jerry gently raise and lower the loaded branches from underneath with the back of a snow shovel or broom, thus shaking off the snow without damaging the brittle branches. When the snow was frozen, Uncle had to wait until it had melted a bit. If the branches were bowed out of shape they were propped up with boxes or notched boards for a few weeks.